WORLD WIDE WEB JOURNAL

SO-EGH-453

Advancing HTML

Style and Substance

Cascading Style Sheets

Web Accessibility for the Disabled

Animation Tools and Tips

Customizing HTML with JavaScript

O'REILLY™

WORLD WIDE WEB JOURNAL

ADVANCING HTML: STYLE AND SUBSTANCE   Volume 2, Issue 1, Winter 1997

Editor: Rohit Khare

Managing Editor: Donna Woonteiler

News Editors: D.C. Denison, Kirsten Alexander

Production Editor: Nancy Crumpton

Technical Illustrator: Chris Reilley

Software Tools Specialist: Mike Sierra

Quality Assurance: Clairemarie Fisher O'Leary

Cover Design: Hanna Dyer

Text Design: Nancy Priest, Marcia Ciro

Subscription Administrator: Marianne Cooke

Photos: Flint Born

ISSN: 1085-2301

ISBN: 1-56592-264-6

1/1/97

W 3 C   P E O P L E

W3C Administration

Jean-François Abramatic
  W3C Chairman and Associate
  Director, MIT Laboratory for
  Computer Science
  jfa@w3.org

Tim Berners-Lee
  Director of the W3C
  timbl@w3.org

Vincent Quint
  Deputy Director for Europe
  Vincent.Quint@w3.org

User Interface

Vincent Quint
  Domain Leader
  Vincent.Quint@w3.org

Bert Bos
  bert@w3.org

Jose Kahan
  Jose.Kahan@w3.org

Yves Lafon
  lafon@w3.org

Hakon Lie
  howcome@w3.org

Chris Lilley
  chris@w3.org

Dave Raggett
  dsr@w3.org

Irene Vatton
  Irene.Vatton@w3.org

Daniel Veillard
  Daniel.Veillard@w3.org

Technology and Society

Jim Miller
  Domain Leader
  Jmiller@w3.org

Eui-Suk Chung
  euisuk@w3.org

Daniel Dardailler
  danield@w3.org

Philip DesAutels
  philipd@w3.org

Rohit Khare
  khare@w3.org

Joseph Reagle
  reagle@w3.org

Architecture

Dan Connolly
  Domain Leader
  connolly@w3.org

Anselm Baird-Smith
  abaird@w3.org

Jim Gettys
  jg@w3.org

Philipp Hoschka
  Philipp.Hoschka@w3.org

Ora Lassila
  lassila@w3.org

Henrik Frystyk Nielsen
  frystyk@w3.org

Cross Areas and Technical Support

Stephane Boyera
  Stephane.Boyera@w3.org

Tom Greene
  tjg@w3.org

Sally Khudairi
  khudairi@w3.org

Luc Ottavj
  ottavj@w3.org

Arthur Secret
  secret@w3.org

Stéphan Montigaud
  montigaud@w3.org

Administrative Support

Beth Curran
  beth@w3.org

Susan Hardy
  susan@w3.org

Josiane Roberts
  Josiane.Roberts@inria.fr

Yukari Mitsuhashi
  Administrative Assistant
  yukari@w3.org

Adobe Systems Inc.

Aérospatiale

AGF.SI

Agfa Division, Bayer Corp.

Alcatel Alsthom Recherche

Alis Technologies, Inc.

America Online, Inc.

American International Group Data Center, Inc. (AIG)

American Internet Corporation

Apple Computer, Inc.

Architecture Projects Management Ltd.

AT&T

BELGACOM

Bellcore

Bitstream, Inc.

British Telecommunications Laboratories

Bull S.A.

Canon, Inc.

Cap Gemini Innovation

Center for Mathematics and Computer Science (CWI)

CIRAD

CMG Information Services

CNR—Instituto Elaborazione dell'Informazione

CNRS/UREC

Commissariat a L'Énergie Atomique (CEA)

CompuServe, Inc.

Computer Answer Line

Council for the Central Laboratory of the Research Councils (CCL)

CyberCash, Inc.

Cygnus Support

Dassault Aviation

Data Research Associates, Inc.

Defense Information Systems Agency (DISA)

Delphi Internet

Deutsche Telekom

Digital Equipment Corporation

DigitalStyle Corporation

Eastman Kodak Company

École Nationale Supérieure d'Informatique et de Mathématiques Appliquées (ENSIMAG)

EDF

EEIG/ERCIM

Electronic Book Technologies, Inc.

ENEL

Enterprise Integration Technology

ERICSSON

ETNOTEAM S.p.A.

First Floor, Inc.

First Virtual Holdings, Inc.

Folio Corporation

Foundation for Research and Technology (FORTH)

France Telecom

FTP Software

Fujitsu Limited

GCTECH, Inc.

General Magic, Inc.

Geoworks

GMD Institute FIT

Grenoble Network Initiative

GRIF S.A.

Groupe ESC Grenoble

Harlequin Inc.

HAVAS

Hewlett Packard Laboratories, Bristol

Hitachi, Ltd.

Hummingbird Communications Ltd.

IBERDROLA S.A.

IBM Corp.

ILOG, S.A.

InContext Systems

Industrial Technology Research Institute

Infopartners S.A.

INRETS

Institut Franco-Russe A.M. Liapunov

Intel Corporation

Internet Profiles Corporation

Joint Info. Systems Comm. of the UK Higher Ed. Funding Council

Justsystem Corporation

Kumamoto Institute of Computer Software, Inc.

Lexmark International, Inc.

Los Alamos National Laboratory

Lotus Development Corporation

Lucent Technologies

Matra Hachette

MCI Telecommunications

Metrowerks Corporation

Michelin

Microsoft Corp.

MITRE Corporation

Mitsubishi Electric Corporation

MTA SZTAKI

National Center for Supercomputing Applications (NCSA)

NEC Corporation

NetMarket

Netscape Communications

NeXT Software, Inc.

Nippon Telegraph & Telephone Corp. (NTT)

NOKIA Mobile Phones

Novell, Inc.

NTT Data Communications Systems Corp.

Nynex Science & Technology, Inc.

O'Reilly & Associates, Inc.

O2 Technology

Object Management Group, Inc. (OMG)

Omron Corporation

Open Market Inc.

Open Software Foundation

Oracle Corp.

ORSTOM

Pacifitech Corporation

PointCast Incorporated

Process Software Corp.

Prodigy Services Company

Progressive Networks

Public IP Exchange, Ltd. (PIPEX)

R.I.S. Technologies

Raptor Systems, Inc.

Reed-Elsevier

Rice University for Nat'l HCPP Software

Royal Hong Kong Jockey Club

Security Dynamics Technologies, Inc.

Sema Group

SICS

Siemens-Nixdorf

Silicon Graphics, Inc.

SLIGOS

SoftQuad

Software 2000

Sony Corporation

Spry, Inc.

Spyglass, Inc.

STET

Sun Microsystems Corporation

SURFnet bv

Swedish Institute for Systems Development (SISU)

Tandem Computers Inc.

Teknema Corporation

Telequip Corporation

Terisa Systems

Thomson-CSF Ventures

TriTeal Corporation

U.S. Web Corporation

UKERNA

Verity, Inc.

Vermeer Technologies Inc.

VTT Information Technology

Wolfram Research, Inc.

Wollongong Group

WWW— KR

X Consortium

Xerox Corporation

C O N T E N T S

The cover photo
montage was
created by
Edie Freedman
and Hanna Dyer.
Copyright ©1997
Photodisc, Inc.

C O N T E N T S

C O N T E N T S

Advancing HTML: Style and Substance

This issue is all about where the "rubber meets the road"—the user interface technologies that make the Web come alive on screen, on paper, in braille, over the phone. We're proud to present the first official W3C Recommendations on HyperText Markup Language 3.2 and Cascading Style Sheets 1.1, users' guides to these new specifications, and technical articles on advanced UI technologies for animated graphics, interactive scripting, and on how to apply these tools with care to build a usable, accessible, attractive, and popular Web experience. *Advancing HTML: Style and Substance* reflects W3J's editorial balance of covering the technology behind powerful new Web UI ideas and advice on how to use these techniques effectively and responsibly.

The specifications and commentary in this issue highlight the work of the User Interface domain at the World Wide Web Consortium. The UI domain is concerned with making the Web effective and attractive through development of software, such as W3C's flagship *Amaya* browser, and through specifications for markup, graphics, layout, fonts, animation, and more. This team also works closely with the Architecture domain on issues like distributed authoring and with the Technology & Society domain to ensure full access for the disabled, collaboration, and content-selection (PICS) interfaces.

W3C Advances HTML and CSS

HTML is the bedrock of the Web user experience—not only for Net surfers accustomed to desktop browsers with graphical HTML formatting conventions, but also for all of the diverse tools which access the Web, from handheld personal communicators to text-to-speech devices. HTML 3.2 defines the core set of current, industry-supported markup usage. It extends standard HTML 2.0 with tables, embedded active objects, control over text flow around images, and more. But more important than its technical decisions, the 3.2 spec reflects a hard-won consensus from W3C's industrial members and marks a milestone in W3C's HTML development process.

The W3C took over stewardship of HTML from IETF in early 1996 because commercial self interest was tearing apart any technical consensus on new HTML feature proposals. W3C acted to harness those industrial interests to the benefit of the whole Web user community through the HTML Editorial Review Board (ERB). The ERB is a unique, neutral forum for W3C technical staff to work closely with experts from Microsoft, Netscape, Sun, IBM, and others to evaluate and specify new markup ideas. HTML 3.2 represents the ERB's first complete overhaul of HTML—find out more in an exclusive behind-the-scenes look at the ERB and its debates in D.C. Denison's "HTML Background" in the first section of this issue.

Style sheets are a natural complement to HTML: a separate language for describing layout and graphical style. Cascading style sheets have been in development for several years at W3C in parallel with HTML to control colors, whitespace, multicolumn layouts, fonts, and more, allowing site designers to leverage document styles without modifying each page. CSS is uniquely powerful because it defines the look-and-feel for a document by annotating its semantic structure. Rather than resorting to a layout-markup approach like PostScript or RTF, CSS says "make all my top-level headings red" rather than "change the color to red, draw these words, change the color back to black," and so on. Browsers can fetch different style sheets to render the exact same HTML file in the sober style of *Scientific American*, the way-out *Wired* look, as a new spoken rendering, or as adapted for wristwatches or laser printers.

To demonstrate the power of these ideas and others, the W3C has deployed a new graphical Web client, Amaya. Not merely a read-only browser, the UI team uses Amaya to experiment with new ideas for style, layout, linking, and exploring new tasks like editing and authoring. In addition to the complete HTML 3.2 and CSS technical specification in the "W3C Reports" section and their respective user guides in "Technical Reports & Papers," this issue includes a look at the Amaya team and their platform.

Beyond HTML

Moving beyond HTML, Web designers have access to a litany of cool new whiz-bang features to delight and amaze Net surfers. Even without asking users to install and configure mysterious plug-in software, many PC browsers already support a number of now-common UI innovations: animated GIF and MNG graphics files, JavaScript interactivity, and multimedia audio/video streams. There are technical

and how-to articles on using each of these technologies in this issue.

At the same time, many of the papers and articles presented here speak directly to the theme of the upcoming Sixth International World Wide Web Conference: *Accessibility*. Consideration for the diverse audiences on the Web is an essential check for responsible use of these new features. Mike Paciello's manifesto declares "People with Disabilities Can't Access the Web!" and outlines several accessibility considerations for Web authors. Usability engineering also helps guide Web development for diverse audiences. Keith Instone presents an overview of the field and its application to Web issues; the dean of usability, Jakob Nielsen, weighs in with his own "Guidelines for Multimedia on the Web." Finally, the audience registers its verdict by voting with their mice: Thomas Novak and Donna Hoffman discuss their model of Web usage measurement in "New Metrics for New Media: Toward the Development of Web Measurement Standards."

Refining W3J's Editorial Mission

Looking back on our first year of publication, we note that this is the last in a series of issues that have presented the latest developments in each of the Web Consortium's three domains. *The Web After Five Years* (Summer 1996) concentrated on the social impact of the Web's explosive growth into a mass, commercial medium and the corresponding interest in (ethically!) mapping its demographics. *Building an Industrial Strength Web* (Fall 1996) outlined the changes ahead for the architecture of the Web's infrastructure, including the landmark IETF Proposed Standard specification of the HyperText Transfer Protocol/1.1. Finally, this issue, *Advancing HTML: Style and Substance* (Winter 1997), reflects the latest advances in user interface technology for the Web and looks ahead to new frontiers for Web applications. Building upon the record of our first volume, the Journal's future issues will strike a similar balance between timely technical specifications, guides to using and developing those technologies, and lively, independent, and articles around a central theme.

Welcome to the second volume of the *World Wide Web Journal*!

Rohit Khare
khare@w3.org
December 1996, Cambridge, Massachusetts

HTML BACKGROUND
SETTING STANDARDS
W3C's ERB reflects on progress, process, and HTML 3.2

The W3C established the HTML Editorial Review Board (ERB) in March 1996, bringing together experts from most of the major companies with significant Web business, including Netscape and Microsoft. One of the first orders of business: to draw up a solid, HTML benchmark, 3.2.

Lou Montulli, Netscape's representative on the ERB, didn't wait long to start horse trading.

"Right off the bat I said that I wouldn't push for <blink> to be part of HTML 3.2, if Microsoft didn't push for the inclusion of <marquee>, an equally ridiculous tag," Montulli recalls.

Microsoft's Thomas Reardon agreed.

"<marquee> was not something that we felt had to be in HTML 3.2," he says dryly. "I was happy to make that deal."

In subsequent weeks and months, the HTML ERB moved onto far weightier matters. The result, HTML 3.2, is available in this issue, starting on page 29. Chuck Musciano's commentary on the spec is available starting on page 127. Also important, however, was the experience of the members of the ERB. How did these various, and often competitive, entities work together? And what does their experience say about future of this group, and other W3C standards groups? D. C. Denison canvassed a group of ERB members and asked them to reflect on their experience.

Set Your Sites . . . Low

"We started with a simple plan," W3C's Dave Raggett explains. "We'd only put in things that were being used as of January 1st, 1996. That isn't a particularly ambitious undertaking, but it got the project off to a good start. Also we decided that the joint spec didn't have to specify everything. It just had to specify things that we felt comfortable about.

"In a sense it was a reverse-engineering assignment," Dan Connolly, the group's chair adds. "We wanted to take what people were already doing and write it up. Basically we had to decide which elements we were going to bless."

By concentrating on existing practice only, the ERB was able to get a non-controversial start. But were they just laying down track after the train had gone by?

"That feels like kind of a negative metaphor," Netscape's Lou Montulli states. "But in fact the history of the Internet is that things have to be working and in place before they get standardized. It allows people to work out problems before setting anything in stone. I think it's a grave mistake to standardize things before there have been substantial implementation efforts. Those kinds of things that are typically designed in a committee, or designed by people without implementation experience— sometimes you go to implement them, and you realize all the problems too late. It's already been set in stone. So the standardization of 3.2 is an extremely important step. It takes the best parts of the market, of what we've had, and gets solid industry support behind those things. And it ties up all the loose ends."

Losing the Competitive Edge

There was no denying the impact of the so-called "browser wars." "Things moved faster," Eric Sink of Spyglass reports. "And there were politics. The representatives from Microsoft and Netscape tended to get a lot of air time in ERB discussions. Since they have relatively distinct agendas, consensus could be tough on some issues."

The competitive overtones were not lost on the major players

"At first I was really sensitive and very political," Thomas Reardon of Microsoft recalls. "But once things got going it became 90 percent technical to 10 percent rather than political. People pretty much checked their agenda at the door and worried about the technology rather than specific product agendas."

"Clearly the two companies are very competitive," W3C's Dave Raggett adds, "but they also come from very different backgrounds as well. Microsoft is very thorough. They aren't exactly flashy. Their software doesn't shine with any unusual brilliance. But they are very good at finishing things, at just doing it. Whereas Netscape is a bit more, well they do things very quickly, and they aren't about attention to details. So you're not just dealing with competitors, you're dealing with different cultures."

Many ERB members report, however, that a number of factors mitigated the competitive atmosphere.

"Microsoft and Netscape do have this reputation as gorillas," according to Steve DeRose, an ERB member representing EBT. "Everybody's very conscious of that. So people tend to jump to the other side. And Microsoft and Netscape scale back."

ERB members often contributed as mediators. Murray Maloney, who represents SoftQuad, a comparatively small Canadian software firm, often ventured a non-partisan opinion.

"I often got involved in trying to resolve disputes," he says. "I'd try to look at the problem from different perspectives to see if there was a way to solve the problem so that politics didn't get in the way. There's a lot of politics in that group.'

And everybody felt the influence of a large, looming presence: customers.

"There's always been a kind of competitive tension to our meeting," Dave Raggett says. "But on the other hand the market reality was that they had to come to some sort of accommodation. Otherwise both companies would get a toasting from the customers."

Still, competition did have its advantages.

"When we had a meeting at Netscape, Lou Montulli took us to an absolutely fantastic restaurant," Dan Connolly recalls. "Six months later, we were at Microsoft, and Thomas Reardon knew he had to do Netscape one better—a nice positive byproduct of competition."

Visions of HTML

All competition aside, the Editorial Review Board also hosted a wide variety of views on the potential of HTML, and how it should grow.

Dan Connolly, for example, does not feel that HTML should be constantly extended.

"I've become a hard core HTML minimalist," he says. "I've come to believe that with features like style sheets and scripting, you don't have to extend HTML to introduce something new to the Web. HTML doesn't have to account for every new graphics format. It could simply evolve into a collection of the common idioms that you need to communicate in this medium: things like paragraphs, links, headers, lists, tables, etc. "

On the other hand, Connolly's W3C colleague, Dave Raggett, has been extending HTML since 1992.

"I'm in favor of extending HTML, and I've quite a bit of work in that area. Ideally, we should be looking at features that people need, or could use, and building them in. Unfortunately, the browser manufacturers today do not take that design approach. The attitude seems to be, 'What additional features can we hack into the next release. And what features introduced by somebody else do we have to recognize.' That's been their model. So they haven't moved forward according to design; it's been much more haphazard, which makes it tough to work on."

And then there's the glue or envelope model: the idea that HTML will eventually evolve into a structure that contains various active and interactive elements. Netscape's Lou Montulli subscribes to this view.

"I think the direction of HTML is more toward the glue aspect, of bringing together active content. And I think it will move more and more towards scriptable active content—a highly interactive, programmable medium. As well as having a lot of the conventions of traditional publishing. It's kind of walking a fine line there."

By contrast, Murray Maloney, of the Web publishers SoftQuad, has been a strong advocate for pushing HTML toward ideas of structured documents and traditional publishing jobs.

"Many members of the ERB are focused on making HTML an environment for programming and doing page layout, which is a little shortsighted," he says. "It's certainly glamorous but misses the point of what the potential for the Web is, in terms of managing information and making information more accessible.

"There's a lot of value in structural and content markup. That is, if you identify information for what it is, it's easier to work with it. It's easier to find a part number when the markup says 'This is a part number' instead of 'This is bold.' A lot more could be done to make HTML a language for managing information. But there's a bend toward programming— making HTML an envelope for a programming environment. That appeals to the software engineers. But there are few people involved in the HTML ERB, or the HTML working group before that, who brought much publishing experience to the table. At times it has been discouraging and frustrating to try to explain simple concepts of document formatting and layout, or how typesetters and typographers use certain metaphors with respect to publishing. The computer scientists basically look at

that and say, 'Yeah, but so what?' I feel like they're basically saying 'so what' to a thousand years of tradition. While tradition alone shouldn't be the thing that guides us in how we approach new problems, it certainly should be a factor.

"The direction that major vendors are taking HTML has very little to do with information anymore," Maloney continues. "Someone recently said that HTML is evolving towards the 'Macintosh of the Web.' It's all about graphic design and interactivity. And that's good, I'm not saying that it shouldn't do that. But for a lot of us this revolution wasn't just

---

"Many members of the ERB seem to be focused on making HTML an environment for programming and doing page layout, which is a little shortsighted."

---

about pretty pictures on the screen—it was about information. Mainstream businesses are trying to get a job done—they have work to do. From a business manager's pont of view, being able to run JavaScripts, and VRML, and watch videos may be cool, that's not what they need. They need the test technician sitting at the bench to be able to easily get to and from repair procedures, schematics, and parts lists. They need structure and semantic markup and strongly typed links."

Maloney is also an advocate for an accessible HTML.

"The Yuri Rubinsky Insight Foundation and the International Committee for Accessible Document Design are concerned with making information accessible to people with disabilities. There are about 25 million people in North America who cannot easily read the stuff that's on the Web because of visual disabilities. Advancing the Web along the lines of more graphical and more visual capabilities is all well and good, but a small effort would also enhance it in favor of people who don't have the ability to deal with that. To make an analogy, we've already seen that sidewalk curbcuts make life easier for people in wheelchairs, on bicycles and roller blades, and people pushing baby carriages. Providing accessible information on the Web is like that—it is a matter of conscious design, and it benefits everyone."

Maloney's caveats notwithstanding, future HTML development is likely to focus more on scripting than structure.

"HTML implementations will become programmable, in the sense that the underlying document structures will be available to scripting languages such as JavaScript," ERB member (and Spyglass representative) Eric Sink says. "This will probably be the next major battlefield."

Can We All Just Get Along?

Despite the differences, consensus won out on HTML 3.2.

"HTML 3.2 says nothing about where HTML is going," according to W3C's Dave Raggett, "It merely says, 'This is a point of consensus at the beginning of '96.'

"HTML 3.2 is basically saying, 'Let's try to develop some kind of agreement about where things are now,'" Raggett continues. "Individual companies will extend things; they are going to keep extending things in a peremptory fashion, and people will implement those extensions. But from the point of view of people who are publishing content that they want to be around for many, many years—they will prefer to have something more stable to point to. Something that is reasonably well defined. Because most of these new extensions are not documented very formally. So, basically, everybody agrees that it's important to have material that everyone regards as a standard, which represents a point of stability, and consensus. Instead of looking to the future, it looks to the near past."

Which makes a stable spec for the distant future.

"Right, in the sense that if the Library of Congress is coding up their documents, HTML 3.2 is something they can use and know that people will be able to read it in 20 years."

And the consensus extends to more than just browsers.

"It's important to realize that the ERB isn't there just for browser vendors," Thomas Reardon of Microsoft says, "HTML is not a browser technology—that's probably the really important part of this whole story. The kinds of people who've been involved, the people who've really added value, like SoftQuad or Novell, were people in areas other than strictly brows-ers. SoftQuad was more from the editing and tool side, the people from Oracle or database centers more tools and back end side. There's as much of a stake in HTML from there as from browser vendors. That's key: looking beyond the needs of browser."

Into the Future

Of course the ERB's job extends beyond HTML 3.2, and the decisions ahead promise to be even more challenging.

"Standards and marketing typically exist in direct conflict," Eric Sink says. "It's somewhat difficult to standardize something which was explicitly designed to create a competitive advantage. Unfortunately, this is the arena where innovation is happening. Most of the people who are qualified to participate in these kind if industry interoperability discus-sions are the ones who have a conflict of inter-est. But the ERB does a good job of mitigating those potential conflicts."

The major challenges are likely to arise as the ERB ventures into newer work, rather than concentrating on conventions that are already in wide use.

"The ERB has been a mixture of codifying existing practice as well as doing new design work, so it's special as standards organizations go," Microsoft's Thomas Reardon says. "You get arguments from some people that you don't do standards until there's lots of existing practice, but W3C hasn't restricted itself to that approach. For example, the ERB has been tackling cascading style sheets, which is all

new. And I think our work on style sheets has been impressive, because it is really all new," Reardon continues. "There wasn't a lot of pub-lic thinking going on around style sheets. In a sense, style sheets are orthogonal to HTML; that's where things get exciting. People were approaching it as a big picture problem, in terms of how do we take HTML into whole new spaces, into the formal document space where you need tighter control over presenta-tion, and into the richer user interface experi-

---

"HTML is not a browser technology—that's probably the really important part of this whole story."

---

ence, when you take a high-end publishing experience on the Web—the Starwaves of the world—and trying to balance those two things. This need for very strict document layout, and also really rich, sexy document presentation. That is exciting, and it will be a real challenge for the ERB."

Doubtless the debate on style sheets will be contentious. Many of the issues ahead are likely to be more fractious than anything the ERB has encountered so far. Fortunately, W3C's Dave Raggett is choosing to take a pos-itive view of the situation.

"Contentiousness is a sign that people care enough about HTML to try to sort things out," he says. "I'd prefer it if we could take a slightly more academic viewpoint: we'd analyze what the needs are, then we'd design for the needs.

But that's not the way this marketplace is working. Everyone thinks very much short term. That's why it's up to W3C, and the ERB, to push things that are in the long-term interest, and not accept things that are not in the long-term interest." ∎

WORK IN PROGRESS
People & Projects
at W3C

IRENE VATTON
MAKING A TEST BED FOR THE WEB

I t's a state-of-the-art Web browser that sup-ports all the features of HTML 3.2, Cascad-ing Style Sheets, the new PNG graphics format, and an extensible API. It also includes an inte-grated WYSIWYG Web editor and supports direct uploading to remote servers and auto-matic link updating. No, this is not the latest beta out of Mountain View, California, or Red-mond, Washington—it's Amaya, the W3C's own Web client, initiated by Irene Vatton and developed by an INRIA in Grenoble.

Amaya is the successor to the Arena browser, previously developed as a W3C test bed for HTML and Cascading Style Sheets. The new Amaya interface is designed for users with a variety of skill levels. Amaya's powerful native editing capabilities mean that it can not only test style sheets, but automatically gener-ate code for them. It's editing interface allows a user to manipulate text on a Web page directly, like a standard word processor docu-ment, with the option to simultaneously view the document structure, HTML source code, and even a "text only" version of the page in separate windows.

Amaya's browser is designed to be cus-tomized by a broad spectrum of users and incorporates innovative features like multiple Web page windows that a user can size and zoom in or out of at will, automatically scaling the text size proportionally. Amaya's API is designed to allow more features and functions to be added easily. Though it is currently available only for Unix platforms, a Windows version is planned for release in mid 1997.

Though Amaya was new to the W3C as of February 1996, it has its roots in a project that has been ongoing for more than a decade, and W3C research engineer Irene Vatton has been involved from the start.

Vatton grew up in Marseille, in the south of France, and attended the University of Grenoble to earn her doctorate in Computer Science, specializing in structured documents and user interface. She started work on the Opera project with Vincent Quint in 1982. Their goal was to create a specification language for the logical structure of documents.

They produced a language very similar to the later SGML standard, except that their "Thot" library specified both a language for document presentation elements like fonts and spacing and an interactive authoring tool. Thot was named for the Egyptian god of the moon and of wisdom and learning, whose symbol is the ibis, which appears in the Thot logo.

Working at INRIA in Grenoble, Vatton and Quint started developing an HTML editor in October of 1994. According to Quint, this original prototype, dubbed "Tamaya," was built on the Thot library and designed "to evaluate the advantages of structured editing for authoring Web documents."

At the third International World Wide Web Conference held in Darmstadt, Germany, in April 1995, Vatton and Quint decided to build a prototype of a Web page editor based on the technology they had developed for the Opera project. Daniel Veillard joined the team in October of 1995 to implement the proposal for Cascading Style Sheets. They presented Tamaya at the fourth International World Wide Web Conference in Boston, Massachusetts, that December.

Based on this presentation, Vatton and Quint were contacted by the W3C team and asked to provide the test bed for the new HTML Web standards the Consortium was developing. They, along with Veillard, joined the W3C team in February 1996, based at INRIA: Vatton as a research engineer, and Quint as both coordinator of the W3C User Interface areas and Deputy Director for European operations.

Tamaya was named, Vatton explains, "after a pleasant tree with beautiful flowers which comes from New Mexico. It was a sacred tree for the old population of that region." The "T" was dropped because the name was already in use by another French company, but the tree still appears in the Amaya logo.

Amaya incorporates much from both Thot and the Opera project browser. As Irene explains, "[Thot] can support any kind of document structure like drawing or mathematics. Amaya just uses a small part of the Thot potential." Amaya also shares many of the distinguishing characteristics of the Opera Web browser, which Vatton continues to participate in developing.

Unlike most other Web browsers, Opera was not built on existing Mosaic code; it was written from scratch. In bypassing the existing C++ libraries, the Opera team is able to produce a program that can be installed from a single diskette while rivaling the functionality of browsers that take up several times as much space. This makes for a very fast browser that runs efficiently even on slower systems with as little as four megabytes of RAM. The innovative design allows users to customize most of the controls according to their own preferences or handicaps. It also allows users to view a number of document windows through a single interface, and zoom in and out of these windows in fine increments, preserving the document formatting and adjusting the size of the display fonts accordingly. Vatton is particularly proud of Opera's incremental formatting engine.

Even though Amaya combines all of the interface options of the Opera browser with very powerful WYSIWYG editing capabilities, the installation file currently weighs in at a trim 1.5 megabytes. With other browser/editors tipping the scales at over twice that much, how is this possible? Amaya is written in C, Vatton explains, and like Opera, uses code economically. "We use the same generic functions to manipulate document items and compute the display image."

What is the biggest challenge of combining these features with the authoring capabilities of the Amaya browser/editor? Vatton says that balancing a powerful feature set with ease of use while maintaining the document display quality is not easy. Vatton sees her future challenges as coping with the time constraints on multimedia content delivery, developing

groupware applications that allow users to collaborate on documents across the Internet, and working on structure transformations.

—*Eileen Foley*

HÅKON LIE
WEB STYLIST

*O*ne of the first things you'll see when you reach Håkon Lie's home page is a sepia toned, filtered photo of himself. With rivet-like circles cutting through it and most definition removed, it's difficult to make out exactly what this guy looks like.

It's just that kind of understated humility you'd expect from someone who casually opens with the sentence, "I work for the guy who invented the Web. His name is Tim."

Over in the right corner of the page, you'll see a strange symbol, looking like a cross between the equation $E=mc^2$ and a WWW logo. The "E" can also be seen as a tilted "W" or the mathematical symbol Sigma, meaning "the sum of all things." To the right is "W3," his symbol for the World Wide Web Consortium. It's an icon of his own making, says Håkon, (pronounced Hoo-kon in Norway, his native country).

The icon is symbolic of the two worlds in which Lie treads—those of art and technology. You see, Lie is also the primary developer of style sheets, a new way of describing how documents will be presented on the Web. Until now, Web designers essentially had to resort to Web tricks—a sort of smoke and mirrors way to make pages appear aesthetically pleasing. Things that are normally easy to do on paper (like indenting paragraphs or setting fonts) are nearly impossible on the Web, unless you turn that text into a graphic, or place invisible pictures as "tabs."

Cascading Style Sheets (CSS), as they're called, work alongside HTML. With CSS, you can specify what fonts, color and white space HTML documents should use. There are actually three different ways of using style sheets: 1) in a one-time only scenario, where a single element (like a paragraph or header) has a specified style; 2) embedded in the document to format an entire page; and 3) linked, so that multiple pages with a similar "look" are linked to the file that describes all of them stylistically.

That's great news for corporations, who often have multiple Web pages with essentially the same design. Just by changing one document—the style sheet—the entire site is altered, without the hassle of going through the site page by page. Using style sheets also helps when you're printing pages from the Web. Paper has different properties from a computer screen and the differences can be accounted for in a style sheet. CSS is also a boon to the visually impaired community. For instance, text displayed as images can't be altered to appear larger or in a different color. Nor can they be read aloud by voice synthesizers. But style sheets allow visually captivating text to appear as just that—text.

Cascading Style Sheets are currently supported by Microsoft Internet Explorer 3.0 and higher. And Netscape announced it will support style sheets in its next browser release. Both Microsoft and Netscape plan to extend the concept of style sheets with scripting languages. Rather than acting as competitors to CSS, the scripting languages will allow dynamic changes to a static style sheet—for example, the color of a font could change over time.

"Web authors should be able to have a stronger influence in how their documents are to be presented," says Lie. "We feel that style sheets will give people the ability to describe the presentation—that means font, color, white space—without resorting to tricks."

In fact, the guru of typographical tricks on the Web, David Siegel, met with Lie and other W3C members to consult on style sheets. (Siegel's mention of Lie in his electronic diary is what Lie calls his "claim to fame.")

"He's been very helpful person coming from the graphic design community," Lie says of Siegel. "He publishes all these 'dirty' tricks that would work in one browser, but not in others. But at the same time, I think he's aware that there are better ways.

"Since 1990 (the beginning of the Web), a lot of people have been wanting to describe the presentation of HTML, and we think style sheets are the correct way of doing so. It's the right technology rather than trying to extend HTML itself.

"I do think style sheets will change the look of the Web. It will bring back aesthetics as an issue." Lie professes an interest in typography and aesthetics in general (check out the painting he did with his two children on the

Web). Though he comes from a highly technical background, Lie says his experience working at MIT's Media Lab served as a "melting pot" for him, bringing together designers, musicians and other artists together with technologists. "I'm not a designer at all, but I have the secret dream of being one."

Lie says this aesthetic element is integral to the Web, especially since so many people spend their time there. "It's a very lightweight technology, but a very powerful one. . . . It will give designers a lot of new toys. And for people who are interested in the content of their documents, it will give them a clear way of presenting their documents."

Lie has been working for the W3C in France at INRIA, the National Institute for Research in Computer Science and Control, since 1995. His main projects there include the development of style sheets and the Arena browser. Although no longer maintained by W3C, Arena served as the testbed for a variety of Web technology, including HTML tables and CSS.

Lie first became involved with networking and the Internet back in 1987, while he was working for Norwegian Telecom Research. A couple years later, he ended up at MIT's Media Lab, working toward his master's degree and with MIT's Electronic Publishing Group trying to develop electronic newspapers. Electronic newspapers may be almost commonplace now, but they certainly weren't back when there wasn't a Web. "The Web suddenly made all sorts of distributed applications possible. But in the beginning, people weren't too concerned with how the documents were pre-sented on the Web. That was the motivation for starting work on CSS," says Lie.

Today, Lie spends his time jet-setting from his work in France to his family in Norway. Along the way, he's trying to learn French. (He confesses the new language is coming slowly, since most everyone at INRIA also speaks English.) That, of course, would add to his other two tongues—English and German.

And if that along with his work doesn't keep him busy enough, he can always fulfill his dream—to build a pipe organ. He doesn't actually play the pipe organ—the computer will have to help him there—but finds the instrument itself very interesting. "It's a very complicated machine. It's a complex, fascinating instrument, just like a computer is."

Until then, Lie's enthusiasm for the Web will keep him working on developing better ways to present information. To him, it's more than just making documents look nice—it's having them available to the public in general. It's this political aspect to the Web that intrigues Lie most.

"The Web as a political phenomena is great: this 'everyone can publish' model—this very liberal medium where tolerance is very high," says Lie. "I think that's an important part of it and why I got interested in the Web before this all turned very commercial. There still is a strong political side to it, but the commercial side is very strong now."

"It's how technology can change the way society works."

— Kimberly Amaral

LILLEY UNGILDED
PNG'ING TRUE COLORS TO THE WEB

Writers are frequently told "don't gild the lily," and in this case, that advice has never been better: Chris Lilley's career and words speak for themselves and make him a fascinating person to talk with about the latest development in Web graphics—particularly Portable Network Graphics (PNG), where there's no need to gild anything—in fact, the goal for PNG is to make everything come through the Web as true and as fast as possible.

A biochemist turned Medical Laboratory Scientific Officer, Lilley's scientific interest took a decidedly graphic swing about eight years ago and he went on to:

- Earn a Masters of Science in Biological Computing.

- Join the Computer Graphics Unit at the University of Manchester.

- Write a set of modular distance learning materials on computer graphics or scientific visualization and become one of the pioneers in using the Web for education.

- Present courses on Scientific Visualization, Internet Skills for Bioinformatics, and Active Web Pages.

- Prepare a number of tutorials and short courses on various aspects of the Web—

portable document design, HTML, HTTP and CGI.

Lilley is interested in the application of color science to computer graphics and the Web, and he sees PNG as bringing lots of benefits to those making Web pages, whether their interests are scientific, business, or aesthetic. Here are his responses as we zeroed in on PNG.

Q: *Let's say I'm a Web developer, what does PNG mean to me?*

A: It gives you control, takes out the uncertainty—no more "can I fudge this so it looks okay on a PC and a Mac? It lets you do 'kewl' things like semi-transparent overlays. It avoids the white halos and lets you reuse graphics on any background. It lets robots search your site and index the graphics by the keywords you put in them. It gives faster download.

Q: *The rationale for PNG mentions its support of "truecolor" images. What are the major advantages of "truecolor," and why is it important that PNG do this?*

A: Truecolor means that each pixel can be any color you want. This is the natural state of graphics, before people start putting them on the Web.

Say we have a simple logo which a designer may say has two colors, russet and teal (if they come from a print background and assume the white as given. Okay, lets say it has three colors). The computer graphic of that logo will have hundreds of colors—all the mixtures of russet fading to white, teal fading to russet, teal fading to white. That's probably the simplest logo. I just mention that because people cite design simplicity as a reason for not needing more than 256 colors.

Given some multicolor line art, say an Illustrator file—modern commercial graphics—you either throw away the sharp edges and smooth color by going to JPEG (and a file like that would not compress well with JPEG) or you throw away most of the colors and get banding and jaggies by going to GIF. PNG gives you a third option that will deal well with that image and keep it pixel-perfect.

Q: *Does this mean, for example, that PNG will display better even on 8-bit systems?*

A: It might, depending on the browser and how it handles color information. At minimum, the browser will do gamma correction so it looks better than a GIF. The PNG will not look worse than the GIF. Sending a truecolor image and letting the browser quantize to it's own palette is a win because you send the best quality you have and the browser only takes away as much quality as it needs to.

Q: *With PNG can I throw away my "browser safe" palettes—those colors that seem to be handled the same by Macs and PCs?*

A: Yes, several browsers use the intersection of the Mac and Win95 palettes, a set of 216 colors. Unix boxes don't use those colors. PC and Mac browsers that are displaying a single image on a page often use a different palette.

And of course those 216 colors don't look the same on the Mac and the PC, they just have the same numerical values.

Once you take an image down to a fixed palette you throw away most of the quality,

you are left with a gross approximation. Of those 216 colors a typical image might use only 30 or 40 of them. (I actually came across some huge GIFs the other day, apparently made by some automatic whatever-to-HTML converter, and they all had the 216 color palette. The actual image contained only two colors, black and white ;-).)

Q: *Can I start using PNG immediately?*

A: Yes, we have at W3C.

Q: *What happens when someone who is using a PNG-challenged browser meets a PNG image?*

A: They get a GIF. It's called content negotiation.

Q: *In a very general way people use GIFs for line art and JPEGs for photos—I know PNG is aimed at replacing GIFs, but I haven't seen explicit statements about whether or not it is best used for line art, best used for photos, or performs equally with either?*

A: It works well with line art because JPEG would give artifacts on the hard edges and GIF would drop most of the colors.

It works well with photos if you ever want to edit them, or if you need any transparency. If those two things don't apply and the subject matter is able to take lossy compression, then use JPEG—the JPEG will be smaller.

It also replaces many common uses of TIFF.

Q: *How long do you think it will take before the majority of Web browsers have PNG capabilities?*

A: About one or two months after the market leader has PNG capabilities.

Q: *The most recent stats I looked at showed that about 10 percent of the users at one popular site were still using Netscape 1.0.*

A: That didn't stop people putting JPEG-only inlines on their pages as soon as a couple of browsers supported it. But it is possible to send out whatever images the browser can handle. Any good server can do this; Apache, the market leader, in fact has two different ways to do it. Of course the CERN server and the W3C Jigsaw server can both do this, too.

Q: *I just recently came across a Web page called "Gif Wizard" which gives you an opportunity to cut the size of a GIF file significantly while making a judgment on how much (and what kind) of quality you're willing to sacrifice. If you're familiar with this, what sort of advantages would you say PNG has over this kind of altered GIF which (I think) allows you a similar level of file size reduction as PNG?*

A: Make me ten GIFs with that page and when you have traded off your quality against size to your satisfaction, send them to me, and I will make ten PNGs, which are smaller and look just the same. If people want to shave bytes and make censy little files with few colors, PNG can do that, too.

So you can either have a PNG that is smaller than your squeezed GIF, or a file that is the same size and looks a bit better.

Q: *Will PNG support (either now or eventually) the kind of poor man's animation of the animated GIF?*

A: No. Sending a ten-frame animation in an animation format that no one ever used to use (because there were much better ones) so that most browsers can only display the first frame (or the last, the GIF spec is unclear) is fairly dumb. It just gives you a massive file.

A better way to do animation is not to use the IMG tag but to use the object tag that was developed by Netscape, Microsoft, Sun, Spyglass, IBM, and other member companies. Put the animation on the object tag and the replacement static picture on an img tag inside the object. Then browsers get the smallest file they need; people can switch off animation download but keep on still image download, for example.

That said, there is a new format in the PNG family called MNG, which is for animations. I have a prototype player on my workstation. It has all the advantages of PNG plus it moves (and the spec is open and freely implementable without freeware authors having to pay royalties on the software they give away!!).

Q: *The battle over standards and the Web (in conflict with commercial interests seeking commercial advantages) seems to be alive and, if anything, heating up. Is it going to be as difficult to get a graphics standard used—such as PNG—as it is to get HTML standards accepted?*

A: Um, actually my crystal ball just dumped core, can you hang on while it reboots?

Q: *From both your writing and your background, it seems that you are interested in graphics primarily as a communications medium and you feel it's important to be able to present graphics accurately so that we com-*

municate things such as scientific drawings, or advertisements of products, accurately.

A: Yes. All graphics is communication. If it doesn't say anything, drop it. Which applies right across the board from scientific visualization to fine art.

Q: *Your comments on this seem to support a very precise, technical approach to graphics. Does the more subjective—perhaps artistic— approach to graphics content interest you as well?*

A: Actually yes. I do have an interest in the graphic arts—first thing I did after graduating in biochemistry was take an exam in Art and Design. Redress the balance, as it were. I took part in some interesting experiments in collaborative artwork on the Net, people taking image files, manipulating them, passing them on to the next one in the group, that sort of thing. And I have been known to spend the odd hour or ten fiddling with Photoshop, GIMP, and so on.

I can appreciate the technical and aesthetic aspects at the same time, with different parts of my head. Of course it is going to be the real artistic sites that benefit most immediately from PNG, coupled with CSS1 the sort of fast loading, knockout-looking stuff that can be done is incredible.

Q: *Your professional biography is pretty incredible—biochemistry, med lab science, computer graphics, distance learning, the Web—what's the common thread here (if, of course, there is one)?*

A: `<Grin>` Last time I wrote a CV I made a convincing case for a planned career path, but hey, I think the common thread is interest and possibilities and real practical applications. At each step it was just a case of trying to see the right path at the time, the most fulfilling direction. Sort of zeroing in on the best thing.

And the social aspects, the interaction, are very important which is where the distance learning thing comes in. Most of the PNG authors have never met, the whole thing was designed and built over the Net. We just decided to do it and there we are.

Q: *What are your personal goals? What excites you—professionally—right now? Do you think what you are doing is important, interesting, revolutionary, ho hum, it's a living? (Choose one, or invent your own.) If so, why?*

A: Being at a crossroads of history. Are we going to end up with a global communication medium that allows any scale of publishing from personal to corporate and spans the globe? Are we going to have something we can learn from, something that helps us learn from each other? It's the chance to make a difference, to have helped, that excites me now. I cannot honestly think of a job I would rather have than the one I am in now. ■

—Greg Stone

Libwww 5.0a Public Release

OCTOBER 10, 1996, *Grenoble, France*
With the public release of version 5.0a, the status of Libwww shifts from a generic Web toolkit toward a playground for experimenting with new Web features. Libwww will be used for extensive experimentation with new features in HTTP and for gathering data with new protocols like W3Mux. W3C is also looking into how the experiences from building the Libwww API can be projected onto other areas such as mobile code and distributed systems. *http://www.w3.org/pub/WWW/ Library/Distribution.html*

PNG Approved as W3C Recommendation

OCTOBER 14, 1996, *Cambridge, Massachusetts*
Responding to a need for faster loading, enhanced quality cross-platform Web graphics, the W3C members vote to endorse the Portable Network Graphics (PNG) specification, a patent-free replacement for GIF, as a W3C Recommendation; CompuServe—original creators of the GIF format and now W3C members and PNG spec development supporters—concur, hoping to see PNG become accepted as the new Internet standard format for lossless graphics. "PNG offers optional full transparency, enabling content with partially transparent overlaid images which will display correctly over any background color or texture," explains W3C's Chris Lilley. *http://www.w3.org/ pub/WWW/Graphics/PNG/Overview.html*

JEPI Specifications Completed

OCTOBER 15, 1996, *Cambridge, Massachusetts and New Orleans, Louisiana*
The World Wide Web Consortium (W3C) and CommerceNet announce that the specifications for Joint Electronic Payments Initiative (JEPI) are complete and that several run-time scenarios are available. This represents a major step toward resolving the industrywide Internet payment challenge. JEPI provides a universal payment platform that will allow merchants and consumers to transact business over the Internet using many different forms of payment. *http://www.w3.org/ pub/WWW/Payment*

Process-ERB Has First Meeting

OCTOBER 23, 1996, *Cambridge, Massachusetts*
The recently elected Process-Editorial Review Board (Process-ERB) was formed to review and redesign the Interim Process now in use by W3C. The board holds its first meeting with all members in attendance. With several other in-person and teleconferences planned, a report is scheduled for release in early December. *http://www.w3.org/pub/WWW/Consortium/Process/*

Digital Signature Initiative First Working Meeting

OCTOBER 28-29, 1996, Darmstadt, Germany

The first of three working meetings, this gathering, hosted by GMD, features Carl Ellison of Cybercash giving an overview of trust management and W3C's Rohit Khare discussing using PICS labels for that task. The team separates into two subgroups to address Signature Block and Trust Management. The group plans two additional meetings before the conclusion of the design phase as well as a presentation of results at the 8th Security Working Group in November, following the second meeting, on November 20, in Stockholm. *http://www.w3.org/pub/WWW/Security/DSig/Overview.html*

Voting Commences on HTML 3.2 Reference Specification as Proposed Recommendation

NOVEMBER 5, 1996, Cambridge, Massachusetts

HTML 3.2 is W3C's specification for HTML, developed in early 1996 together with vendors including IBM, Microsoft, Netscape, Novell, SoftQuad, Spyglass, and Sun Microsystems. HTML 3.2 adds widely deployed features such as tables, applets, and text flow around images, while providing full backwards compatibility with the existing standard HTML 2.0. W3C is continuing to work with vendors on extensions for multimedia objects, scripting, style sheets, layout, forms, math, and internationalization. W3C plans on incorporating this work into further versions of HTML. Member voting runs through December 15. *http://www.w3.org/pub/WWW/TR/PR-html32-961105*

AMAYA Alpha 0.9 Released to Public

NOVEMBER 14, 1996, Grenoble, France

The latest version of Amaya, which seamlessly integrates browsing and editing, includes full support of HTML 3.2 and other enhancements. This version also supports stylesheets and OBJECT embedding. Amaya is now available to the public in binary form for Linux and Sun/Solaris. *http://www.w3.org/pub/WWW/Amaya/*

Symposium: A Comparison of DCOM and CORBA

NOVEMBER 18, 1996, *Cambridge, Massachusetts*
The Consortium continues to be interested in the issue of distributed objects and mobile code. W3C invited two experts to this educational symposium, preceded by a dinner and reception the night before. For purposes of comparison, Nat Brown, who is Microsoft's Lead Program Manager, OLE/COM and Annrai O'Toole, the Chief Technical Officer of IONA Technologies, each present very detailed technical explanations of Microsoft's DCOM and OMG's CORBA systems, respectively. *http://www.w3.org/pub/WWW/OOP/96-symposium/cfp*

Technology & Society Projects: Orientation on DSig and JEPI2

NOVEMBER 21-22, *Stockholm, Sweden*
Hosted by Ericsson, the objective of this meeting is to discuss participation opportunities for the second phase of the JEPI project and for the implementation and evaluation phase of the Digital Signature Initiative. The entire staff of the T&S attends in order to meet with companies interested in future participation. The DSig Design Team appraised attendees of its current plans for trust management and cryptographic signature labels. The Working group decides to consider using the Signature Block in current PICS development and to request formal participation in the DSig Implementation phase by January 24, 1997. *http://www.w3.org/pub/WWW/Security/Group/961122_Workshop/*

European Commission's ESPRIT Project Invites Presentation

NOVEMBER 25-27, 1996, *Brussels, Belgium*
At the invitation of the European Commission's ESPRIT project, W3C presents its work on PICS (Platform for Internet Content Selection) at the European Information Technology Conference. During this high visibility presentation, W3C explains how the PICS specifications, recently announced as a W3C Recommendation, allow for content filtering without state censorship.

Distributed Authoring: Present, and Future

DECEMBER 4-5, 1996, *Sunnyvale, CA*
This two-day symposium features presentations and demonstrations by Netscape, Microsoft, America Online, Continuus, W3C/INRIA, GMD FIT, and U.C. Irvine on such topics as distributed HTML authoring, intranet-enabled tools, Web page hosting services, configuration management of a Web site, collaborative authoring and awareness over the Web, and Web-based software development. *http://www.w3.org/pub/WWW/Authoring961001/Call.html*

W3C Member Review for CSS1

DECEMBER 11, 1996,
After extensive review by the HTML Editorial Review Board and following the W3C interim Recommendation process, the Cascading Stylesheet level 1 (CSS1) specification is submitted to members for review and comments as a Proposed Recommendation, with final responses due on this date. *http://www.w3.org/pub/WWW/TR/PR-CSS1-961112*

Advisory Committee Meeting

JANUARY 15-16,1997, *London, UK*
Official member representatives convene to hear updates from the W3C's director and staff on various areas of activity and plans for the future.

Sixth International World Wide Web Conference

APRIL 7-11, 1997, *Santa Clara, California*
Subscribe to the WWW6 Mailing List, start planning that super Birds of a Feather session, and find out about WWW6 collaborative conferences, Hypertext 97 and the W3C's conference track. Confirmed speakers at WWW6 include Paul Saffo and Howard Rheingold. W3C will organize the traditional closing Developers' Day. *http://www6conf.slac.stanford.edu/*

The title of this issue reflects the central role of HTML and CSS in the Web user experience. The subtler message, though, is that the Web Consortium believes firmly in the separation of Style *and* Substance—*semantic markup is the key insight that makes the Web a knowledge representation system instead of a video game. Instead of confounding these two principles like so many of its predecessor formats (including PostScript, Rich Text Format, and troff), the Web uses the HyperText Markup Language to encode the concepts and ideas in a document with a style sheet language to render them. Together, they liberate the Web from the tyranny of WYSIWYG documents that presume the printed paper form is the only, final form.*

HTML 3.2 reflects no revolutions in semantic markup; it reflects the existing consensus in the industry and provides a stable place in which to "plant a flag" for the rapid progress of future HTML development. This section presents the Proposed Recommendation for HTML 3.2 as approved by the W3C Advisory Council. (Please note that final Recommendation's appendices on access for the disabled were not available by press time.)

Though Cascading Style Sheets is a new technology, it represents a very traditional solution. A CSS style sheet can indicate that all H1 headlines should be purple and, say, 12 points larger than usual, or that H2 headlines of a certain kind should be in red. Moving beyond the usual word processor metaphors for style tags, though, CSS uses cascading to successively compose different style sheets. Each new style sheet can add or subtract style definitions and make relative statements about color, font, placement, layout, and so on. Soon, CSS will also be able to control the layering ("z-ordering") of the various elements of a Web page. For now, however, the first Recommendation for CSS is a milestone release from the W3C that starts the process rolling (including its own ERB for its future evolution). It's reassuring to note that with today's release of CSS-compliant browsers, the Web has recaptured the visual control and customizability of NeXUS, the NeXTSTEP client that Tim Berners-Lee created five years ago.

HTML 3.2 REFERENCE
SPECIFICATION

Dave Raggett

Abstract

[W3C Proposed Recommendation; PR-html32-961105; November 5, 1996]

The HyperText Markup Language (HTML) is a simple markup language used to create hypertext documents that are portable from one platform to another. HTML documents are SGML documents with generic semantics that are appropriate for representing information from a wide range of applications. This specification defines HTML version 3.2. HTML 3.2 aims to capture recommended practice as of early 1996 and as such to be used as a replacement for HTML 2.0 (RFC 1866).

While HTML 3.2 does not contain all the new features in discussion at the World Wide Web Consortium, it provides a firm basis for more extensive specifications that are in preparation. HTML 3.2 is an important specification for applications in which wide cross-platform interoperability is required, and for documents that may have long lifetimes, independent of individual technology suppliers.

Status of This Document

This document is in the course of review by the members of the World Wide Web Consortium. This is a stable document derived from the working draft *WD-html32-960924.html*. Details of this review have been distributed to members' representatives.

HTML 3.2 represents the collaboration, consensus, and commitment of support of the W3C HTML ERB participants, which represent a significant portion of the market in HTML-related products.

To encourage access by the visually impaired, W3C expects to add an appendix to the specification that defines an SGML LPD to enable automated support for conversion of HTML 3.2 documents into ICADD—e.g., for output to Braille. This requires no changes to HTML 3.2 user agents.

The review period will end on December 15, 1996. Within 14 days from that time, the document's disposition will be announced. It may become a W3C Recommendation (possibly with minor changes), or it may revert to Working Draft status, or it may be dropped as a W3C work item. This document does not at this time imply any endorsement by the Consortium's staff or member organizations.

A list of current W3C Proposed Recommendations and Working Drafts can be found at *http://www.w3.org/pub/WWW/TR*.

Introduction to HTML 3.2

HTML 3.2 is W3C's specification for HTML, developed in early 1996 together with vendors including IBM, Microsoft, Netscape Communications Corporation, Novell, SoftQuad, Spyglass, and Sun Microsystems. HTML 3.2 adds widely deployed features such as tables, applets, and text flow around images, while providing full backwards compatibility with the existing standard HTML 2.0.

W3C is continuing to work with vendors on extensions for multimedia objects, scripting, style sheets, layout, forms, math, and internationalization. W3C plans on incorporating this work in further versions of HTML.

HTML as an SGML Application

HTML 3.2 is an SGML application conforming to International Standard ISO 8879—Standard Generalized Markup Language. As an SGML application, the syntax of conforming HTML 3.2 documents is defined by the combination of the SGML declaration and the document type definition (DTD). This specification defines the intended interpretation of HTML 3.2 elements and places further constraints on the permitted syntax that are otherwise inexpressible in the DTD. The SGML declaration and the DTD for use with HTML 3.2 are given in appendices. Guidelines for parsing HTML are given in *WD-html-lex*, which was published in Volume 1, Issue 3 of the *World Wide Web Journal*.

Note that some user agents require attribute minimization for the following attributes: **compact**, **ismap**, **checked**, **nowrap**, **noshade**, and **nohref**. These user agents don't accept syntax such as `compact=compact` or `ismap=ismap`, although this is legitimate according to the HTML 3.2 DTD.

The Structure of HTML Documents

HTML 3.2 documents start with a <!DOCTYPE> declaration followed by an HTML element containing a HEAD and then a BODY element:

```
<!DOCTYPE HTML PUBLIC "-//W3C//
    DTD HTML 3.2 Draft//EN">
<HTML>
<HEAD>
<TITLE>A study of population
    dynamics</TITLE>
... other head elements
</HEAD>
<BODY>
... document body
</BODY>
</HTML>
```

In practice, the HTML, HEAD, and BODY start and end tags can be omitted from the markup as these can be inferred in all cases by parsers conforming to the HTML 3.2 DTD.

Every conforming HTML 3.2 document *must* start with the <!DOCTYPE> declaration that is needed to distinguish HTML 3.2 documents from other versions of HTML. Every HTML 3.2 document must also include the descriptive title element. A minimal HTML 3.2 document thus looks like:

```
<!DOCTYPE HTML PUBLIC "-//W3C//
    DTD HTML 3.2 Draft//EN">
<TITLE>A study of population
    dynamics</TITLE>
```

NOTE

The word "draft" will be replaced by the word "final" when the HTML 3.2 specification is fully ratified by the W3C member organizations.

The HEAD Element

This contains the document head, but you can always omit both the start and end tags for HEAD.

- The TITLE element
- The ISINDEX element
- The BASE element
- The META element
- The LINK element
- The TITLE element

```
<!ENTITY % head.content "TITLE &
    ISINDEX? & BASE?">
<!ENTITY % head.misc
    "SCRIPT|STYLE|META|LINK">

<!ELEMENT HEAD O O  (%head.content)
    +(%head.misc)>
```

The `%head.misc` entity is used to allow the associated elements to occur multiple times at arbitrary positions within the HEAD. The following elements can be part of the document head:

TITLE
    Defines the document title and is always needed.

ISINDEX
    For simple keyword searches, see **prompt** attribute.

BASE

Defines base URL for resolving relative URLs.

SCRIPT

Reserved for future use with scripting languages.

STYLE

Reserved for future use with style sheets.

META

Used to supply meta info as name/value pairs.

LINK

Used to define relationships with other documents.

TITLE, SCRIPT and STYLE are containers and require both start and end tags. The other elements are not containers so that end tags are forbidden. Note that conforming browsers won't render the contents of SCRIPT and STYLE elements.

The TITLE Element

TITLE is described in the HTML 3.2 DTD as:

```
<!ELEMENT TITLE - -  (#PCDATA)* -
    (%head.misc)>
```

Every HTML 3.2 document *must* have exactly one TITLE element in the document's HEAD. It provides an advisory title that can be displayed in a user agent's window caption, etc. The content model is PCDATA. As a result, character entities can be used for accented characters and to escape special characters such as & and <. Markup is not permitted in the content of a TITLE element.

Example TITLE element:

```
<TITLE>A study of population
    dynamics</TITLE>
```

The STYLE and SCRIPT Elements

STYLE and SCRIPT are described in the HTML 3.2 DTD as:

```
<!ELEMENT STYLE  - - CDATA --
    placeholder for style info -->
<!ELEMENT SCRIPT - - CDATA --
    placeholder for script
    statements -->
```

These are place holders for the introduction of style sheets and client-side scripts in future versions of HTML. User agents should hide the contents of these elements.

These elements are defined with CDATA as the content type. As a result, they may contain only SGML characters. All markup characters or delimiters are ignored and passed as data to the application, except for ETAGO (</) delimiters followed immediately by a name character (a-zA-Z). This means that the element's end tag (or that of an element in which it is nested) is recognized, while an error occurs if the ETAGO is invalid.

The ISINDEX Element

ISINDEX is described in the HTML 3.2 DTD as:

```
<!ELEMENT ISINDEX - O EMPTY>
<!ATTLIST ISINDEX
    prompt CDATA #IMPLIED -- prompt
        message -->
```

The ISINDEX element indicates that the user agent should provide a single line text input field for entering a query string. There are no restrictions on the number of characters that can be entered. The PROMPT attribute can be used to specify a prompt string for the input field, as follows:

```
<ISINDEX PROMPT="Search Phrase">
```

The semantics for ISINDEX are currently well defined only when the base URL for the enclosing document is an HTTP URL. Typically, when the user presses the Enter (Return) key, the query string is sent to the server identified by the base URL for this document. For example, if the query string entered is "ten green apples" and the base URL is *http://www.acme.com/*, the query generated is *http://www.acme.com/?ten+green+apples"*

Note that space characters are mapped to + characters and that normal URL character escaping mechanisms apply. For further details see the HTTP specification.

NOTE

In practice, the query string is restricted to Latin-1 because there is no current mechanism for the URL to specify a character set for the query.

The BASE Element

BASE is described in the HTML 3.2 DTD as:

```
<!ELEMENT BASE - O EMPTY>
<!ATTLIST BASE
     href %URL  #REQUIRED
     >
```

The BASE element gives the base URL for dereferencing relative URLs, using the rules given by the URL specification, as follows:

```
<BASE href="http://www.acme.com/
    intro.html">
...
<IMG SRC="icons/logo.gif">
```

The image is dereferenced to *http://www.acme.com/icons/logo.gif.*

In the absence of a BASE element, the document URL should be used. Note that this is not necessarily the same as the URL used to request the document, as the base URL may be overridden by an HTTP header accompanying the document.

The META Element

META is described in the HTML 3.2 DTD as:

```
<!ELEMENT META - O EMPTY     --
    Generic Metainformation -->
<!ATTLIST META
        http-equiv  NAME
         #IMPLIED  -- HTTP response
         header name  --
    name        NAME
         #IMPLIED  --
         metainformation name   --
    content     CDATA
         #REQUIRED -- associated
         information     --
        >
```

The META element can be used to include name/value pairs describing properties of the document, such as author, expiry date, a list of key words, etc. The NAME attribute specifies the property name while the CONTENT attribute specifies the property value, as follows:

```
<META NAME="Author" CONTENT="Dave
    Raggett">
```

The HTTP-EQUIV attribute can be used in place of the NAME attribute and has a special significance when documents are retrieved via the Hypertext Transfer Protocol (HTTP). HTTP servers may use the property name specified by the HTTP-EQUIV attribute to create an RFC 822 style header in the HTTP response. This can't be used to set certain HTTP headers though. See the HTTP specification for details. The following:

```
<META HTTP-EQUIV="Expires"
    CONTENT="Tue, 20 Aug 1996
    14:25:27 GMT">
```

will result in the HTTP header:

```
Expires: Tue, 20 Aug 1996 14:25:27
    GMT
```

This can be used by caches to determine when to fetch a fresh copy of the associated document.

The LINK Element

LINK provides a media-independent method for defining relationships with other documents and resources. LINK has been part of HTML since the very early days although few browsers as yet take advantage of it (most still ignore LINK elements).

LINK elements (see Example 1) can be used in principle:

- For document-specific navigation toolbars/menus when used with the LINK element in a document head.

- To control how collections of HTML nodes are rendered into printed documents.

href

Specifies a URL designating the linked resource.

rel

> The forward relationship also known as the "link type."

rev

> This defines a reverse relationship. A link from document A to document B with `rev=relation` expresses the same relationship as a link from B to A with `rel=relation`. `rev=made` is sometimes used to identify the document author—either the author's email address with a *mailto* URL or a link to the author's home page.

title

> An advisory title for the linked resource.

See Internet Draft *draft-ietf-html-relrev-00.txt* for information on proposed relationship values. Some of the more common are:

`rel=contents`

> The link references a document serving as a table of contents.

`rel=index`

> The link references a document providing an index for the current document.

`rel=glossary`

> The link references a document providing a glossary of terms that pertain to the current document.

`rel=copyright`

> The link references a copyright statement for the current document.

`rel=next`

> The link references the next document to visit in a guided tour.

`rel=previous`

> The link references the previous document in a guided tour.

`rel=help`

> The link references a document offering help—e.g., describing the wider context and offering further links to relevant documents. This is aimed at reorienting users who have lost their way.

`rel=bookmark`

> Bookmarks are used to provide direct links to key entry points into an extended document. The **title** attribute may be used to label the bookmark. Several bookmarks may be defined in each document and provide a means for orienting users in extended documents.

Example LINK elements:

```
<LINK REL=Contents HREF-toc.html>
<LINK REL=Previous HREF=doc31.html>
<LINK REL=Next HREF=doc33.html>
```

The BODY Element

This contains the document body. Both start and end tags for BODY may be omitted. The body can contain a wide range of elements:

- Headings (H1–H6)
- The ADDRESS element
- Block-level elements
- Text-level elements

Example 1

```
<!ELEMENT LINK - O EMPTY>
<!ATTLIST LINK
        href    %URL    #IMPLIED    -- URL for linked resource --
        rel     CDATA   #IMPLIED    -- forward link types --
        rev     CDATA   #IMPLIED    -- reverse link types --
        title   CDATA   #IMPLIED    -- advisory title string --
        >
```

Example 2

```
<!ENTITY % body.content "(%heading | %text | %block | ADDRESS)*">

<!ENTITY % color "CDATA" -- a color specification: #HHHHHH @@ details? -->

<!ENTITY % body-color-attrs "
        bgcolor %color #IMPLIED
        text %color #IMPLIED
        link %color #IMPLIED
        vlink %color #IMPLIED
        alink %color #IMPLIED
        ">

<!ELEMENT BODY O O  %body.content>
<!ATTLIST BODY
        background %URL #IMPLIED  -- texture tile for document background --
        %body-color-attrs;  -- bgcolor, text, link, vlink, alink --
        >
```

The key attributes are **background, bgcolor, text, link, vlink,** and **alink**. These can be used to set a repeating background image, plus background and foreground colors for normal text and hypertext links. Example 2 illustrates the use of these attributes.

Example:

```
<body bgcolor=white text=black
    link=red vlink=maroon
    alink=fuschia>
```

bgcolor

Specifies the background color for the document body. See below for the syntax of color values.

text

Specifies the color used to stroke the document's text. This is generally used when you have changed the background color with the **bgcolor** or **background** attributes.

link

Specifies the color used to stroke the text for unvisited hypertext links.

vlink

Specifies the color used to stroke the text for visited hypertext links.

alink

Specifies the highlight color used to stroke the text for hypertext links at the moment the user clicks on the link.

background

Specifies a URL for an image that will be used to tile the document background.

Colors are given in the sRGB color space as hexadecimal numbers (e.g., `color="#C0FFC0"`) or as one of 16 widely understood color names. These colors were originally picked as being the standard 16 colors supported with the Windows VGA palette and are listed in Table 1.

Block- and Text-Level Elements

Most elements that can appear in the document body fall into one of two groups: block-level elements that cause paragraph breaks and text-level elements that don't. Common block-level elements include H1 to H6 (headers), P (paragraphs), LI (list items), and HR (horizontal rules). Common text-level elements include EM, I, B and FONT (character emphasis), A (hypertext links), IMG and APPLET (embedded objects), and BR (line breaks). Note that block elements generally act as containers for text-level and other block-level elements (excluding headings and address

Table 1   Color Names and sRGB Values

Black = "#000000"	Green = "#008000"
Silver = "#C0C0C0"	Lime = "#00FF00"
Gray = "#808080"	Olive = "#808000"
White = "#FFFFFF"	Yellow = "#FFFF00"
Maroon = "#800000"	Navy = "#000080"
Red = "#FF0000"	Blue = "#0000FF"
Purple = "#800080"	Teal = "#008080"
Fuchsia = "#FF00FF"	Aqua = "#00FFFF"

elements), while text-level elements can only contain other text-level elements. The exact model depends on the element.

Headings

Headings are described in the HTML 3.2 DTD as:

```
<!--
   There are six levels of headers
   from H1 (the most important)
   to H6 (the least important).
-->

<!ELEMENT ( %heading )   - -
   (%text;)*>
<!ATTLIST ( %heading )
      align  (left|center|right)
      #IMPLIED
      >
```

H1, H2, H3, H4, H5, and H6 are used for document headings. You always need the start and end tags. H1 elements are more important than H2 elements and so on, so that H6 elements define the least important level of headings. More important headings are generally rendered in a larger font than less important ones. Use the optional ALIGN attribute to set the text alignment within a heading, as follows:

```
<H1 ALIGN=CENTER> <i>... centered
   heading ...</i> </H1>
```

The default is left alignment, but this can be over-ridden by an enclosing DIV or CENTER element.

ADDRESS

ADDRESS is described in the HTML 3.2 DTD as:

```
<!ENTITY % address.content
"((%text;) | P)*">

<!ELEMENT ADDRESS - - %address.
content>
```

The ADDRESS element requires start and end tags and specifies information such as authorship and contact details for the current document. User agents should render the content with paragraph breaks before and after. Note that the content is restricted to paragraphs, plain text, and text-like elements as defined by the **%text** entity.

Example:

```
<ADDRESS>
Newsletter editor<BR>
J.R. Brown<BR>
8723 Buena Vista, Smallville, CT
   01234&t;BR>
Tel: +1 (123) 456 7890
</ADDRESS>
```

Block Elements

P (paragraphs)
  The paragraph element requires a start tag, but the end tag can always be omitted. Use the **align** attribute to set the text alignment within a paragraph—e.g., <P ALIGN=RIGHT>.

UL (unordered lists)
  Requires start and end tags and contains one or more LI elements representing individual list items.

OL (ordered [i.e., numbered] lists)

Requires start and end tags and contains one or more LI elements representing individual list items.

DL (definition lists)

Requires start and end tags. It contains DT elements that give the terms and DD elements that give corresponding definitions.

PRE (preformatted text)

Requires start and end tags. These elements are rendered with a monospaced font and preserve layout defined by whitespace and line break characters.

DIV (document divisions)

Requires start and end tags. It is used with the **align** attribute to set the text alignment of the block elements it contains. **align** can be one of **left**, **center**, or **right**.

CENTER (text alignment)

Requires start and end tags. It is used to center text lines enclosed by the CENTER element. See DIV for a more general solution.

BLOCKQUOTE (quoted passage)

Requires start and end tags. It is used to enclose extended quotations and is typically rendered with indented margins.

FORM (fill-out forms)

Requires start and end tags. This element is used to define a fill-out form for processing by HTTP servers. The attributes are **action**, **method**, and **enctype**. Form elements can't be nested.

ISINDEX (primitive HTML forms)

Not a container, so the end tag is forbidden. This predates FORM and is used for simple kinds of forms that have a single text input field, implied by this element. A single ISINDEX can appear in the document head or body.

HR (horizontal rules)

Not a container, so the end tag is forbidden. Attributes are **align**, **noshade**, **size**, and **width**.

TABLE (can be nested)

Requires start and end tags. Each table starts with an optional CAPTION followed by one or more TR elements defining table rows. Each row has one or more cells defined by TH or TD elements. Attributes for TABLE elements are **width**, **border**, **cellspacing**, and **cellpadding**.

Paragraphs

The P element is described in the HTML 3.2 DTD as:

```
<!ELEMENT P      - O (%text)*>
<!ATTLIST P
    align  (left|center|right)
     #IMPLIED
      >
```

The P element is used to mark up paragraphs. It is a container and requires a start tag. The end tag is optional as it can always be inferred by the parser. User agents should place paragraph breaks before and after P elements. The rendering is user agent dependent, but text is generally wrapped to fit the space available.

Example:

```
<P>This is the first paragraph.
<P>This is the second paragraph.
```

Paragraphs are usually rendered flush left with a ragged right margin. The **align** attribute can be used to explicitly specify the horizontal alignment:

align=left

The paragraph is rendered flush left.

align=center

The paragraph is centered.

align=right

The paragraph is rendered flush right.

For example:

```
<p align=center>This is a centered
    paragraph.
<p align=right>and this is a flush
    right paragraph.
```

The default is left alignment, but this can be overridden by an enclosing DIV or CENTER element.

Lists

List items can contain block- and text-level items, including nested lists, although headings and address elements are excluded. This limitation is defined via the %flow entity.

Unordered Lists

Unordered lists are described in the HTML 3.2 DTD as shown in Example 3.

Unordered lists take the form:

```
<UL>
  <LI> <i>... first list item</i>
  <LI> <i>... second list item</i>
  ...
</UL>
```

The UL element is used for unordered lists. Both start and end tags are always needed. The LI element is used for individual list items. The end tag for LI elements can always be omitted. Note that LI elements can contain nested lists. The **compact** attribute can be used as a hint to the user agent to render lists in a more compact style.

The **type** attribute can be used to set the bullet style on UL and LI elements. The permitted values are disc, square, or circle. The default generally depends on the level of nesting for lists.

- With `<li type=disc>`

□ With `<li type=square>`

o With `<li type=circle>`

NOTE

This list was chosen to cater for the original bullet shapes used by Mosaic in 1993.

Ordered Lists (Numbered Lists)

Ordered lists are described in the HTML 3.2 DTD as shown in Example 4.

Ordered (numbered) lists take the form:

```
<OL>
  <LI> <i>... first list item</i>
  <LI> <i>... second list item</i>
  ...
</OL>
```

The **ol start** attribute can be used to initialize the sequence number (by default it is initialized to 1). You can set it later on with the **value** attribute on LI elements. Both of these attributes expect inte

Example 3

```
<!ELEMENT UL - -  (LI)+>
   <!ENTITY % ULStyle "disc|square|circle">

   <!ATTLIST UL -- unordered lists --
       type    (%ULStyle)    #IMPLIED    -- bullet style --
       compact (compact)     #IMPLIED    -- reduced interitem spacing --
       >

   <!ELEMENT LI - O %flow -- list item -->
   <!ATTLIST LI
       type    (%LIStyle)    #IMPLIED    -- list item style --
       >
```

Example 4

```
<!ELEMENT OL - -  (LI)+>
   <!ATTLIST OL -- ordered lists --
       type        CDATA       #IMPLIED    -- numbering style --
       start       NUMBER      #IMPLIED    -- starting sequence number --
       compact     (compact)   #IMPLIED    -- reduced interitem spacing --
       >

   <!ELEMENT LI - O %flow -- list item -->
   <!ATTLIST LI
       type        CDATA       #IMPLIED    -- list item style --
       value       NUMBER      #IMPLIED    -- set sequence number --
       >
```

ger values. You can't indicate that numbering should be continued from a previous list or toskip missing values without giving an explicit number.

The **compact** attribute can be used as a hint to the user agent to render lists in a more compact style. The **ol type** attribute allows you to set the numbering style for list items. Table 2 lists the various numbering styles.

Definition Lists

Definition lists are described in the HTML 3.2 DTD as shown in Example 5.

Definition lists take the form:

```
<DL>
  <DT> <i>term name</i>
  <DD> <i>term definition</i>
  . . .
</DL>
```

DT elements can act as containers only for text-level elements, while DD elements can hold block-level elements as well, excluding headings and address elements.

For example:

```
<DL>
<DT>Term 1<dd>This is the
        definition of the first term.
<DT>Term 2<dd>This is the
        definition of the second term.
</DL>
```

which could be rendered as:

Term 1

    This is the definition of the first term.

Term 2

    This is the definition of the second term.

The **compact** attribute can be used with the DL element as a hint to the user agent to render lists in a more compact style.

Table 2   Numbering Styles for Ordered Lists

Type	Numbering Style	
1	Arabic numbers	1, 2, 3, . . .
a	Lower alpha	a, b, c, . . .
A	Upper alpha	A, B, C, . . .
i	Lower roman	i, ii, iii, . . .
I	Upper roman	I, II, III, . . .

Example 5

```
<!-- definition lists - DT for term, DD for its definition -->

<!ELEMENT DL      - -  (DT|DD)+>
<!ATTLIST DL
        compact (compact) #IMPLIED -- more compact style --
        >

<!ELEMENT DT - O  (%text)*>
<!ELEMENT DD - O  %flow;>
```

DIR and MENU

DIR and MENU are described in the HTML 3.2 DTD as:

```
<!ELEMENT (DIR|MENU) - -  (LI)+ -
    (%block)>
<!ATTLIST (DIR|MENU)
            compact (compact) #IMPLIED
            >
```

These elements have been part of HTML from the early days. They are intended for unordered lists similar to UL elements. User agents are recommended to render DIR elements as multicolumn directory lists, and MENU elements as single column menu lists. In practice, Mosaic and most other user agents ignored this advice and instead rendered DIR and MENU in an identical way to UL elements.

Preformatted text

Preformatted text is described in the HTML 3.2 DTD as:

```
<!ELEMENT PRE - -  (%text)* -(%pre.
    exclusion)>
<!ATTLIST PRE
            width NUMBER #implied
            >
```

The PRE element can be used to include preformatted text. User agents render this in a fixed pitch font, preserving spacing associated with whitespace characters, such as space and newline characters. Automatic word wrap should be disabled within PRE elements.

Note that the SGML standard requires that the parser remove a newline immediately following the start tag or immediately preceding the end tag.

PRE has the same content model as paragraphs, excluding images and elements that produce changes in font size—e.g., IMG, BIG, SMALL, SUB, SUP, and FONT.

A few user agents support the **width** attribute. It provides a hint to the user agent of the required width in characters. The user agent can use this to select an appropriate font size or to indent the content appropriately.

Here is an example of a PRE element—a verse from Shelley ("To a Skylark"):

```
<PRE>
Higher still and higher
    From the earth thou springest
Like a cloud of fire;
    The blue deep thou wingest,
And singing still dost soar, and
    soaring ever singest.
</PRE>
```

which is rendered as:

```
Higher still and higher
    From the earth thou springest
Like a cloud of fire;
    The blue deep thou wingest,
And singing still dost soar, and
    soaring ever singest.
```

The horizontal tab character (encoded in Unicode, US ASCII, and ISO 8859-1 as decimal 9) should be interpreted as the smallest non-zero number of spaces that will leave the number of characters so far on the line as a multiple of 8. Its use is strongly discouraged since it is common practice when editing to set the tab spacing to other values, leading to misaligned documents.

XMP, LISTING, and PLAINTEXT

XMP, LISTING, and PLAINTEXT are described in the HTML 3.2 DTD as shown in Example 6.

These are obsolete tags for preformatted text that predate the introduction of PRE. User agents may support these for backwards compatibility. Authors should avoid using them in new documents!

DIV and CENTER

DIV and CENTER are described in the HTML 3.2 DTD as:

```
<!ELEMENT DIV - - %body.content>
<!ATTLIST DIV
        align   (left|center|right)
    #IMPLIED -- alignment of
    following text --
        >

<!-- CENTER is a shorthand for DIV
    with ALIGN=CENTER -->
<!ELEMENT center - - %body.content>
```

DIV elements can be used to structure HTML documents as a hierarchy of divisions. The **align** attribute can be used to set the default horizontal alignment for elements within the content of the DIV element. Its value is restricted to left, center, or right and is defined in the same way as for the paragraph element <P>.

Note that because DIV is a block-like element, it will terminate an open P element. Other than this, user agents are *not* expected to render paragraph breaks before and after DIV elements. CENTER is directly equivalent to DIV with `align=center`. Both DIV and CENTER require start and end tags.

NOTE

CENTER was introduced by Netscape before they added support for the HTML 3.0 DIV element. It is retained in HTML 3.2 on account of its widespread deployment.

BLOCKQUOTE

BLOCKQUOTE is described in the HTML 3.2 DTD as:

```
<!ELEMENT BLOCKQUOTE - - %body.
    content>
```

This is used to enclose block quotations from other works. Both the start and end tags are required. It is often rendered indented, as follows:

They went in single file, running like hounds on a strong scent, and an eager light was in their eyes. Nearly due west the broad swath of the marching Orcs tramped its ugly slot; the sweet grass of Rohan had been bruised and blackened as they passed.

—from The Two Towers
by J.R.R. Tolkien

Example 6

```
<![ %HTML.Deprecated [

<!ENTITY % literal "CDATA"
        -- historical, non-conforming parsing mode where
           the only markup signal is the end tag
           in full
        -->

<!ELEMENT (XMP|LISTING) - -  %literal>
<!ELEMENT PLAINTEXT - O %literal>

]]>
```

FORM

FORM is described in the HTML 3.2 DTD as shown in Example 7.

This is used to define an HTML form, and you can have more than one form in the same document. Both the start and end tags are required. For very simple forms, you can also use the ISINDEX element. Forms can contain a wide range of HTML markup including several kinds of form fields such as single and multi-line text fields, radio button groups, checkboxes, and menus.

action

> This specifies a URL that will be used to invoke a server-side forms handler. This is either an HTTP server or a *mailto* URL. The latter allows you to post forms via email— e.g., `action="mailto:foo@bar.com"`.

method

> When the **action** attribute specifies an HTTP server, the **method** attribute determines which HTTP method will be used to send the form's contents to the server. It can be either GET or POST and defaults to GET.

enctype

> This determines the mechanism used to encode the form's contents. It defaults to *application/x-www-form-urlencoded.*

Further details on handling forms are given in RFC 1867.

HR

Horizontal rules may be used to indicate a change in topic. In a speech-based user agent, the rule could be rendered as a pause.

```
<!ELEMENT HR       - O EMPTY>
<!ATTLIST HR
        align (left|right|center)
  #IMPLIED
        noshade (noshade) #IMPLIED
        size  %Pixels #IMPLIED
        width %Length #IMPLIED
        >
```

HR elements are not containers, so the end tag is forbidden. The attributes are **align**, **noshade**, **size**, and **width**.

align

> This determines whether the rule is placed at the left, center, or right of the space between the current left and right margins for `align=left`, `align=center`, or `align= right`, respectively. By default, the rule is centered.

noshade

> This attribute requests the user agent to render the rule in a solid color rather than as the traditional two color "groove."

size

> This can be used to set the height of the rule in pixels.

width

> This can be used to set the width of the rule in pixels (e.g., `width=100`) or as the percentage between the current left and right margins (e.g., `width="50%"`). The default is 100 percent .

Example 7

```
<!ENTITY % HTTP-Method "GET | POST"
       -- as per HTTP specification
       -->

<!ELEMENT FORM - - %body.content -(FORM)>
<!ATTLIST FORM
        action %URL #IMPLIED  -- server-side form handler --
        method (%HTTP-Method) GET -- see HTTP specification --
        enctype %Content-Type; "application/x-www-form-urlencoded"
        >
```

Tables

HTML 3.2 includes a widely deployed subset of the specification given in RFC 1942 and can be used to mark up tabular material or for layout purposes. Note that the latter role typically causes problems when rendering to speech or to text only user agents (see Example 8).

Example 8

```
<!-- horizontal placement of table relative to window -->
<!ENTITY % Where "(left|center|right)">

<!-- horizontal alignment attributes for cell contents -->
<!ENTITY % cell.halign
        "align  (left|center|right) #IMPLIED"
        >

<!-- vertical alignment attributes for cell contents -->
<!ENTITY % cell.valign
        "valign  (top|middle|bottom|baseline)  #IMPLIED"
        >

<!ELEMENT table - - (caption?, tr+)>
<!ELEMENT tr - O (th|td)*>
<!ELEMENT (th|td) - O %body.content>

<!ATTLIST table                         -- table element --
        align     %Where;    #IMPLIED   -- table position relative to window --
        width     %Length    #IMPLIED   -- table width relative to window --
        border    %Pixels    #IMPLIED   -- controls frame width around table --
        cellspacing %Pixels  #IMPLIED   -- spacing between cells --
        cellpadding %Pixels  #IMPLIED   -- spacing within cells --
        >

<!ELEMENT CAPTION - - (%text;)* -- table or figure caption -->
<!ATTLIST CAPTION
        align (top|bottom) #IMPLIED
        >

<!ATTLIST tr                            -- table row --
        %cell.halign;                   -- horizontal alignment in cells --
        %cell.valign;                   -- vertical alignment in cells --
        >

<!ATTLIST (th|td)                       -- header or data cell --
        nowrap (nowrap)   #IMPLIED      -- suppress word wrap --
        rowspan NUMBER    1             -- number of rows spanned by cell --
        colspan NUMBER    1             -- number of cols spanned by cell --
        %cell.halign;                   -- horizontal alignment in cells --
        %cell.valign;                   -- vertical alignment in cells --
        width    %Pixels  #IMPLIED      -- suggested width for cell --
        height   %Pixels  #IMPLIED      -- suggested height for cell --
        >
```

Tables take the general form:

```
<TABLE BORDER=3 CELLSPACING=2
    CELLPADDING=2 WIDTH="80%">
<CAPTION><i> ... table caption ...</
    i> </CAPTION>
<TR><TD> <i>first cell</i> <TD>
    <i>second cell</i>
<TR> ...
...
</TABLE>
```

The attributes for TABLE are all optional. By default, the table is rendered without a surrounding border. The table is generally sized automatically to fit the contents, but you can also set the table width using the **width** attribute. **border, cellspacing**, and **cellpadding** provide further control over the table's appearence. Captions are rendered at the top or bottom of the table depending on the **align** attribute.

Each table row is contained in a TR element, although the end tag can always be omitted. Table cells are defined by TD elements for data and TH elements for headers. Like TR, these are containers and can be given without trailing end tags. TH and TD support several attributes: **align** and **valign** for aligning cell content, **rowspan** and **colspan** for cells that span more than one row or column. A cell can contain a wide variety of other block- and text-level elements including form fields and other tables.

The TABLE element always requires both start and end tags. It supports the following attributes:

align

This takes one of the case-insensitive values: LEFT, CENTER, or RIGHT. It specifies the horizontal placement of the table relative to the current left and right margins. It defaults to left alignment, but this can be overridden by an enclosing DIV or CENTER element.

width

In the absence of this attribute, the table width is automatically determined from the table contents. You can use the **width** attribute to set the table width to a fixed value in pixels (e.g., `width=212`) or as a per-

centage of the space between the current left and right margins (e.g., `width="80%"`).

border

This attribute can be used to specify the width of the outer border around the table to a given number of pixels (e.g., `border=4`). The value can be set to zero to suppress the border altogether. In the absence of this attribute, the border should be suppressed. Note that some browsers also accept `<TABLE BORDER>` with the same semantics as `border=1`.

cellspacing

In traditional desktop publishing software, adjacent table cells share a common border. This is not the case in HTML. Each cell is given its own border that is separated from the borders around neighboring cells. This separation can be set in pixels using the **cellspacing** attribute, (e.g., `cellspacing=10`). The same value also determines the separation between the table border and the borders of the outermost cells.

cellpadding

This sets the padding in pixels between the border around each cell and the cell's contents.

Note that pixel values refer to screen pixels and should be multiplied by an appropriate factor when rendering to very high resolution devices such as laser printers. For instance, if a user agent has a display with 75 pixels per inch and is rendering to a laser printer with 600 dots per inch, the pixel values given in HTML attributes should be multiplied by a factor of 8.

A common approach, introduced by Netscape, renders tables in bas-relief, raised up with the outer border as a bevel, and individual cells inset into this raised surface. Borders around individual cells are drawn only if the cell has explicit content. Whitespace doesn't count for this purpose with the exception of ` `.

The CAPTION element has one attribute, **align**, which can be either `align=top` or `align=bottom`. This can be used to force the caption to be placed above the top or below the bottom of the table, respectively. Most user agents default to placing the caption above the table. CAPTION always requires both start and end tags. Captions are limited to plain text and text-level elements as defined by the `%text` entity. Block-level elements are not permitted.

The TR or table row element requires a start tag, but the end tag can always be left out. TR acts as a container for table cells. It has two attributes:

align

Sets the default horizontal alignment of cell contents. It takes one of the case-insensitive values—LEFT, CENTER, or RIGHT—and plays the same role as the **align** attribute on paragraph elements.

valign

This can be used to set the default vertical alignment of cell contents within each cell. It takes one of the case-insensitive values—TOP, MIDDLE, or BOTTOM—to position the cell contents at the top, middle, or bottom of the cell, respectively.

Two elements define table cells: TH is used for header cells, and TD for data cells. This distinction allows user agents to render header and data cells in different fonts and enables speech-based browsers to do a better job. The start tags for TH and TD are always needed, but the end tags can be left out. Table cells can have the following attributes:

nowrap

The presence of this attribute disables automatic word wrap within the contents of this cell (e.g., `<TD NOWRAP>`). This is equivalent to using the `&ampnbsp;` entity for non-breaking spaces within the content of the cell.

rowspan

This takes a positive integer value specifying the number of rows spanned by this cell. It defaults to one.

colspan

This takes a positive integer value specifying the number of columns spanned by this cell. It defaults to one.

align

Specifies the default horizontal alignment of cell contents and overrides the **align** attribute on the table row. It takes the same values—LEFT, CENTER, and RIGHT. If you don't specify an **align** attribute value on the cell, the default is left alignment for `<td>` and center alignment for `<th>`, although you can override this with an **align** attribute on the TR element.

valign

Specifies the default vertical alignment of cell contents, overriding the **valign** attribute on the table row. It takes the same values—TOP, MIDDLE, and BOTTOM. If you don't specify a **valign** attribute value on the cell, the default is MIDDLE, although you can override this with a **valign** attribute on the TR element.

width

Specifies the suggested width for cell content in pixels excluding the cell padding. This value will normally be used except when it conflicts with the width requirements for other cells in the same column.

height

Specifies the suggested height for cell content in pixels excluding the cell padding. This value will normally be used except when it conflicts with the height requirements for other cells in the same row.

The algorithms used to automatically size tables should take into account the minimum and maximum width requirements for each cell. This is used to determine the minimum and maximum width requirements for each column and hence for the table itself.

Cells spanning more than one column contribute to the widths of each of the columns spanned. One approach is to evenly apportion the cell's minimum and maximum width between these columns; another is to weight the apportioning according to the contributions from cells that don't span multiple columns.

For some user agents, it may be necessary or desirable to break text lines within words. In such cases, a visual indication that this has occurred is advised.

The minimum and maximum width of nested tables contribute to the minimum and maximum width of the cell in which they occur. Once the width requirements are known for the top-level table, the column widths for that table can be assigned. This allows the widths of nested tables to be assigned and, hence in turn, the column widths of such tables. If practical, all columns should be assigned at least their minimum widths. It is suggested that any surplus space is then shared out proportional to the difference between the minimum and maximum width requirements of each column.

Note that pixel values for width and height refer to screen pixels and should be multiplied by an appropriate factor when rendering to very high resolution devices such as laser printers. For instance, if a user agent has a display with 75 pixels per inch and is rendering to a laser printer with 600 dots per inch, the pixel values given in HTML attributes should be multiplied by a factor of 8.

Text-Level Elements

These don't cause paragraph breaks. Text-level elements that define character styles can generally be nested. They can contain other text-level elements, such as those in the following list, but not block-level elements.

- Font-style elements

- Phrase elements
- Form fields
- The A (anchor) element
- IMG—inline images
- APPLET (Java applets)
- FONT elements
- BASEFONT elements
- BR—line breaks
- MAP—client-side image maps

Font-Style Elements

These all require start and end tags, as follows:

```
This has some <B>bold text</B>.
```

Text-level elements must be properly nested. The following example is in error.

```
This has some <B>bold and <I>
    </B>italic text</I>.
```

User agents should do their best to respect nested emphasis, as follows:

```
This has some <B>bold and <I>italic
    text</I></B>.
```

Where the available fonts are restricted or for speech output, alternative means should be used for rendering differences in emphasis.

TT
 Teletype or monospaced text

I

 Italic text style

B

 Bold text style

U

 Underlined text style

STRIKE
 Strike-through text style

BIG
 Places text in a large font

SMALL

> Places text in a small font

SUB

> Places text in subscript style

SUP

> Places text in superscript style

NOTE

STRIKE may be phased out in favor of the more concise *S* tag from HTML 3.0.

Phrase Elements

These all require start and end tags, as follows:

```
This has some <EM>emphasized
    text</EM>.
```

EM

> Basic emphasis typically rendered in an italic font

STRONG

> Strong emphasis typically rendered in a bold font

DFN

> Defining instance of the enclosed term

CODE

> Used for extracts from program code

SAMP

> Used for sample output from programs, scripts, etc.

KBD

> Used for text to be typed by the user

VAR

> Used for variables or arguments to commands

CITE

> Used for citations or references to other sources

Form Fields

INPUT, SELECT, and TEXTAREA are only allowed within FORM elements. INPUT can be used for a variety of form fields including single line text fields, password fields, checkboxes, radio buttons, submit and reset buttons, hidden fields, file upload, and image buttons. SELECT elements are used for single or multiple choice menus. TEXTAREA elements are used to define multi-line text fields. The content of the element is used to initialize the field.

INPUT (Text Fields, Radio Buttons, Checkboxes, etc.)

INPUT elements are not containers, so the end tag is forbidden (see Example 9).

Example 9

```
<!ENTITY % InputType
        "(TEXT | PASSWORD | CHECKBOX | RADIO | SUBMIT
          | RESET | FILE | HIDDEN | IMAGE)">

<!ELEMENT INPUT - O EMPTY>
<!ATTLIST INPUT
          type %InputType TEXT    -- what kind of widget is needed --
          name  CDATA #IMPLIED    -- required for all but submit and reset --
          value CDATA #IMPLIED    -- required for radio and checkboxes --
          checked (checked) #IMPLIED -- for radio buttons and checkboxes --
          size CDATA  #IMPLIED    -- specific to each type of field --
          maxlength NUMBER #IMPLIED
          src   %URL #IMPLIED     -- for fields with background images --
          align  (top|middle|bottom|left|right) top -- image alignment --
          >
```

type

Used to set the type of input field:

type=text (the default)

A single line text field whose visible size can be set using the **size** attribute—e.g., `size=40` for a 40-character wide field. Users should be able to type more than this limit though with the text scrolling through the field to keep the input cursor in view. You can enforce an upper limit on the number of characters that can be entered with the **maxlength** attribute. The **name** attribute is used to name the field, while the **value** attribute can be used to initialize the text string shown in the field when the document is first loaded.

```
<input type=text size=40
       name=user value="your
       name">
```

type=password

This is like **type=text** but echoes characters using a character like * to hide the text from prying eyes when entering passwords. You can use **size** and **maxlength** attributes to control the visible and maximum length exactly as per regular text fields.

```
<input type=password size=12
       name=pw>
```

type=checkbox

Used for simple Boolean attributes or for attributes that can take multiple values at the same time. The latter is represented by several checkbox fields with the same **name** and a different **value** attribute. Each checked checkbox generates a separate name/value pair in the submitted data, even if this results in duplicate names. Use the **checked** attribute to initialize the checkbox to its checked state.

```
<input type=checkbox checked
       name=uscitizen value=yes>
```

type=radio

Used for attributes that can take a single value from a set of alternatives. Each radio button field in the group should be given the same name. Radio buttons require an explicit **value** attribute. Only the checked radio button in the group generates a name/value pair in the submitted data. One radio button in each group should be initially checked using the **checked** attribute.

```
<input type=radio name=age
       value="0-12">
<input type=radio name=age
       value="13-17">
<input type=radio name=age
       value="18-25">
<input type=radio name=age
       value="26-35" checked>
<input type=radio name=age
       value="36-">
```

type=submit

This defines a button that users can click to submit the form's contents to the server. The button's label is set from the **value** attribute. If the **name** attribute is given, the Submit button's name/value pair will be included in the submitted data. You can include several submit buttons in the form. See **type=image** for graphical Submit buttons.

```
<input type=submit value="Party
       on ...">
```

type=image

This is used for graphical Submit buttons rendered by an image rather than a text string. The URL for the image is specified with the **src** attribute. The image alignment can be specified with the **align** attribute. In this respect, graphical Submit buttons are treated identically to IMG elements, so you can set align to left, right, top, middle, or bottom. The **name** and **value** attributes are treated the same as for textual Submit buttons and should be provided for the benefit of nongraphical user agents.

```
<input type=image src=partyon.
    gif value="Party on ...">
```

type=reset

This defines a button that users can click to reset form fields to their initial state when the document was first loaded. You can set the label by providing a **value** attribute. Reset buttons are never sent as part of the form's contents.

```
<input type=reset value="Start
    over ...">
```

type=file

This provides a means for users to attach a file to the form's contents. It is generally rendered by text field and an associated button that when clicked invokes a file browser to select a filename. The filename can also be entered Just like **type=text** you can use the **size** attribute to set the visible width of this field in average character widths. You can set an upper limit to the length of filenames using the **maxlength** attribute. Some user agents support the ability to restrict the kinds of files that can be attached to ones matching a comma-separated list of MIME content types given with the **accept** attribute—e.g., **accept="image/*"** restricts files to images. Further information can be found in RFC 1867.

```
<input type=file name=photo
    size=20 accept="image/*">
```

type=hidden

These fields should not be rendered and provide a means for servers to store state information with a form. This will be passed back to the server when the form is submitted, using the name/value pair defined by the corresponding attributes. This is a workaround for the

statefulness of HTTP. Another approach is to use Cookies.

```
<input type=hidden
    name=customerid
    value="c2415-345-8563">
```

name

Used to define the property name that will be used to identify this field's content when it is submitted to the server.

value

Used to initialize the field or to provide a textual label for Submit and Reset buttons.

checked

The presence of this attribute is used to initialize checkboxes and radio buttons to their checked state.

size

Used to set the visible size of text fields to a given number of average character widths—e.g., **size=20**.

maxlength

Sets the maximum number of characters permitted in a text field.

src

Specifies a URL for the image to use with a graphical Submit button.

align

Used to specify image alignment for graphical submit buttons. It is defined just like the IMG **align** attribute and takes one of the values TOP, MIDDLE, BOTTOM, LEFT, or RIGHT, defaulting to BOTTOM.

SELECT (Menus)

SELECT is described in the HTML 3.2 DTD as:

```
<!ELEMENT SELECT - - (OPTION+)>
<!ATTLIST SELECT
    name CDATA #REQUIRED
    size NUMBER #IMPLIED
    multiple (multiple) #IMPLIED
    >

<!ELEMENT OPTION - O (#PCDATA)*>
```

```
<!ATTLIST OPTION
      selected (selected) #IMPLIED
      value   CDATA   #IMPLIED --
      defaults to element content --
      >
```

SELECT is used to define select one from many or many from many menus. SELECT elements require start and end tags and contain one or more OPTION elements that define menu items. One from many menus are generally rendered as drop-down menus while many from many menus are generally shown as list boxes.

Example:

```
<SELECT NAME="flavor">
<OPTION VALUE=a>Vanilla
<OPTION VALUE=b>Strawberry
<OPTION VALUE=c>Rum and Raisin
<OPTION VALUE=d>Peach and Orange
</SELECT>
```

SELECT attributes:

name

Specifies a property name that is used to identify the menu choice when the form is submitted to the server. Each selected option results in a property name/value pair being included as part of the form's contents.

size

Sets the number of visible choices for many from many menus.

multiple

Signifies that the users can make multiple selections. By default only one selection is allowed.

OPTION attributes:

selected

When this attribute is present, the option is selected when the document is initially loaded. It is an error for more than one option to be so selected for one from many menus.

value

Specifies the property value to be used when submitting the form's content. This is com-

bined with the property name as given by the name attribute of the parent SELECT element.

TEXTAREA (Multi-Line Text Fields)

TEXTAREA is described in the HTML 3.2 DTD as:

```
<!-- Multi-line text input field.
     -->

<!ELEMENT TEXTAREA - - (#PCDATA)*>
<!ATTLIST TEXTAREA
          name CDATA #REQUIRED
          rows NUMBER #REQUIRED
          cols NUMBER #REQUIRED
          >
```

TEXTAREA elements require start and end tags. The content of the element is restricted to text and character entities. It is used to initialize the text that is shown when the document is first loaded.

Example:

```
<TEXTAREA NAME=address ROWS=4
    COLS=40&gt;
Your address here ...
</TEXTAREA>
```

It is recommended that user agents canonicalize line endings to CR, LF (ASCII decimal 13, 10) when submitting the field's contents. The character set for submitted data should be ISO Latin-1, unless the server has previously indicated that it can support alternative character sets.

name

Specifies a property name that is used to identify the textarea field when the form is submitted to the server.

rows

Specifies the number of visible text lines. Users should be able to enter more lines that this, so user agents should provide some means to scroll through the contents of the textarea field when the contents extend beyond the visible area.

cols

Specifies the visible width in average character widths. Users should be able to enter longer lines that this, so user agents should provide some means to scroll through the contents of the textarea field when the contents extend beyond the visible area. User agents may wrap visible text lines to keep long lines visible without the need for scrolling.

Special Text-Level Elements

A (anchor), IMG, APPLET, FONT, BASEFONT, BR, and MAP.

The A (anchor) element

The A element is described in the HTML 3.2 DTD as:

```
<!ELEMENT A - - (%text)* -(A)>
<!ATTLIST A
        name      CDATA    #IMPLIED
-- named link end --
        href     %URL      #IMPLIED
-- URL for linked resource --
        rel       CDATA    #IMPLIED
-- forward link types --
        rev       CDATA    #IMPLIED
-- reverse link types --
        title    CDATA     #IMPLIED
-- advisory title string --
        >
```

Anchors can't be nested and always require start and end tags. They are used to define hypertext links and also to define named locations for use as targets for hypertext links, as follows:

```
The way to <a href="hands-on.
html">happiness</a>.
```

Anchors are also used to define named locations for use as targets for hypertext links, as follows:

```
<h2><a name=mit>545 Tech Square -
Hacker s Paradise</a></h2>
```

name

This should be a string defining unique name for the scope of the current HTML document. **name** is used to associate a name

with this part of a document for use with URLs that target a named section of a document.

href

Specifies a URL acting as a network address for the linked resource. This could be another HTML document, a PDF file, an image, etc.

rel

The forward relationship also known as the "link type." It can be used to determine to how deal with the linked resource when printing out a collection of linked resources.

rev

This defines a reverse relationship. A link from document A to document B with **rev=relation** expresses the same relationship as a link from B to A with **rel=relation**. **rev=made** is sometimes used to identify the document author, either the author's email address with a *mailto* URL or a link to the author's home page.

title

An advisory title for the linked resource.

IMG (inline images)

IMG is described in the HTML 3.2 DTD as shown in Example 10.

Used to insert images. IMG is an empty element, and so the end tag is forbidden. Images can be positioned vertically relative to the current text line or floated to the left or right. See BR with the **clear** attribute for control over text flow.

Example:

```
<IMG SRC="canyon.gif" ALT="Grand
Canyon">
```

IMG elements support the following attributes:

src

Required for every IMG element. It specifies a URL for the image resource—for instance, a GIF, JPEG, or PNG image file.

Example 10

```
<!ENTITY % IAlign "(top|middle|bottom|left|right)">

<!ELEMENT IMG    - O EMPTY --  Embedded image -->
<!ATTLIST IMG
          src    %URL     #REQUIRED  -- URL of image to embed --
          alt    CDATA    #IMPLIED   -- for display in place of image --
          align  %IAlign  #IMPLIED   -- vertical or horizontal alignment --
          height %Pixels  #IMPLIED   -- suggested height in pixels --
          width  %Pixels  #IMPLIED   -- suggested width in pixels --
          border %Pixels  #IMPLIED   -- suggested link border width --
          hspace %Pixels  #IMPLIED   -- suggested horizontal gutter --
          vspace %Pixels  #IMPLIED   -- suggested vertical gutter --
          usemap %URL     #IMPLIED   -- use client-side image map --
          ismap  (ismap)  #IMPLIED   -- use server image map --
          >
```

alt

Provides a text description of the image and is vital for interoperability with speech-based and text only user agents.

align

Specifies how the image is positioned relative to the current text line in which it occurs:

`Align=top`

Positions the top of the image with the top of the current text line. User agents vary in how they interpret this. Some take into account only what has occurred on the text line prior to the IMG element and ignore what happens after it.

`Align=middle`

Aligns the middle of the image with the baseline for the current text line.

`Align=bottom`

Is the default and aligns the bottom of the image with the baseline.

`Align=left`

Floats the image to the current left margin, temporarily changing this margin, so that subsequent text is flowed along the image's right-hand side. The rendering depends on whether there is any left-aligned text or images that appear in the markup. Such text (but not images) generally forces left-aligned images to wrap to a new line, with the subsequent text continuing on the former line.

`Align=right`

Floats the image to the current right margin, temporarily changing this margin, so that subsequent text is flowed along the image's left-hand side. The rendering depends on whether there is any right-aligned text or images that appear in the markup. Such text (but not images) generally forces right-aligned images to wrap to a new line, with the subsequent text continuing on the former line.

Note that some browsers (e.g., IE 2.0 and 3.0) introduce spurious spacing with multiple left- or right-aligned images. As a result, authors can't depend on this being the same for browsers from different vendors. See BR for ways to control text flow.

width

Specifies the intended width of the image in pixels. When given together with the height, this allows user agents to reserve screen space for the image before the image data has arrived over the network.

height

Specifies the intended height of the image in pixels. When given together with the width, this allows user agents to reserve screen space for the image before the image data has arrived over the network.

border

When the IMG element appears as part of a hypertext link, the user agent will generally indicate this by drawing a colored border (typically blue) around the image. This attribute can be used to set the width of this border in pixels. Use `border=0` to suppress the border altogether.

hspace

This can be used to provide whitespace to the immediate left and right of the image. The HSPACE attribute sets the width of this whitespace in pixels. By default HSPACE is a small non-zero number.

vspace

This can be used to provide whitespace above and below the image. The **vspace** attribute sets the height of this whitespace in pixels. By default 9.0 pt is a small non-zero number.

usemap

This can be used to give a URL fragment identifier for a client-side image map defined with the MAP element.

ismap

When the IMG element is part of a hypertext link and the user clicks on the image, the **ismap** attribute causes the location to be passed to the server.

Here is an example of how you use **ismap**:

```
<a href="/cgibin/navbar.map"><img
    src=navbar.gif ismap border=0>
    </a>
```

The location clicked is passed to the server as follows. The user agent derives a new URL from the URL specified by the HREF attribute by appending ? the x coordinate , and the y coordinate of the location in pixels. The link is then followed using the new URL. For instance, if the user clicked at at the location x=10, y=27, the derived URL will be: */cgibin/navbar.map?10,27*. It is generally a good idea to suppress the border and use graphical idioms to indicate that the image is clickable.

Note that pixel values refer to screen pixels and should be multiplied by an appropriate factor when rendering to very high resolution devices such as laser printers. For instance, if a user agent has a display with 75 pixels per inch and is rendering to a laser printer with 600 dots per inch, the pixel values given in HTML attributes should be multiplied by a factor of 8.

APPLET (Java Applets)

APPLET is described in the HTML 3.2 DTD as shown in Example 11.

Requires start and end tags. This element is supported by all Java-enabled browsers. It allows you to embed a Java applet into HTML documents. APPLET uses associated PARAM elements to pass parameters to the applet. Following the PARAM elements, the content of APPLET elements should be used to provide an alternative to the applet for user agents that don't support Java. It is restricted to text-level markup as defined by the `%text` entity in the DTD. Java-compatible browsers ignore this extra HTML code. You can use it to show a snapshot of the applet running, with text explaining what the applet does. Other possibilities for this area are a link to a page that is more useful for the Java-ignorant browser or text that taunts the user for not having a Java-compatible browser.

Here is a simple example of a Java applet:

```
<applet code="Bubbles.class"
    width=500 height=500>
Java applet that draws animated
    bubbles.
</applet>
```

Example 11

```
<!ELEMENT APPLET - - (PARAM | %text)*>
<!ATTLIST APPLET
        codebase  %URL      #IMPLIED   -- code base --
        code      CDATA     #REQUIRED  -- class file --
        alt       CDATA     #IMPLIED   -- for display in place of applet --
        name      CDATA     #IMPLIED   -- applet name --
        width     %Pixels   #REQUIRED  -- suggested width in pixels --
        height    %Pixels   #REQUIRED  -- suggested height in pixels --
        align     %IAlign   #IMPLIED   -- vertical or horizontal alignment --
        hspace    %Pixels   #IMPLIED   -- suggested horizontal gutter --
        vspace    %Pixels   #IMPLIED   -- suggested vertical gutter --
        >

<!ELEMENT PARAM - O EMPTY>
<!ATTLIST PARAM
    name     NAME      #REQUIRED   -- The name of the parameter --
    value    CDATA     #IMPLIED    -- The value of the parameter --
    >
```

Here is another one using a PARAM element:

```
<applet code="AudioItem" width=15
  height=15>
<param name=snd value="Hello.
  au|Welcome.au">
Java applet that plays a welcoming
  sound.
</applet>
```

codebase = *codebaseURL*

This optional attribute specifies the base URL of the applet—the directory or folder that contains the applet's code. If this attribute is not specified, the document's URL is used.

code = *appletFile*

This required attribute gives the name of the file that contains the applet's compiled applet subclass. This file is relative to the base URL of the applet. It cannot be absolute.

alt = *alternateText*

This optional attribute specifies any text that should be displayed if the browser understands the APPLET tag but can't run Java applets.

name = *appletInstanceName*

This optional attribute specifies a name for the applet instance, which makes it possible for applets on the same page to find (and communicate with) each other.

width = *pixels*

height = *pixels*

These required attributes give the initial width and height (in pixels) of the applet display area, not counting any windows or dialogs that the applet brings up.

align = *alignment*

This required attribute specifies the alignment of the applet. The possible values of this attribute are the same (and have the same effects) as those for the IMG tag: LEFT, RIGHT, TOP, TEXTTOP, MIDDLE, ABSMIDDLE, BASELINE, BOTTOM, and ABSBOTTOM.

vspace = *pixels*

hspace = *pixels*

These optional attributes specify the number of pixels above and below the applet (**vspace**) and on each side of the applet (**hspace**). They're treated the same way as the IMG tag's **vspace** and **hspace** attributes.

The PARAM element is used to pass named parameters to APPLET:

<PARAM NAME = *appletParameter* **VALUE**

```
        = value>PARAM elements are the
```
only way to specify applet-
specific parameters. Applets
read user-specified values for
parameters with the
`getParameter()` method.

name = *applet parameter name*
value = *parameter value*

SGML character entities such as é, ", and ¹ are expanded before the parameter value is passed to the applet.

FONT

Font is described in the HTML 3.2 DTD as shown in Example 12.

Requires start and end tags. This allows you to change the font size and/or color for the enclosed text. The attributes are **size** and **color**. Font sizes are given in terms of a scalar range defined by the user agent with no direct mapping to point sizes, etc.

size

Sets the font size for the contents of the font element. You can set size to an integer ranging from 1 to 7 for an absolute font size or specify a relative font size with a signed integer value—e.g., `size="+1"` or `size="-2"`. This is mapped to an absolute font size by adding the current base font size as set by the BASEFONT element (see below).

color

Sets the color to stroke the text. Colors are given as RGB in hexadecimal notation or as one of 16 widely understood color names defined as per the **bgcolor** attribute on the BODY element.

NOTE

Some user agents also support a face attribute that accepts a comma-separated list of font names in order of preference. This is used to search for an installed font with the corresponding name.

Figure 1 shows the effects of setting FONT to absolute sizes.

Figure 2 shows the effect of relative font sizes using a base font size of 3.

Figure 3 shows the effect of relative font sizes using a base font size of 6.

BASEFONT

BASEFONT is described in the HTML 3.2 DTD as shown in Example 13.

Example 12

```
<!ELEMENT FONT - - (%text)*      -- local change to font -->
<!ATTLIST FONT
      size     CDATA     #IMPLIED    -- [+]nn e.g. size="+1", size=4 --
      color    CDATA     #IMPLIED    -- #RRGGBB in hex, e.g. red: color="#FF0000" --
      >
```

The following shows the effects of setting font to absolute sizes:

size=1 size=2 size=3 size=4 size=5 size=6 size=7

Figure 1   Setting font to absolute sizes

The following shows the effect of relative font sizes using a base font size of 3:

size=-4 size=-3 size=-2 size=-1 size=+1 **size=+2** size=+3 size=+4

Figure 2   Base font size of 3

Used to set the base font size. BASEFONT is an empty element so the end tag is forbidden. The SIZE attribute is an integer value ranging from 1 to 7. The base font size applies to the normal and preformatted text but not to headings, except where these are modified using the FONT element with a relative font size.

BR

Used to force a line break. This is an empty element so the end tag is forbidden. The **clear** attribute can be used to move down past floating images on either margin. `<BR CLEAR=LEFT>` moves down past floating images on the left margin, `<BR CLEAR=RIGHT>` does the same for floating images on the right margin, while `<BR CLEAR=ALL>` does the same for such images on both left and right margins.

MAP

The MAP element provides a mechanism for client-side image maps. These can be placed in the same document or grouped in a separate document although this isn't yet widely supported. The MAP element requires start and end tags. It contains one or more AREA elements that specify hot zones on the associated image and bind these hot zones to URLs.

MAP is described in the HTML 3.2 DTD as shown in Example 14.

The following shows the effect of relative font sizes using a base font size of 6:

size=-4 size=-3 size=-2 **size=-1** size=+1
size=+2 size=+3 size=+4

Figure 3   Base font size of 6

Example 13

```
<!ELEMENT BASEFONT - O EMPTY    -- base font size (1 to 7)-->
<!ATTLIST BASEFONT
    size    CDATA   #IMPLIED    -- e.g. size=4, defaults to 3--
    >
```

Here is a simple example for a graphical navigational toolbar:

```
<img src="navbar.gif" border=0
   usemap="#map1">

<map name="map1">
 <area href=guide.html alt="Access
   Guide" shape=rect
   coords="0,0,118,28">
 <area href=search.html
   alt="Search" shape=rect
   coords="184,0,276,28">
 <area href=shortcut.html alt="Go"
   shape=rect
   coords="118,0,184,28">
 <area href=top10.html alt="Top
   Ten" shape=rect
   coords="276,0,373,28">
 </map>
```

The MAP element has one attribute **name** that is used to associate a name with a map. This is then used by the **usemap** attribute on the IMG element to reference the map via a URL fragment identifier. Note that the value of the **name** attribute is case sensitive.

The AREA element is an empty element, so the end tag is forbidden. It takes the following attributes: **shape**, **coords**, **href**, **nohref**, and **alt**. The **shape** and **coords** attributes define a region on the image. If the **shape** attribute is omitted, `shape="rect"` is assumed.

```
shape=rect coords="left-x, top-y,
   right-x, bottom-y"
shape=circle coords="center-x,
   center-y, radius"
shape=poly coords="x1,y1, x2,y2,
   x3,y3, . . ."
```

Where x and y are measured in pixels from the left/top of the associated image. If x and y values are given with a percent sign as a suffix, the values should be interpreted as percentages of the image's width and height, respectively. For example:

```
SHAPE=RECT COORDS="0, 0, 50%, 100%"
```

The **href** attribute gives a URL for the target of the hypertext link. The **nohref** attribute is used when you want to define a region that doesn't act as a hot zone. This is useful when you want to cut a hole in an underlying region acting as a hot zone.

If two or more regions overlap, the region defined first in the map definition takes precedence over subsequent regions. This means that AREA elements with **nohref** should generally be placed before ones with the **href** attribute. AREA elements with `shape=default` should be placed last of all; otherwise, none of the other AREA elements will have any effect.

Example 14

```
<!ENTITY % SHAPE "(rect|circle|poly)">
<!ENTITY % COORDS "CDATA" -- comma separated list of numbers -->

<!ELEMENT MAP - - (AREA)+>
<!ATTLIST MAP
    name    CDATA    #IMPLIED
    >

<!ELEMENT AREA - O EMPTY>
<!ATTLIST AREA
    shape    %SHAPE   rect
    coords   %COORDS  #IMPLIED  -- always needed except for shape=default --
    href     %URL     #IMPLIED  -- this region acts as hypertext link --
    nohref   (nohref) #IMPLIED  -- this region has no action --
    alt      CDATA    #REQUIRED
    >
```

Example A

```
PUBLIC "-//W3C//DTD HTML 3.2 Draft 19960821//EN" HTML32.dtd
PUBLIC "-//W3C//DTD HTML 3.2 Draft//EN" HTML32.dtd
PUBLIC "-//W3C//DTD HTML 3.2 Final//EN" HTML32.dtd
PUBLIC "-//W3C//DTD HTML 3.2//EN" HTML32.dtd
PUBLIC "ISO 8879-1986//ENTITIES Added Latin 1//EN//HTML" ISOlat1.ent
```

The **alt** attribute is used to provide text labels that can be displayed in the status line as the mouse or other pointing device is moved over hot zones, or for constructing a textual menu for non-graphical user agents. Authors are strongly recommended to provide meaningful **alt** attributes to support interoperability with speech-based or text-only user agents.

Appendix A: Sample SGML Open Catalog for HTML 3.2

This can be used with an SGML parser like nsgmls to verify that files conform to the HTML 3.2 DTD. It assumes that the DTD has been saved as the file *HTML32.dtd* and that the Latin-1 entities are in the file *ISOlat1.ent*.

Appendix B: SGML Declaration for HTML 3.2

This uses the 8-bit ISO Latin-1 character set. The size limits on properties like literals and tag names have been considerably increased from their HTML 2.0 values, but it is recommended that user agents avoid imposing arbitrary length limits.

Example B

```
<!SGML  "ISO 8879:1986"
    --

        SGML Declaration for HyperText Markup Language version 3.2

        With support for Unicode UCS-2 and increased limits
        for tag and literal lengths etc.

    --

    CHARSET
        BASESET   "ISO 646:1983//CHARSET
                   International Reference Version
                   (IRV)//ESC 2/5 4/0"
        DESCSET   0    9    UNUSED
                  9    2    9
                  11   2    UNUSED
                  13   1    13
                  14   18   UNUSED
                  32   95   32
                  127  1    UNUSED
        BASESET   "ISO Registration Number 100//CHARSET
                   ECMA-94 Right Part of
                   Latin Alphabet Nr. 1//ESC 2/13 4/1"
        DESCSET   128  32   UNUSED
                  160  96   32

    CAPACITY    SGMLREF
                TOTALCAP      200000
```

Example B *(continued)*

```
            GRPCAP           150000
            ENTCAP           150000


SCOPE     DOCUMENT
SYNTAX
    SHUNCHAR CONTROLS 0 1 2 3 4 5 6 7 8 9 10 11 12 13 14 15 16
            17 18 19 20 21 22 23 24 25 26 27 28 29 30 31 127
    BASESET  "ISO 646:1983//CHARSET
            International Reference Version
            (IRV)//ESC 2/5 4/0"
    DESCSET  0 128 0

    FUNCTION
            RE              13
            RS              10
            SPACE           32
            TAB SEPCHAR      9

    NAMING    LCNMSTRT ""
              UCNMSTRT ""
              LCNMCHAR ".-"
              UCNMCHAR ".-"
              NAMECASE GENERAL YES
                       ENTITY  NO
    DELIM     GENERAL  SGMLREF
              SHORTREF SGMLREF
    NAMES     SGMLREF
    QUANTITY  SGMLREF
              ATTSPLEN 65536
              LITLEN   65536
              NAMELEN  65536
              PILEN    65536
              TAGLVL   100
              TAGLEN   65536
              GRPGTCNT 150
              GRPCNT   64


FEATURES
  MINIMIZE
    DATATAG   NO
    OMITTAG   YES
    RANK      NO
    SHORTTAG  YES
  LINK
    SIMPLE    NO
    IMPLICIT  NO
    EXPLICIT  NO
  OTHER
    CONCUR    NO
    SUBDOC    NO
    FORMAL    YES
APPINFO       NONE
>
```

Appendix C: HTML 3.2 Document Type Definition

Example C is the HTML 3.2 DTD.

Example C

```
<!--

        W3C Document Type Definition for the HyperText Markup Language
        This version is code named Wilbur, and also as "HTML 3.2".

        Draft: Tuesday September 18th 1996

        Author: Dave Raggett <dsr@w3.org>

        This is subject to change, pending final approval by the W3C
        member companies.

        HTML 3.2 aims to capture recommended practice as of early 1996
        and as such to be used as a replacement for HTML 2.0 (RFC 1866).
        Widely deployed rendering attributes are included where they
        have been shown to be interoperable. SCRIPT and STYLE are
        included to smooth the introduction of client-side scripts
        and style sheets. Browsers must avoid showing the contents
        of these element Otherwise support for them is not required.
        ID, CLASS and STYLE attributes are not included in this version
        of HTML.

        The next version of HTML after Wilbur is code named Cougar and
        will add support for <OBJECT>, client-side scripting, style
        sheets, and extensions to fill-out forms.
-->

<!ENTITY % HTML.Version
        "-//W3C//DTD HTML 3.2 Draft 19960821//EN"

        -- Typical usage:

            <!DOCTYPE HTML PUBLIC "-//W3C//DTD HTML 3.2 Draft 19960821//EN">
            <html>
            ...
            </html>
        --
        >

<!--================== Deprecated Features Switch ==========================-->

<!ENTITY % HTML.Deprecated "INCLUDE">

<!--================== Imported Names ======================================-->

<!ENTITY % Content-Type "CDATA"
        -- meaning a MIME content type, as per RFC1521
        -->
```

Example C *(continued)*

```
<!ENTITY % HTTP-Method "GET | POST"
        -- as per HTTP specification
        -->

<!ENTITY % URL "CDATA"
        -- The term URL means a CDATA attribute
           whose value is a Uniform Resource Locator,
           See RFC1808 (June 95) and RFC1738 (Dec 94).
        -->

<!-- Parameter Entities -->

<!ENTITY % head.misc "SCRIPT|STYLE|META|LINK" -- repeatable head elements -->

<!ENTITY % heading "H1|H2|H3|H4|H5|H6">

<!ENTITY % list "UL | OL | DIR | MENU">

<![ %HTML.Deprecated [
    <!ENTITY % preformatted "PRE | XMP | LISTING">
]]>

<!ENTITY % preformatted "PRE">

<!--=============== Character mnemonic entities ===========================-->

<!ENTITY % ISOlat1 PUBLIC
        "ISO 8879-1986//ENTITIES Added Latin 1//EN//HTML">
%ISOlat1;

<!--=============== Entities for special symbols ===========================-->
<!-- &trade &shy and &cbsp are not widely deployed and so not included here -->

<!ENTITY copy    CDATA "&#169"    -- copyright sign    -->
<!ENTITY reg     CDATA "&#174"    -- registered sign   -->
<!ENTITY amp     CDATA "&#38;"    -- ampersand         -->
<!ENTITY gt      CDATA "&#62;"    -- greater than      -->
<!ENTITY lt      CDATA "&#60;"    -- less than         -->
<!ENTITY quot    CDATA "&#34;"    -- double quote      -->
<!ENTITY nbsp    CDATA " "   -- non breaking space -->

<!--=================== Text Markup ===========================================-->

<!ENTITY % font "TT | I | B | U | STRIKE | BIG | SMALL | SUB | SUP">

<!ENTITY % phrase "EM | STRONG | DFN | CODE | SAMP | KBD | VAR | CITE">

<!ENTITY % special "A | IMG | APPLET | FONT | BASEFONT | BR | SCRIPT | MAP">

<!ENTITY % form "INPUT | SELECT | TEXTAREA">

<!ENTITY % text "#PCDATA | %font | %phrase | %special | %form">
```

Example C *(continued)*

```
<!ELEMENT (%font|%phrase) - - (%text)*>

<!-- there are also 16 widely known color names although
  the resulting colors are implementation dependent:

   aqua, black, blue, fuchsia, gray, green, lime, maroon,
   navy, olive, purple, red, silver, teal, white, and yellow

 These colors were originally picked as being the standard
 16 colors supported with the Windows VGA palette.
 -->

<!ELEMENT FONT - - (%text)*     -- local change to font -->
<!ATTLIST FONT
    size    CDATA    #IMPLIED    -- [+]nn e.g. size="+1", size=4 --
    color   CDATA    #IMPLIED    -- #RRGGBB in hex, e.g. red: color="#FF0000" --
    >

<!ELEMENT BASEFONT - O EMPTY    -- base font size (1 to 7)-->
<!ATTLIST BASEFONT
    size    CDATA    #IMPLIED    -- e.g. size=3 --
    >

<!ELEMENT BR     - O EMPTY    -- forced line break -->
<!ATTLIST BR
        clear (left|all|right|none) none -- control of text flow --
        >

<!--================= HTML content models ================================-->
<!--
    HTML has three basic content models:

        %text       character level elements and text strings
        %flow       block-like elements e.g. paragraphs and lists
        %bodytext   as (b) plus headers and ADDRESS
-->

<!ENTITY % block
    "P | %list | %preformatted | DL | DIV | CENTER |
    BLOCKQUOTE | FORM | ISINDEX | HR | TABLE">

<!-- %flow is used for DD and LI -->

<!ENTITY % flow "(%text | %block)*">

<!--================= Document Body ========================================-->

<!ENTITY % body.content "(%heading | %text | %block | ADDRESS)*">

<!ENTITY % color "CDATA" -- a color specification: #HHHHHH @@ details? -->

<!ENTITY % body-color-attrs "
```

Example C *(continued)*

```
          bgcolor %color #IMPLIED
          text %color #IMPLIED
          link %color #IMPLIED
          vlink %color #IMPLIED
          alink %color #IMPLIED
          ">

<!ELEMENT BODY O O  %body.content>
<!ATTLIST BODY
          background %URL #IMPLIED  -- texture tile for document background --
          %body-color-attrs;  -- bgcolor, text, link, vlink, alink --
          >

<!ENTITY % address.content "((%text;) | P)*">

<!ELEMENT ADDRESS - - %address.content>

<!ELEMENT DIV - - %body.content>
<!ATTLIST DIV
          align   (left|center|right) #IMPLIED -- alignment of following text --
          >

<!-- CENTER is a shorthand for DIV with ALIGN=CENTER -->
<!ELEMENT center - - %body.content>

<!--=================== The Anchor Element =====================================-->

<!ELEMENT A - - (%text)* -(A)>
<!ATTLIST A
          name    CDATA   #IMPLIED    -- named link end --
          href    %URL    #IMPLIED    -- URL for linked resource --
          rel     CDATA   #IMPLIED    -- forward link types --
          rev     CDATA   #IMPLIED    -- reverse link types --
          title   CDATA   #IMPLIED    -- advisory title string --
          >

<!--=================== Client-side image maps ===========================-->

<!-- These can be placed in the same document or grouped in a
     separate document although this isn t yet widely supported -->

<!ENTITY % SHAPE "(rect|circle|poly)">
<!ENTITY % COORDS "CDATA" -- comma separated list of numbers -->

<!ELEMENT MAP - - (AREA)*>
<!ATTLIST MAP
     name    CDATA   #IMPLIED
     >

<!ELEMENT AREA - O EMPTY>
<!ATTLIST AREA
     shape   %SHAPE  rect
     coords  %COORDS #IMPLIED  -- always needed except for shape=default --
```

Example C *(continued)*

```
    href    %URL    #IMPLIED  -- this region acts as hypertext link --
    nohref (nohref) #IMPLIED  -- this region has no action --
    alt     CDATA   #REQUIRED
    >


<!--================== The LINK Element =====================================-->

<!ENTITY % Types "CDATA"
        -- See Internet Draft: draft-ietf-html-relrev-00.txt
           LINK has been part of HTML since the early days
           although few browsers as yet take advantage of it.

           Relationship values can be used in principle:

                a) for document specific toolbars/menus when used
                   with the LINK element in document head:
                b) to link to a separate style sheet (rel=stylesheet)
                c) to make a link to a script (rel=script)
                d) by stylesheets to control how collections of
                   html nodes are rendered into printed documents
                e) to make a link to a printable version of this document
                   e.g. a postscript or pdf version (rel=print)
-->

<!ELEMENT LINK - O EMPTY>
<!ATTLIST LINK
        id      ID      #IMPLIED    -- SGML ID attribute --
        href    %URL    #IMPLIED    -- URL for linked resource --
        rel     %Types  #IMPLIED    -- forward link types --
        rev     %Types  #IMPLIED    -- reverse link types --
        title   CDATA   #IMPLIED    -- advisory title string --
        >


<!--================== Images ===============================================-->

<!ENTITY % Length "CDATA"    -- nn for pixels or nn% for percentage length -->
<!ENTITY % Pixels "NUMBER"   -- integer representing length in pixels -->

<!-- Suggested widths are used for negotiating image size
     with the module responsible for painting the image.
     align=left or right cause image to float to margin
     and for subsequent text to wrap around image -->

<!ENTITY % IAlign "(top|middle|bottom|left|right)">

<!ELEMENT IMG    - O EMPTY -- Embedded image -->
<!ATTLIST IMG
        src     %URL    #REQUIRED   -- URL of image to embed --
        alt     CDATA   #IMPLIED    -- for display in place of image --
        align   %IAlign #IMPLIED    -- vertical or horizontal alignment --
        height  %Pixels #IMPLIED    -- suggested height in pixels --
        width   %Pixels #IMPLIED    -- suggested width in pixels --
        border  %Pixels #IMPLIED    -- suggested link border width --
```

Example C *(continued)*

```
        hspace  %Pixels  #IMPLIED   -- suggested horizontal gutter --
        vspace  %Pixels  #IMPLIED   -- suggested vertical gutter --
        usemap  %URL     #IMPLIED   -- use client-side image map --
        ismap   (ismap)  #IMPLIED   -- use server image map --
        >

<!-- USEMAP points to a MAP element which may be in this document
  or an external document, although the latter is not widely supported -->

<!--=================== Java APPLET tag =======================================-->
<!--
  This tag is supported by all Java enabled browsers. Applet resources
  (including their classes) are normally loaded relative to the document
  URL (or <BASE> element if it is defined). The CODEBASE attribute is used
  to change this default behavior. If the CODEBASE attribute is defined then
  it specifies a different location to find applet resources. The value
  can be an absolute URL or a relative URL. The absolute URL is used as is
  without modification and is not effected by the documents <BASE> element.
  When the codebase attribute is relative, then it is relative to the
  document URL (or <BASE> tag if defined).
-->
<!ELEMENT APPLET - - (PARAM | %text)*>
<!ATTLIST APPLET
        codebase %URL     #IMPLIED   -- code base --
        code     CDATA    #REQUIRED  -- class file --
        alt      CDATA    #IMPLIED   -- for display in place of applet --
        name     CDATA    #IMPLIED   -- applet name --
        width    %Pixels  #REQUIRED  -- suggested width in pixels --
        height   %Pixels  #REQUIRED  -- suggested height in pixels --
        align    %IAlign  #IMPLIED   -- vertical or horizontal alignment --
        hspace   %Pixels  #IMPLIED   -- suggested horizontal gutter --
        vspace   %Pixels  #IMPLIED   -- suggested vertical gutter --
        >

<!ELEMENT PARAM - O EMPTY>
<!ATTLIST PARAM
        name     NAME     #REQUIRED  -- The name of the parameter --
        value    CDATA    #IMPLIED   -- The value of the parameter --
        >


<!--
Here is an example:

    <applet codebase="applets/NervousText"
        code=NervousText.class
        width=300
        height=50>
    <param name=text value="Java is Cool!">
    <img src=sorry.gif alt="This looks better with Java support">
    </applet>
-->


<!--=================== Horizontal Rule =======================================-->
```

Example C *(continued)*

```
<!ELEMENT HR    - O EMPTY>
<!ATTLIST HR
        align (left|right|center) #IMPLIED
        noshade (noshade) #IMPLIED
        size  %Pixels #IMPLIED
        width %Length #IMPLIED
        >
<!--================== Paragraphs==========================================-->

<!ELEMENT P    - O (%text)*>
<!ATTLIST P
        align   (left|center|right) #IMPLIED
        >

<!--================== Headings ===========================================-->

<!--
  There are six levels of headers from H1 (the most important)
  to H6 (the least important).
-->

<!ELEMENT ( %heading )  - -  (%text;)*>
<!ATTLIST ( %heading )
        align  (left|center|right) #IMPLIED
        >

<!--================== Preformatted Text ==================================-->

<!-- excludes images and changes in font size -->

<!ENTITY % pre.exclusion "IMG|BIG|SMALL|SUB|SUP|FONT">

<!ELEMENT PRE - - (%text)* -(%pre.exclusion)>
<!ATTLIST PRE
        width NUMBER #implied -- is this widely supported? --
        >

<![ %HTML.Deprecated [

<!ENTITY % literal "CDATA"
        -- historical, non-conforming parsing mode where
           the only markup signal is the end tag
           in full
        -->

<!ELEMENT (XMP|LISTING) - - %literal>
<!ELEMENT PLAINTEXT - O %literal>

]]>

<!--================== Block-like Quotes ==================================-->
```

Example C *(continued)*

```
<!ELEMENT BLOCKQUOTE - - %body.content>

<!--=================== Lists ===================================================-->

<!--
    HTML 3.2 allows you to control the sequence number for ordered lists.
    You can set the sequence number with the START and VALUE attributes.
    The TYPE attribute may be used to specify the rendering of ordered
    and unordered lists.
-->

<!-- definition lists - DT for term, DD for its definition -->

<!ELEMENT DL     - -   (DT|DD)+>
<!ATTLIST DL
        compact (compact) #IMPLIED -- more compact style --
        >

<!ELEMENT DT - O  (%text)*>
<!ELEMENT DD - O  %flow;>

<!-- Ordered lists OL, and unordered lists UL -->
<!ELEMENT (OL|UL) - -  (LI)+>

<!--
        Numbering style
    1    arabic numbers     1, 2, 3, ...
    a    lower alpha        a, b, c, ...
    A    upper alpha        A, B, C, ...
    i    lower roman        i, ii, iii, ...
    I    upper roman        I, II, III, ...

    The style is applied to the sequence number which by default
    is reset to 1 for the first list item in an ordered list.

    This can t be expressed directly in SGML due to case folding.
-->

<!ENTITY % OLStyle "CDATA" -- constrained to: [1|a|A|i|I] -->

<!ATTLIST OL -- ordered lists --
        type      %OLStyle   #IMPLIED   -- numbering style --
        start     NUMBER     #IMPLIED   -- starting sequence number --
        compact  (compact)   #IMPLIED   -- reduced interitem spacing --
        >

<!-- bullet styles -->

<!ENTITY % ULStyle "disc|square|circle">

<!ATTLIST UL -- unordered lists --
        type      (%ULStyle)  #IMPLIED   -- bullet style --
        compact (compact)      #IMPLIED   -- reduced interitem spacing --
```

Example C *(continued)*

```
        >

<!ELEMENT (DIR|MENU) - -   (LI)+ -(%block)>
<!ATTLIST DIR
        compact (compact) #IMPLIED
        >
<!ATTLIST MENU
        compact (compact) #IMPLIED
        >

<!-- <DIR>               Directory list                -->
<!-- <DIR COMPACT>        Compact list style            -->
<!-- <MENU>               Menu list                     -->
<!-- <MENU COMPACT>       Compact list style            -->

<!-- The type attribute can be used to change the bullet style
     in unordered lists and the numbering style in ordered lists -->

<!ENTITY % LIStyle "CDATA" -- constrained to: "(%ULStyle|%OLStyle)" -->

<!ELEMENT LI - O %flow -- list item -->
<!ATTLIST LI
        type    %LIStyle    #IMPLIED    -- list item style --
        value   NUMBER      #IMPLIED    -- reset sequence number --
        >

<!--=============== Forms =================================================-->

<!ELEMENT FORM - - %body.content -(FORM)>
<!ATTLIST FORM
        action %URL #IMPLIED  -- server-side form handler --
        method (%HTTP-Method) GET -- see HTTP specification --
        enctype %Content-Type; "application/x-www-form-urlencoded"
        >

<!ENTITY % InputType
        "(TEXT | PASSWORD | CHECKBOX | RADIO | SUBMIT
          | RESET | FILE | HIDDEN | IMAGE)">

<!ELEMENT INPUT - O EMPTY>
<!ATTLIST INPUT
        type %InputType TEXT      -- what kind of widget is needed --
        name  CDATA #IMPLIED      -- required for all but submit and reset --
        value CDATA #IMPLIED      -- required for radio and checkboxes --
        checked (checked) #IMPLIED -- for radio buttons and check boxes --
        size CDATA  #IMPLIED      -- specific to each type of field --
        maxlength NUMBER #IMPLIED
        src   %URL  #IMPLIED      -- for fields with background images --
        align (top|middle|bottom|left|right) top -- image alignment --
        >

<!ELEMENT SELECT - - (OPTION+)>
<!ATTLIST SELECT
```

Example C *(continued)*

```
        name CDATA #REQUIRED
        size NUMBER #IMPLIED
        multiple (multiple) #IMPLIED
        >

<!ELEMENT OPTION - O (#PCDATA)*>
<!ATTLIST OPTION
        selected (selected) #IMPLIED
        value  CDATA  #IMPLIED -- defaults to element content --
        >

<!-- Multi-line text input field. -->

<!ELEMENT TEXTAREA - - (#PCDATA)*>
<!ATTLIST TEXTAREA
        name CDATA #REQUIRED
        rows NUMBER #REQUIRED
        cols NUMBER #REQUIRED
        >

<!--====================== Tables ========================================-->

<!-- Widely deployed subset of the full table standard, see RFC 1942
     e.g. at http://www.ics.uci.edu/pub/ietf/html/rfc1942.txt -->

<!-- horizontal placement of table relative to window -->
<!ENTITY % Where "(left|center|right)">

<!-- horizontal alignment attributes for cell contents -->
<!ENTITY % cell.halign
        "align  (left|center|right) #IMPLIED"
        >

<!-- vertical alignment attributes for cell contents -->
<!ENTITY % cell.valign
        "valign  (top|middle|bottom|baseline)  #IMPLIED"
        >

<!ELEMENT table - - (caption?, tr+)>
<!ELEMENT tr - O (th|td)*>
<!ELEMENT (th|td) - O %body.content>

<!ATTLIST table                       -- table element --
        align     %Where;   #IMPLIED  -- table position relative to window --
        width     %Length   #IMPLIED  -- table width relative to window --
        border    %Pixels   #IMPLIED  -- controls frame width around table --
        cellspacing %Pixels #IMPLIED  -- spacing between cells --
        cellpadding %Pixels #IMPLIED  -- spacing within cells --
        >

<!ELEMENT CAPTION - - (%text;)* -- table or figure caption -->
<!ATTLIST CAPTION
        align (top|bottom) #IMPLIED
```

Example C *(continued)*

```
        >

<!ATTLIST tr                            -- table row --
        %cell.halign;                   -- horizontal alignment in cells --
        %cell.valign;                   -- vertical alignment in cells --
        >

<!ATTLIST (th|td)                       -- header or data cell --
        nowrap (nowrap)  #IMPLIED       -- suppress word wrap --
        rowspan NUMBER    1             -- number of rows spanned by cell --
        colspan NUMBER    1             -- number of cols spanned by cell --
        %cell.halign;                   -- horizontal alignment in cell --
        %cell.valign;                   -- vertical alignment in cell --
        width   %Pixels  #IMPLIED       -- suggested width for cell --
        height  %Pixels  #IMPLIED       -- suggested height for cell --
        >

<!--=============== Document Head ========================================-->

<!-- %head.misc defined earlier on as "SCRIPT|STYLE|META|LINK" -->

<!ENTITY % head.content "TITLE & ISINDEX? & BASE?">

<!ELEMENT HEAD O O  (%head.content) +(%head.misc)>

<!ELEMENT TITLE - -  (#PCDATA)* -(%head.misc)
                -- The TITLE element is not considered part of the flow of text.
                   It should be displayed, for example as the page header or
                   window title.
                -->

<!ELEMENT ISINDEX - O EMPTY>
<!ATTLIST ISINDEX
        prompt CDATA #IMPLIED -- prompt message -->

<!--
    The BASE element gives an absolute URL for dereferencing relative
    URLs, e.g.

            <BASE href="http://foo.com/index.html">
            ...
            <IMG SRC="images/bar.gif">

    The image is deferenced to

            http://foo.com/images/bar.gif

  In the absence of a BASE element the document URL should be used.
  Note that this is not necessarily the same as the URL used to
  request the document, as the base URL may be overridden by an HTTP
  header accompanying the document.
-->
```

Example C *(continued)*

```
<!ELEMENT BASE - O EMPTY>
<!ATTLIST BASE
        href %URL   #REQUIRED
        >


<!ELEMENT META - O EMPTY -- Generic Metainformation -->
<!ATTLIST META
        http-equiv  NAME    #IMPLIED  -- HTTP response header name  --
        name        NAME    #IMPLIED  -- metainformation name       --
        content     CDATA   #REQUIRED -- associated information      --
        >


<!-- SCRIPT/STYLE are place holders for transition to next version of HTML -->

<!ELEMENT STYLE   - - (#PCDATA)* -(%head.misc) -- style info -->
<!ELEMENT SCRIPT  - - (#PCDATA)* -(%head.misc) -- script statements -->


<!--================ Document Structure ======================================-->

<!ENTITY % version.attr "VERSION CDATA #FIXED  %HTML.Version; ">

<![ %HTML.Deprecated [
    <!ENTITY % html.content "HEAD, BODY, PLAINTEXT?">
]]>

<!ELEMENT HTML O O  (%html.content)>
<!ATTLIST HTML
        %version.attr;
        >
```

Appendix D: Character Entities
for ISO Latin-1

Example D provides the character entities for ISO
Latin-1.

Example D

```
<!-- (C) International Organization for Standardization 1986
     Permission to copy in any form is granted for use with
     conforming SGML systems and applications as defined in
     ISO 8879, provided this notice is included in all copies.
-->
<!-- Character entity set. Typical invocation:
     <!ENTITY % ISOlat1 PUBLIC
       "ISO 8879-1986//ENTITIES Added Latin 1//EN//HTML">
     %ISOlat1;
-->
<!-- Modified for use in HTML
        $Id: ISOlat1.sgml,v 1.2 1994/11/30 23:45:12 connolly Exp $ -->
<!ENTITY AElig  CDATA "&#198;" -- capital AE diphthong (ligature) -->
<!ENTITY Aacute CDATA "&#193;" -- capital A, acute accent -->
<!ENTITY Acirc  CDATA "&#194;" -- capital A, circumflex accent -->
```

Example D *(continued)*

```
<!ENTITY Agrave CDATA "&#192;" -- capital A, grave accent -->
<!ENTITY Aring  CDATA "&#197;" -- capital A, ring -->
<!ENTITY Atilde CDATA "&#195;" -- capital A, tilde -->
<!ENTITY Auml   CDATA "&#196;" -- capital A, dieresis or umlaut mark -->
<!ENTITY Ccedil CDATA "&#199;" -- capital C, cedilla -->
<!ENTITY ETH    CDATA "&#208;" -- capital Eth, Icelandic -->
<!ENTITY Eacute CDATA "&#201;" -- capital E, acute accent -->
<!ENTITY Ecirc  CDATA "&#202;" -- capital E, circumflex accent -->
<!ENTITY Egrave CDATA "&#200;" -- capital E, grave accent -->
<!ENTITY Euml   CDATA "&#203;" -- capital E, dieresis or umlaut mark -->
<!ENTITY Iacute CDATA "&#205;" -- capital I, acute accent -->
<!ENTITY Icirc  CDATA "&#206;" -- capital I, circumflex accent -->
<!ENTITY Igrave CDATA "&#204;" -- capital I, grave accent -->
<!ENTITY Iuml   CDATA "&#207;" -- capital I, dieresis or umlaut mark -->
<!ENTITY Ntilde CDATA "&#209;" -- capital N, tilde -->
<!ENTITY Oacute CDATA "&#211;" -- capital O, acute accent -->
<!ENTITY Ocirc  CDATA "&#212;" -- capital O, circumflex accent -->
<!ENTITY Ograve CDATA "&#210;" -- capital O, grave accent -->
<!ENTITY Oslash CDATA "&#216;" -- capital O, slash -->
<!ENTITY Otilde CDATA "&#213;" -- capital O, tilde -->
<!ENTITY Ouml   CDATA "&#214;" -- capital O, dieresis or umlaut mark -->
<!ENTITY THORN  CDATA "&#222;" -- capital THORN, Icelandic -->
<!ENTITY Uacute CDATA "&#218;" -- capital U, acute accent -->
<!ENTITY Ucirc  CDATA "&#219;" -- capital U, circumflex accent -->
<!ENTITY Ugrave CDATA "&#217;" -- capital U, grave accent -->
<!ENTITY Uuml   CDATA "&#220;" -- capital U, dieresis or umlaut mark -->
<!ENTITY Yacute CDATA "&#221;" -- capital Y, acute accent -->
<!ENTITY aacute CDATA "&#225;" -- small a, acute accent -->
<!ENTITY acirc  CDATA "&#226;" -- small a, circumflex accent -->
<!ENTITY aelig  CDATA "&#230;" -- small ae diphthong (ligature) -->
<!ENTITY agrave CDATA "&#224;" -- small a, grave accent -->
<!ENTITY aring  CDATA "&#229;" -- small a, ring -->
<!ENTITY atilde CDATA "&#227;" -- small a, tilde -->
<!ENTITY auml   CDATA "&#228;" -- small a, dieresis or umlaut mark -->
<!ENTITY ccedil CDATA "&#231;" -- small c, cedilla -->
<!ENTITY eacute CDATA "&#233;" -- small e, acute accent -->
<!ENTITY ecirc  CDATA "&#234;" -- small e, circumflex accent -->
<!ENTITY egrave CDATA "&#232;" -- small e, grave accent -->
<!ENTITY eth    CDATA "&#240;" -- small eth, Icelandic -->
<!ENTITY euml   CDATA "&#235;" -- small e, dieresis or umlaut mark -->
<!ENTITY iacute CDATA "&#237;" -- small i, acute accent -->
<!ENTITY icirc  CDATA "&#238;" -- small i, circumflex accent -->
<!ENTITY igrave CDATA "&#236;" -- small i, grave accent -->
<!ENTITY iuml   CDATA "&#239;" -- small i, dieresis or umlaut mark -->
<!ENTITY ntilde CDATA "&#241;" -- small n, tilde -->
<!ENTITY oacute CDATA "&#243;" -- small o, acute accent -->
<!ENTITY ocirc  CDATA "&#244;" -- small o, circumflex accent -->
<!ENTITY ograve CDATA "&#242;" -- small o, grave accent -->
<!ENTITY oslash CDATA "&#248;" -- small o, slash -->
<!ENTITY otilde CDATA "&#245;" -- small o, tilde -->
<!ENTITY ouml   CDATA "&#246;" -- small o, dieresis or umlaut mark -->
<!ENTITY szlig  CDATA "&#223;" -- small sharp s, German (sz ligature) -->
<!ENTITY thorn  CDATA "&#254;" -- small thorn, Icelandic -->
```

Example D *(continued)*

```
<!ENTITY uacute CDATA "&#250;" -- small u, acute accent -->
<!ENTITY ucirc  CDATA "&#251;" -- small u, circumflex accent -->
<!ENTITY ugrave CDATA "&#249;" -- small u, grave accent -->
<!ENTITY uuml   CDATA "&#252;" -- small u, dieresis or umlaut mark -->
<!ENTITY yacute CDATA "&#253;" -- small y, acute accent -->
<!ENTITY yuml   CDATA "&#255;" -- small y, dieresis or umlaut mark -->
```

0	32		64	@	96	'	128	160		192	À	224	à
1	33	!	65	A	97	a	129	161	¡	193	Á	225	á
2	34	"	66	B	98	b	130	162	¢	194	Â	226	â
3	35	#	67	C	99	c	131	163	£	195	Ã	227	ã
4	36	$	68	D	100	d	132	164	¤	196	Ä	228	ä
5	37	%	69	E	101	e	133	165	¥	197	Å	229	å
6	38	&	70	F	102	f	134	166	¦	198	Æ	230	æ
7	39	'	71	G	103	g	135	167	§	199	Ç	231	ç
8	40	(	72	H	104	h	136	168	¨	200	È	232	è
9	41	)	73	I	105	i	137	169	©	201	É	233	é
10	42	*	74	J	106	j	138	170	ª	202	Ê	234	ê
11	43	+	75	K	107	k	139	171	«	203	Ë	235	ë
12	44	,	76	L	108	l	140	172	¬	204	Ì	236	ì
13	45	–	77	M	109	m	141	173	-	205	Í	237	í
14	46	.	78	N	110	n	142	174	®	206	Î	238	î
15	47	/	79	O	111	o	143	175	¯	207	Ï	239	ï
16	48	0	80	P	112	p	144	176	°	208	Ð	240	ð
17	49	1	81	Q	113	q	145	177	±	209	Ñ	241	ñ
18	50	2	82	R	114	r	146	178	²	210	Ò	242	ò
19	51	3	83	S	115	s	147	179	³	211	Ó	243	ó
20	52	4	84	T	116	t	148	180	´	212	Ô	244	ô
21	53	5	85	U	117	u	149	181	µ	213	Õ	245	õ
22	54	6	86	V	118	v	150	182	¶	214	Ö	246	ö
23	55	7	87	W	119	w	151	183	·	215	×	247	÷
24	56	8	88	X	120	x	152	184	¸	216	Ø	248	ø
25	57	9	89	Y	121	y	153	185	¹	217	Ù	249	ù
26	58	:	90	Z	122	z	154	186	º	218	Ú	250	ú
27	59	;	91	[	123	{	155	187	»	219	Û	251	û
28	60	<	92	\	124	|	156	188	¼	220	Ü	252	ü
29	61	=	93	]	125	}	157	189	½	221	Ý	253	ý
30	62	>	94	^	126	~	158	190	¾	222	Þ	254	þ
31	63	?	95	_	127		159	191	¿	223	ß	255	ÿ

Table E   Printable Latin-1 Character Codes

Appendix E: Table of Printable Latin-1 Character Codes

Table E provides a list of printable Latin-1 character codes. ∎

References

1. Anderson, Mathew, Ricardo Motta, Srinivasan Chandrasekar, and Michael Stokes. "Proposal for a Standard Color Space for the Internet (sRGB)," April 1996, *http://www.w3.org/pub/WWW/Printing/motta/W3Color.html*. Provides a precise definition for RGB that allows sRGB images to be reproduced accurately on different platforms and media in varying lighting conditions.

2. Berners-Lee, Tim, and Dan Connolly. "HTML 2.0" (RFC 1866), November 1995, *ftp://ds.internic.net/rfc/rfc1866.txt*. Defines the Hypertext Markup Language Specification version 2.0. Further information can be found at *http://www.w3.org/pub/WWW/MarkUp/*

3. **Connolly, Dan.** "A Lexical Analyzer for HTML and Basic SGML," June 1996, *http://www.w3.org/pub/WWW/TR/WD-html-lex*. Describes lexical considerations for parsing HTML documents.

4. Nebel, E., and L. Masinter. **"Form-based File Upload in HTML" (RFC 1867)**, November 1995, *ftp://ds.internic.net/rfc/rfc1867.txt*. Describes extensions to HTML 2.0 (RFC 1866) to support file upload from HTML forms.

5. **Raggett, Dave.** "HTML Tables" (RFC 1942), May 1996, *ftp://ds.internic.net/rfc/rfc1942.txt*. Defines the HTML table model, which is a superset of the table model defined by HTML 3.2. Available as a W3C working draft at *http://www.w3.org/pub/WWW/TR/WD-tables*.

About the Author

Dave Raggett
MIT Laboratory for Computer Science
545 Technology Square
Cambridge, MA 02139
dsr@w3.org

Dave currently works at the World Wide Web Consortium (W3C) on secondment from Hewlett Packard's Corporate Research Laboratories in Bristol, England. His work is heavily involved with developing standards for the World Wide Web: as author of the HTML 3.0 draft specification and earlier the HTML+ Internet Draft, as the creator of the Arena browser, and as co-chair of the IETF working group for HTTP. He is also working on ideas for downloadable fonts, style sheets, and non-proprietary public domain protocols for micropayments (without export restrictions).

CASCADING STYLE SHEETS

LEVEL 1

Håkon Wium Lie, Bert Bos

Abstract

[W3C Proposed Recommendation; PR-CSS1-961112; November 12, 1996]

This document specifies Level 1 of the Cascading Style Sheet mechanism (CSS1). CSS1 is a simple style sheet mechanism that allows authors and readers to attach style (e.g., fonts, colors, and spacing) to HTML documents. The CSS1 language is human readable and writable and expresses style in common desktop publishing terminology.

One of the fundamental features of CSS is that style sheets cascade; authors can attach a preferred style sheet, while the reader may have a personal style sheet to adjust for human or technological handicaps. The rules for resolving conflicts between different style sheets are defined in this specification.

Status of This Document

This document is in the course of review by the members of the World Wide Web Consortium. This is a stable document derived from internal working drafts of the W3C HTML Editorial Review Board and the public working draft WD-css1-960911. Details of this review have been distributed to member's representatives. Comments by non-members should be sent to *www-style@w3.org*.

The review period will end on December 11, 1996, 24:00 GMT. Within 14 days from that time, the document's disposition will be announced. It may become a W3C Recommendation (possibly with minor changes), or it may revert to Working Draft status, or it may be dropped as a W3C work item. This document does not at this time imply any endorsement by the Consortium's staff or member organizations.

This document is part of the W3C (*http://www.w3.org/*) Style Sheets activity.

A list of current W3C Recommendations, Proposed Recommendations, and Working Drafts can be found at *http://www.w3.org/pub/WWW/TR*

Terminology

author
> The author of an HTML document.

block-level element
> An element that has a line break before and after (e.g., 'H1' in HTML).

canvas
> The part of the UA's drawing surface onto which documents are rendered.

contextual selector
> A selector that matches elements based on their position in the document structure. A contextual selector consists of several simple selectors. For example, the contextual selector 'H1.initial B' consists of two simple selectors, 'H1.initial' and 'B'.

CSS
> Cascading Style Sheets.

CSS1
> Cascading Style Sheets, Level 1. This document defines CSS1, which is a simple style sheet mechanism for the Web.

CSS1 core features
> The part of CSS1 that is required in all CSS1-compliant UAs.

CSS1 advanced features
> Features that are described in this specification but labeled as not among the CSS1 core features.

declaration
> A property (e.g., 'font-size') and a corresponding value (e.g. '12pt').

designer
> The designer of a style sheet.

document
> HTML document.

element
> HTML element.

fictional tag sequence
> A tool for describing the behavior of pseudo-classes and pseudo-elements.

font size
> The size for which a font is designed. Typically, the size of a font is approximately equal to the distance from the bottom of the lowest letter with a descender to the top of the tallest letter with an ascender and (optionally) with a diacritical mark.

HTML
> Hypertext Markup Language (13), an application of SGML.

HTML extension
> Markup introduced by UA vendors, most often to support certain visual styles. The FONT, CENTER, and BLINK elements are examples of HTML extensions, as is the BGCOLOR attribute. One of the goals of CSS is to provide an alternative to HTML extensions.

inline element
> An element that does not have a line break before and after (e.g. 'STRONG' in HTML).

intrinsic dimensions
> The width and height as defined by the element itself, not imposed by the surroundings. In this specification we assume that all replaced elements—and only replaced elements—come with intrinsic dimensions.

pseudo-element
> Pseudo-elements are used in CSS selectors to address typographical items (e.g., the first line of an element) rather than structural elements.

pseudo-class
> Pseudo-classes are used in CSS selectors to allow information external to the HTML source (e.g., the fact that an anchor has been visited or not) to classify elements.

property
> A stylistic parameter that can be influenced through CSS. This specification defines a list of properties and their corresponding values.

reader
> The person for whom the document is rendered.

replaced element
> An element that the CSS formatter only knows the intrinsic dimensions of. In HTML, 'IMG', 'INPUT', 'TEXTAREA', 'SELECT', and 'OBJECT' elements can be examples of replaced elements. For example, the content of the IMG element is often replaced by the image that the SRC attribute points to. CSS1 does not define how the intrinsic dimensions are found.

rule
> A declaration (e.g., 'font-family: helvetica') and its selector (e.g., 'H1').

selector
> A string that identifies what elements the corresponding rule applies to. A selector can either be a simple selector (e.g., 'H1') or a contextual selector (e.g., 'H1 B'), which consists of several simple selectors.

SGML
> Standard Generalized Markup Language (11), of which HTML is an application.

simple selector
> A selector that matches elements based on their type or attributes, e.g, 'H1.initial'.

style sheet
> A collection of rules.

tag
> HTML tag, e.g., 'H1'.

UA
> User Agent, often a Web browser or Web client.

user
> Synonymous with *reader*.

weight
> The priority of a rule.

In the text of this specification, single quotes ('. . .') denote HTML and CSS excerpts.

1. Basic Concepts

Designing simple style sheets is easy. One needs only to know a little HTML and some basic desktop publishing terminology. For example, to set the text color of 'H1' elements to blue, one can say:

```
H1 { color: blue }
```

The example above is a simple CSS rule. A rule consists of two main parts: selector ('H1') and declaration ('color: blue'). The declaration has two parts: property ('color') and value ('blue'). While the example above tries to influence only one of the properties needed for rendering an HTML document, it qualifies as a style sheet on its own. Combined with other style sheets (one fundamental feature of CSS is that style sheets can be combined), it will determine the final presentation of the document.

The selector is the link between the HTML document and the style, and all HTML tags are possible selectors. HTML tags are defined in the HTML specification (13), and the CSS1 specification defines a syntax for how to address them.

The 'color' property is one of approximately 35 properties that determine the presentation of an HTML document. The list of properties and their possible values is defined in this specification.

HTML authors need to write style sheets only if they want to suggest a specific style for their documents. Each user agent (UA, often a Web browser or Web client) will have a default style sheet that presents documents in a reasonable, but arguably mundane, manner. Appendix A contains a sample style sheet to present HTML documents as suggested in the HTML 2.0 specification.

1.1 Containment in HTML

In order for the style sheets to influence the presentation, the UA must be aware of their existence. Another forthcoming W3C specification, HTML 3 and Style Sheets (8), specifies how to link HTML with style sheets. This section is therefore informative but not normative:

```
<HTML>
  <HEAD>
    <TITLE>title</TITLE>
    <LINK REL=STYLESHEET TYPE=
        "text/css"
        HREF="http://style.com/cool"
    TITLE="Cool">
    <STYLE TYPE="text/css">
      @import url(http://style.com/
        basic);
      H1 { color: blue }
    </STYLE>
  </HEAD>
  <BODY>
    <H1>Headline is blue</H1>
    <P STYLE="color: green">While
        the paragraph is green.
  </BODY>
</HTML>
```

The example shows four ways to combine style and HTML: using the 'LINK' element to link an external style sheet, a 'STYLE' element inside the 'HEAD' element, an imported style sheet using the CSS '@import' notation, and a 'STYLE' attribute on an element inside 'BODY'. The latter option mixes style with content and loses the corresponding advantages of traditional style sheets.

The 'LINK' element references alternative style sheets that the reader can select, while imported style sheets are automatically merged with the rest of the style sheet.

Traditionally, UAs have silently ignored unknown tags. As as result, old UAs will ignore the 'STYLE' element, but its content will be treated as part of the document body and rendered as such. During a transition phase, 'STYLE' element content may be hidden using SGML comments:

```
<STYLE TYPE="text/css"><!--
    H1 { color: green }
--></STYLE>
```

Since the 'STYLE' element is declared as CDATA in the DTD (as defined in [8]), conformant SGML parsers will not consider the above style sheet to be a comment that is to be removed.

1.2 Grouping

To reduce the size of style sheets, one can group selectors in comma-separated lists:

```
H1, H2, H3 { font-family: helvetica
    }
```

Similarly, declarations can be grouped:

```
H1 {
    font-weight: bold;
    font-size: 12pt;
    line-height: 14pt;
    font-family: helvetica;
    font-style: normal
    }
```

In addition, some properties have their own grouping syntax:

```
H1 { font: 12pt/14pt helvetica }
```

The above example sets the 'font-size', 'line-height', and 'font-family' properties.

1.3 Inheritance

In the first example, the color of 'H1' elements was set to blue. Suppose we have an 'H1' element with an emphasized element inside:

```
<H1>The headline <EM>is</EM>
    important!</H1>
```

If no color has been assigned to 'EM', the emphasized "is" will inherit the color of the parent element—it will also appear in blue. Other style properties are likewise inherited—e.g., 'font-family' and 'font-size'.

To set a default style property for a document, one can set the property on an element from which all visible elements descend. In HTML documents, the 'BODY' element can serve this function:

```
BODY {
    color: black;
    background: url(texture.gif)
        white;
    }
```

This will work even if the author has omitted the 'BODY' tag (which is legal) since the parser will infer the missing tag. The example above sets the text color to be black and the background to be an image. The background will be white if the image is not available. (See the description of the 'background' property for more on this.)

Some style properties are not inherited from the parent element to the child element. Most often it is intuitive why this is not the case. For example, the 'background' property does not inherit, but the parent element's background will shine through by default.

Often, the value of a property is a percentage that refers to another property:

```
P { font-size: 10pt }
P { line-height: 120% }  /*
    relative to font-size , i.e.
    12pt */
```

For each property that allows percentage values, it is defined what property it refers to. Children elements of 'P' will inherit the computed value of 'line-height' (i.e., 12pt), not the percentage.

1.4 Class as Selector

To increase the granularity of control over elements, HTML 3 (8) (9) proposes a new attribute—'CLASS'. All elements inside the

'BODY' element can be classed, and the class can be addressed in the style sheet:

```
<HTML>
 <HEAD>
  <TITLE>Title</TITLE>
  <STYLE TYPE="text/css">
    H1.punk { color: #00FF00 }
  </STYLE>
 </HEAD>
 <BODY>
  <H1 CLASS=punk>Way too green</H1>
 </BODY>
</HTML>
```

The normal inheritance rules apply to classed elements; they inherit values from their parent in the document structure.

One can address all elements of the same class by omitting the tag name in the selector:

```
.punk { color: green }  /* all
      elements with CLASS punk */
```

Only one class can be specified per selector. 'P.punk.rap' is therefore an invalid selector in CSS1. (Contextual selectors, described below, can have one class per simple selector.)

CSS gives so much power to the CLASS attribute that in many cases it doesn't even matter what HTML element the class is set on. You can make any element emulate almost any other. Relying on this power is not recommended, since it removes the level of structure that has a universal meaning (HTML elements). A structure based on CLASS is only useful within a restricted domain, where the meaning of a class has been mutually agreed upon.

1.5 ID as Selector

HTML 3 also introduces the 'ID' attribute, which is guaranteed to have a unique value over the document. It can therefore be of special importance as a style sheet selector and can be addressed with a preceding '#':

```
#z098y { letter-spacing: 0.3em }

<P ID=z098y>Wide text</P>
```

By using the ID attribute as selector, one can set style properties on a per-element basis. While style sheets have been designed to augment document structure, this feature will allow authors to create documents that present well on the canvas without taking advantage of the structural elements of HTML. This use of style sheets is discouraged.

1.6 Contextual Selectors

Inheritance saves CSS designers from having to type. Instead of setting all style properties, one can create defaults and then list the exceptions. To give 'EM' elements within 'H1' a different color, one may specify:

```
H1 { color: blue }
EM { color: red }
```

When this style sheet is in effect, all emphasized sections within or outside 'H1' will turn red. Probably, one wanted only 'EM' elements within 'H1' to turn red, and this can be specified with:

```
H1 EM { color: red }
```

The selector is now a search pattern on the stack of open elements, and this type of selector is referred to as a "contextual selector." Contextual selectors consist of several simple selectors separated by whitespace (all selectors described up to now have been simple selectors). Only elements that match the last simple selector (in this case, the 'EM' element) are addressed, and only if the search pattern matches. Contextual selectors in CSS1 look for ancestor relationships, but other relationships (e.g., parent-child) may be introduced in later revisions. In the example above, the search pattern matches if 'EM' is a descendant of 'H1'—i.e., if 'EM' is inside an 'H1' element.

```
UL LI    { font-size: small }
UL UL LI { font-size: x-small }
```

Here, the first selector matches 'LI' elements with at least one 'UL' ancestor. The second selector matches a subset of the first—i.e., 'LI' elements with at least two 'UL' ancestors. The conflict is resolved by the second selector being more specific because of the longer search pattern. See section "3.2 Cascading Order" for more information.

Contextual selectors can look for tags, classes, IDs, or combinations of these:

```
DIV P           { font: small sans-
    serif }
.reddish H1     { color: red }
#x78y CODE      { background: blue }
DIV.sidenote H1 { font-size: large }
```

The first selector matches all 'P' elements that have a 'DIV' among the ancestors. The second selector matches all 'H1' elements that have an ancestor of class 'reddish'. The third selector matches all 'CODE' elements that are descendants of the element with 'ID=x78y'. The fourth selector matches all 'H1' elements that have a 'DIV' ancestor with class 'sidenote'.

Several contextual selectors can be grouped together:

```
H1 B, H2 B, H1 EM, H2 EM { color:
    red }
```

The example above is equivalent to:

```
H1 B  { color: red }
H2 B  { color: red }
H1 EM { color: red }
H2 EM { color: red }
```

1.7 Comments

Textual comments in CSS style sheets are similar to those in the C programming language:

```
EM { color: red }  /* red, really
    red!! */
```

Comments cannot be nested.

2. Pseudo-Classes and Pseudo-Elements

In CSS1, style is normally attached to an element based on its position in the document structure. This simple model is sufficient for a wide variety of styles but doesn't cover some common effects. The concept of pseudo-classes and pseudo-elements extends addressing in CSS1 to allow external information to influence the formatting process.

Pseudo-classes and pseudo-elements can be used in CSS selectors but do not exist in the HTML source. Rather, they are "inserted" by the UA under certain conditions to be used for addressing in style sheets. They are referred to as "classes" and "elements" since this is a convenient way of describing their behavior. More specifically, their behavior is defined by a "fictional tag sequence" where they have a well-defined order.

Pseudo-elements are used to address sub-parts of elements, while pseudo-classes allow style sheets to differentiate between different element types.

2.1 Anchor Pseudo-Classes

User agents commonly display newly visited anchors differently from older ones. In CSS1, this is handled through pseudo-classes on the 'A' element:

```
A:link { color: red }       /*
    unvisited link */
A:visited { color: blue }   /*
    visited links */
A:active { color: lime }    /*
    active links */
```

All 'A' elements with an 'HREF' attribute will be put into one and only one of these groups (i.e., target anchors are not affected). UAs may choose to move an element from 'visited' to 'link' after a certain time. An 'active' link is one that the reader is currently selecting (e.g., by a mouse button press) by the reader.

The formatting of an anchor pseudo-class is as if the class had been inserted manually. A UA is not required to reformat a currently displayed document due to anchor pseudo-class transitions. For example, a style sheet can legally specify that the 'font-size' of an 'active' link should be larger that a 'visited' link, but the UA is not required to dynamically reformat the document when the reader selects the 'visited' link.

Pseudo-class selectors do not match normal classes, and vice versa. The style rule in the following example will therefore not have any influence:

```
A:link { color: red }
```

```
<A CLASS=link NAME=target5> .. </A>
```

Anchor pseudo-classes have no effect on elements other than 'A'.

Pseudo-classes can be used in contextual selectors:

```
A:link IMG { border: solid blue }
```

Also, pseudo-classes can be combined with normal classes:

```
A.external:visited { color: blue }
```

```
<A CLASS=external HREF="http://out.
    side/">external link</A>
```

If the link in the above example has been visited, it will be rendered in blue. Note that normal class names precede pseudo-classes in the selector.

2.2 Typographical Pseudo-Elements

Some common typographical effects are associated not with structural elements but rather with typographical items as formatted on the canvas. In CSS1, two such typographical items can be addressed through pseudo-elements: the first line of an element and the first letter.

NOTE

CSS1 core: UAs may ignore all rules with ':first-line' or ':first-letter' in the selector or, alternatively, only support a subset of the properties on these pseudo-elements. (See section 7.)

2.3 The 'first-line' Pseudo-Element

The 'first-line' pseudo-element is used to apply special styles to the first line as formatted on the canvas:

```
<STYLE TYPE="text/css">
```

```
    P:first-line { font-style:
        small-caps }
</STYLE>
```

```
<P>The first line of an article in
    Newsweek.
```

On a text-based UA, this could be formatted as:

```
THE FIRST LINE OF AN
article in Newsweek.
```

The fictional tag sequence in the above example is:

```
<P>
 <P:first-line> The first line of
   an </P:first-line> article in
   Newsweek.
</P>
```

The 'first-line' end tag is inserted at the end of the first line as formatted on the canvas.

The 'first-line' pseudo-element can be attached only to a block-level element.

The 'first-line' pseudo-element is similar to an inline element but with certain restrictions. Only the following properties apply to a 'first-line' element: font properties, color and background properties, 'text-decoration', 'vertical-align', 'text-transform', 'line-height', and 'clear' (see corresponding sections 5.2–5.5.7).

2.4 The 'first-letter' Pseudo-Element

The 'first-letter' pseudo-element is used for initial caps and drop caps, which are common typographical effects. It is similar to an inline element if its 'float' property is 'none'; otherwise, it is similar to a floating element. These are the properties that apply to 'first-letter' pseudo-elements: font properties, color and background properties, 'text-decoration, 'vertical-align (only if 'float' is 'none'), 'text-transform', 'line-height', margin properties, padding properties, border properties, 'float', and 'clear' (see corresponding sections 5.2–5.5.7).

Example 1 shows how you could make a drop cap initial letter span two lines.

Example 1

```
<HTML>
 <HEAD>
  <TITLE>Title</TITLE>
  <STYLE TYPE="text/css">
   P              { font-size: 12pt; line-height: 12pt }
   P:first-letter { font-size: 200%; float: left }
   SPAN           { text-transform: uppercase }
  </STYLE>
 </HEAD>
 <BODY>
  <P><SPAN>The first</SPAN> few words of an article in The Economist.</P>
 </BODY>
</HTML>
```

(The 'SPAN' element is being proposed as a new character-level element.)

If an text-based UA supports the 'first-letter' pseudo-element (we do not expect this to be the case), Example 1 could be formatted as shown in Figure 1.

The fictional tag sequence in Figure 1 is:

```
 <P>
  <SPAN>
   <P:first-letter> T
   </P:first-letter>
     he first
  </SPAN>
     few words of an article in the
     Economist.
 </P>
```

Note that the 'first-letter' pseudo-element tags abut the content (i.e., the initial character), while the 'first-line' pseudo-element start tag is inserted right after the start tag of the element it is attached to.

The UA defines what characters are inside the 'first-letter' element. Normally, quotes that pre-cede the first letter should be included, as shown in Figure 2.

When the paragraph starts with other punctuation (e.g., parentheses and ellipses) or other characters that are normally not considered letters (e.g., digits and mathematical symbols), 'first-letter' pseudo-elements are usually ignored.

Some languages may have specific rules about how to treat certain letter combinations. In Dutch, for example, if the letter combination "ij" appears at the beginning of a word, both letters should be considered within the 'first-letter' pseudo-element.

The 'first-letter' pseudo-element can only be attached to a block-level element.

2.5 Pseudo-Elements in Selectors

In a contextual selector, pseudo-elements are allowed only in the last simple selector:

```
BODY P:first-letter { color:
    purple }
```

THE FIRST few words of an article in the Economist.

Figure 1   Format of Example 1

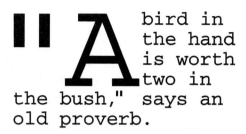

Figure 2   Quotes are included in the 'first-letter' element

Pseudo-elements can be combined with classes in selectors:

```
P.initial:first-letter
    { color: red }
```

```
<P CLASS=initial>First paragraph</A>
```

The above example would make the first letter of all 'P' elements with 'CLASS=initial' red. When combined with classes or pseudo-classes, pseudo-elements must be specified at the end of the selector. Only one pseudo-element can be specified per selector.

2.6 Multiple Pseudo-Elements

Several pseudo elements can be combined:

```
P { color: red; font-size: 12pt }
P:first-letter { color: green; font-
    size: 200% }
P:first-line { color: blue }
```

```
<P>Some text that ends up on two
lines</P>
```

In this example, the first letter of each 'P' element would be green with a font size of 24 points. The rest of the first line (as formatted on the canvas) would be blue while the rest of the paragraph would be red. Assuming that a line break will occur before the word "ends," the fictional tag sequence is:

```
<P>
 <P:first-line>
  <P:first-letter> S
```

```
 </P:first-letter>
 ome text that
 <P:/first-line>
  ends up on two lines
</P>
```

Note that the 'first-letter' element is inside the 'first-line' element. Properties set on 'first-line' will be inherited by 'first-letter' but are overridden if the same property is set on 'first-letter'.

If a pseudo-element breaks up a real element the necessary extra tags must be regenerated in the fictional tag sequence. For example, if a SPAN element spans over a `</P:first-line>` tag, a set of SPAN end and start tags must be regenerated and the fictional tag sequence becomes:

```
<P>
 <P:first-line>
  <SPAN> This text is inside a long
  </SPAN>
 </P:first-line>
 <SPAN> span element
 </SPAN>
```

3. The Cascade

In CSS, more than one style sheet can influence the presentation simultaneously. The two main reasons for this feature are modularity and author/reader balance.

modularity

A style sheet designer can combine several (partial) style sheets to reduce redundancy:

```
@import url(http://www.style.
    org/punk);
```

```
@import url(http://www.style.
    org/funk);

H1 { color: red }      /*
    override imported sheets
    */
```

author/reader balance

Both readers and authors can influence the presentation through style sheets. To do so, they use the same style sheet language thus reflecting a fundamental feature of the Web: everyone can become a publisher. The UA is free to choose the mechanism for referencing personal style sheets.

Sometimes conflicts will arise between the style sheets that influence the presentation. Conflict resolution is based on each style rule having a weight. By default, the weights of the reader's rules are less than the weights of rules in the author's documents. That is, if the style sheets of an incoming document conflict with the reader's personal sheets, the author's rules will be used. Both reader and author rules override the UA's default values.

3.1 'important'

Style sheet designers can increase the weights of their declarations:

```
H1 { color: black ! important;
    background: white ! important }
P  { font-size: 12pt ! important;
    font-style: italic }
```

In the example above, the first three declarations have increased weight, while the last declaration has normal weight.

A reader rule with an important declaration will override an author rule with a normal declaration. An author rule with an important declaration will override a reader rule with an important declaration.

3.2 Cascading Order

Conflicting rules are intrinsic to the CSS mechanism. To find the value for an element/property

combination, the following algorithm must be followed:

1. Find all declarations that apply to the element/property in question. Declarations apply if the selector matches the element in question. If no declarations apply, the inherited value is used. If there is no inherited value (this is the case on the root element and for properties that do not inherit), the initial value is used.

2. Sort the declarations by explicit weight: declarations marked '!important' carry more weight than unmarked (normal) declarations.

3. Sort by origin: the author's style sheets override the reader's style sheets, which override the UA's default values. An imported style sheet has the same origin as the style sheet from which it is imported.

4. Sort by specificity of selector: more specific selectors will override more general ones. To find the specificity, count the number of ID attributes in the selector (a), the number of CLASS attributes in the selector (b), and the number of tag names in the selector (c). Concatenating the three numbers (in a number system with a large base) gives the specificity. Some examples:

```
LI           {...}  /* a=0 b=0
    c=1 -> specificity =    1
    */
UL LI        {...}  /* a=0 b=0
    c=2 -> specificity =    2
    */
UL OL LI     {...}  /* a=0 b=0
    c=3 -> specificity =    3
    */
LI.red       {...}  /* a=0 b=1
    c=1 -> specificity =   11
    */
UL OL LI.red {...}  /* a=0 b=1
    c=3 -> specificity =   13
    */
#x34y        {...}  /* a=1 b=0
    c=0 -> specificity =  100
    */
```

Pseudo-elements and pseudo-classes are counted as normal elements and classes, respectively.

5. Sort by order specified: if two rules have the same weight, the latter specified wins. Rules in imported style sheets are considered specified at the place of the '@import' statement.

The search for the property value can be terminated whenever one rule has a higher weight than the other rules that apply to the same element/property combination.

This strategy gives author's style sheets considerably higher weight than those of the reader. It is therefore important that the reader has the ability to turn off the influence of a certain style sheet, e.g., through a pull-down menu.

A declaration in the 'STYLE' attribute of an element (see section 1.1 for an example) has the same weight as a declaration with an ID-based selector that is specified at the end of the style sheet:

```
<STYLE TYPE="text/css">
    #x97z { color: blue }
```

```
</STYLE>

<P ID=x97z STYLE="color: red">
```

In the above example, the color of the 'P' element would be red. Although the specificity is the same for both declarations, the declaration in the 'STYLE' attribute will override the one in the 'STYLE' element because of cascading rule number 5.

The UA may choose to honor other stylistic HTML attributes—for example, 'ALIGN'. If so, these attributes are translated to the corresponding CSS rules with specificity equal to 1. The rules are assumed to be at the start of the author style sheet and may be overridden by subsequent style sheet rules. In a transition phase, this policy will make it easier for stylistic attributes to coexist with style sheets.

4. Formatting Model

CSS1 assumes a simple box-oriented formatting model where each element results in one or more boxes. All boxes have a core content area with optional surrounding padding, border, and margin areas, as shown in Figure 3.

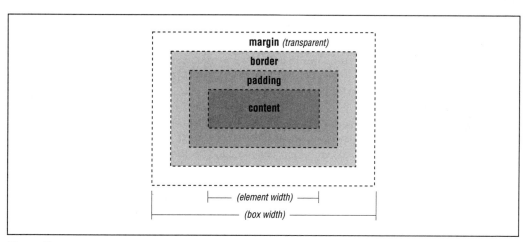

Figure 3   CSS1 box-oriented formatting model

The size of the margin, border, and padding are set with the 'margin', 'border', and 'padding' properties, respectively. The padding area uses the same background as the element itself (set with the 'background' property). The color and style for the border is set with the 'border' properties. The margins are always transparent, so the parent element will shine through.

The size of the box is the sum of the element width (i.e., formatted text or image) and padding, border, and margin areas.

From the formatter's point of view, the two main types of elements are block-level and inline.

4.1 Block-Level Elements

Elements with a 'display' value of 'block' or 'list-item' are block-level elements. Also, floating elements (elements with a 'float' value other than 'none') are formatted as block-level elements.

Example 2 shows how margins and padding format a 'UL' element with two children. To simplify the diagram there are no borders.

The UL element with two children is shown in Figure 4.

Technically, padding and margin properties are not inherited. But, as Example 2 shows, the placement of an element is relative to ancestors and siblings, so these elements' padding and margin properties have an effect on their children.

If the border width had been set (the default value is '0'), the border would have appeared between the padding and the margins.

Figure 5 introduces some useful terminology. The *left outer edge* is the edge of an element with its padding, border, and margin taken into account. The *left inner edge* is the edge of the content only, inside any padding, border, or margin. Ditto for right. The *top* is the top of the object including any padding, border, and margin; it is only defined for inline and floating elements, not for nonfloating block elements. The *inner top* is the top of the content, inside any padding, border, or margin. The *bottom* is the bottom of the element, outside any padding, border, and margin. The *inner bottom* is the bottom of the element, inside any padding, border, and margin.

Example 2

```
<STYLE TYPE="text/css">
  UL {
    background: red;
    margin: A B C D;       /* let s pretend we have constants in CSS1 */
    padding: E F G H;      /* let s pretend we have constants in CSS1 */
  }
  LI {
    color: white;
    background: blue;      /* so text is white on blue */
    margin: a b c d;       /* let s pretend we have constants in CSS1 */
    padding: e f g h;      /* let s pretend we have constants in CSS1 */
    }
</STYLE>
..
<UL>
   <LI>1st element of list
   <LI>2nd element of list
</UL>
```

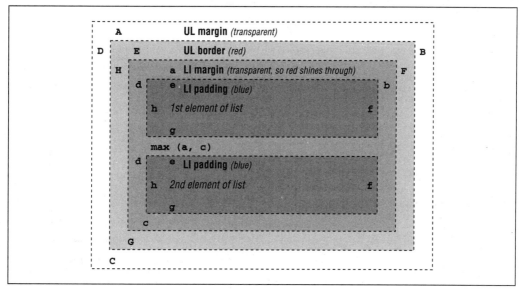

Figure 4   The UL element with two children

The *width* of an element is the width of the content—i.e., the distance between left inner edge and right inner edge. The *height* is the height of the content—i.e., the distance from inner top to inner bottom.

4.1.1 Vertical formatting

The width of the margin on nonfloating block-level elements specifies the minimum distance to the edges of surrounding boxes. Two or more adjoining vertical margins (i.e., with no border, padding, or content between them) are collapsed to use the maximum of the margin values. In most cases, the result is visually more pleasing and closer to what the designer expects. In the example above, the margins between the two 'LI' elements are collapsed by using the maximum of the first LI element's 'margin-bottom' and the second LI element's 'margin-top'. Similarly, if the padding between the 'UL' and the first 'LI' element (the E constant) had been zero, the margins of the UL and first LI elements should have been collapsed.

In the case of negative margins, the absolute maximum of the negative adjoining margins is deducted from the maximum of the positive adjoining margins. If there are no positive margins, the absolute maximum of the negative adjoining margins is deducted from zero.

4.1.2 Horizontal formatting

The horizontal position and size of a nonfloating, block-level element is determined by seven properties: 'margin-left', 'border-left', 'padding-left', 'width', 'padding-right', 'border-right', and 'margin-right'. The sum of these seven is always equal to the 'width' of the parent element.

By default, the 'width' of an element is 'auto'. If the element is not a replaced element, this means that the 'width' is calculated by the UA so that the sum of the seven properties mentioned above is equal to the parent width. If the element is a replaced element, a value of 'auto' for 'width' is automatically replaced by the element's intrinsic width.

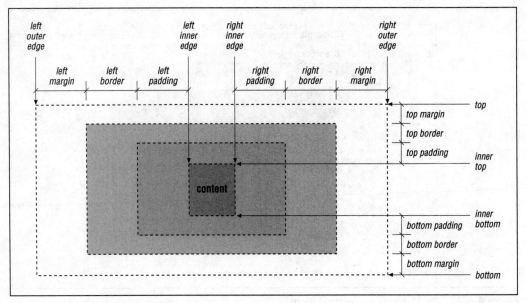

Figure 5   Terminology used to describe block-level elements

Three of the seven properties can be set to 'auto': 'margin-left', 'width', and 'margin-right'. Since a value of 'auto' on 'width' is replaced by the intrinsic width, for replaced elements there can only be two 'auto' values.

The 'width' has a non-negative UA-defined minimum value (which may vary from element to element and even depend on other properties). If 'width' goes below this limit, either because it was set explicitly or because it was 'auto' and the rules below would make it too small, the value will be replaced with the minimum value instead.

If *exactly one* of 'margin-left', 'width', or 'margin-right' is 'auto', the UA will assign that property a value that will make the sum of the seven equal to the parent's width.

If *none* of the properties are 'auto', the value of 'margin-right' will be ignored, and 'margin-right' will be treated as if it were 'auto'.

If *more than one* of the three is 'auto', and one of them is 'width', the others ('margin-left' and/or 'margin-right') will be set to zero, and 'width' will

get the value needed to make the sum of the seven equal to the parent's width.

Otherwise, if both 'margin-left' and 'margin-right' are 'auto', they will be set to equal values. This will center the element inside its parent.

If 'auto' is set as the value for one of the seven properties in an element that is inline or floating, it will be treated as if it were set to zero.

Unlike vertical margins, horizontal margins are not collapsed.

4.1.3 List-item elements

Elements with a 'display' property value of 'list-item' are formatted as block-level elements but preceded by a label. The type of label is determined by the 'list-style' property. The label is placed according to the value of the 'list-style' property:

```
<STYLE TYPE="text/css">
  UL          { list-style: outside }
  UL.compact { list-style: inside }
</STYLE>
```

```
<UL>
   <LI>first list item comes first
   <LI>second list item comes second
</UL>

<UL CLASS=COMPACT>
   <LI>first list item comes first
   <LI>second list item comes second
</UL>
```

The above example may be formatted as:

```
* first list item
  comes first

* second list item
  comes second

* first list
  item comes first

* second list
  item comes second
```

4.1.4 Floating elements

Using the 'float' property, an element can be declared to be outside the normal flow of elements and is then formatted as a block-level element. For example, by setting the 'float' property of an image to 'left', the image is moved to the left until the margin, padding, or border of another block-level element is reached. The normal flow will wrap around on the right side. The margins, borders, and padding of the element itself will be honored, and the margins never collapse with the margins of adjacent elements.

A floating element is positioned subject to the following constraints (see section 4.1 for an explanation of the terms):

1. The left outer edge of a left-floating element may not be to the left of the left inner edge of its parent element. Analogously for right-floating elements.

2. The left outer edge of a left-floating element must be to the right of the right outer edge of every earlier (in the HTML source) left-floating element, or the top of the former must be lower than the bottom of the latter. Analogously for right-floating elements.

3. The right outer edge of a left-floating element may not be to the right of the left outer edge of any right-floating element that is to the right of it. Analogously for right-floating elements.

4. A floating element's top may not be higher than the inner top of its parent.

5. A floating element's top may not be higher than the top of any earlier floating or block-like element.

6. A floating element's top may not be higher than the top of any text line that precedes the floating element in the HTML source.

7. A floating element must be placed as high as possible.

8. A left-floating element must be put as far to the left as possible, a right-floating element as far to the right as possible. A higher position is preferred over one that is farther to the left/right.

```
<STYLE TYPE="text/css">
   IMG { float: left }
   BODY, P, IMG { margin: 2em }
</STYLE>

<BODY>
   <IMG SRC=img.gif>
   <P>Some sample text has no
      other..
</BODY>
```

The above example could be formatted as shown in Figure 6.

Floating elements can overlap with the margin, border, and padding areas of another element when:

- The floating element has a negative margin. Negative margins on floating elements are honored as on other block-level elements.

- The floating element is wider or higher than the element it is inside.

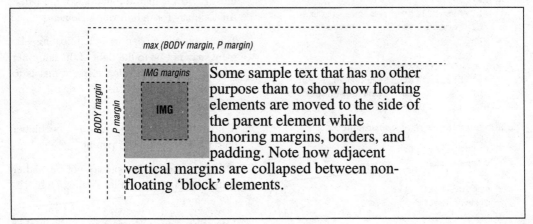

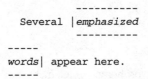

Some sample text that has no other purpose than to show how floating elements are moved to the side of the parent element while honoring margins, borders, and padding. Note how adjacent vertical margins are collapsed between non-floating 'block' elements.

Figure 6   Format of a left-floating element

4.2 Inline Elements

Elements that are not block-level are inline elements. An inline element can share line space with other elements. Consider this example:

```
<P>Several <EM>emphasized</EM>
    words <STRONG>appear</STRONG>.
</P>
```

The 'P' element is normally block level, while 'EM' and 'STRONG' are inline elements. If the 'P' element is wide enough to format the whole element on one line, there will be two inline elements on the line:

Several *emphasized* words **appear.**

If there is not enough room on one line, an inline element will be split into several boxes:

```
<P>Several <EM>emphasized
    words</EM> appear here.</P>
```

The above example may be formatted as:

Several *emphasized*
    words appear here.

If the inline element has attached margins, borders, padding, or text decorations, these will have no effect where the element is broken:

```
          ----------
Several  |emphasized
          ----------
-----
words|  appear here.
-----
```

The example above is slightly distorted due to the use of ASCII graphics. See section 4.4 for a description of how to calculate the height of lines.

4.3 Replaced Elements

A replaced element is an element that is replaced by content pointed to from the element. For example, in HTML, the IMG element is replaced by the image pointed to by the SRC attribute. One can assume that replaced elements come with their own intrinsic dimensions. If the CSS value for 'width' is 'auto', the intrinsic width is used as the width of the element. If a value other than 'auto' is specified in the style sheet, this value is used, and the replaced element is resized accordingly. (The resize method will depend on the media type.) The 'height' property is used in the same manner.

Replaced elements can be either block-level or inline.

4.4 The Height of Lines

All elements other than replaced elements have a 'line-height' property that, in principle, gives the total height of a line of text. Space is added above and below the text of the line to arrive at that line height. For example, if the text is 12 point high and 'line-height' is set to '14pt', an extra space of 2 points is added, namely 1 point above and 1 point below the line. Empty elements influence these calculations just as elements with content.

The difference between the font size and the 'line-height' is called the *leading*. Half the leading is called the *half-leading*. After formatting, each line will form a rectangular *line-box*.

If a line of text contains sections with different 'line-height' values (because there are inline elements on the line), each of those sections has its own half-leading above and below. The height of the line-box is from the top of the highest section to the bottom of the lowest one. (Note that the top and bottom do not necessarily correspond to the tallest element, since elements can be positioned vertically with the 'vertical-align' property.) To form a paragraph, each line-box is stacked immediately below the previous line.

Note that any padding, border, or margin above and below inline elements does not influence the height of the line. In other words, if the 'line-height' is too small for the chosen padding or border, it will overlap with text on other lines.

Replaced elements (e.g., images) on the line can make the line-box bigger, if the top of the replaced element (including all of its padding, border, and margin) is above the tallest text section, or if the bottom is below the lowest.

In the normal case, when there is only one value of 'line-height' throughout a paragraph, and no tall images, the definition above will ensure that baselines of successive lines are exactly 'line-height' apart. This is important when columns of text in different fonts have to be aligned—for example, in a table.

Note that this doesn't preclude the text on two adjacent lines from overlapping. The 'line-height' may be smaller than the height of the text, in which case the leading will be negative. This is actually quite useful if you know that the text will not contain descenders (because it contains only uppercase letters), so the lines can be placed closer together.

4.5 The Canvas

The canvas is the part of the UA's drawing surface onto which documents are rendered. No structural element of a document corresponds to the canvas, and this raises two issues when formatting a document:

- From where should the dimensions of the canvas be set?

- When the document doesn't cover the whole canvas, how should this area be rendered?

A reasonable answer to the first question is that the initial size of the canvas is based on the window size, but CSS1 leaves this issue for the UA to decide. It is also reasonable to expect the UA to change the canvas size when the window is resized, but this is also outside the scope of CSS1.

HTML extensions have set a precedent for the second question: attributes on the 'BODY' element set the background of the whole canvas. To support designers' expectations, CSS1 introduces a special rule to find the canvas background:

> If the background value of the HTML element is different from transparent, use it; otherwise, use the background value of the BODY element. If the resulting value is transparent, the rendering is undefined.

This rule allows:

```
<HTML STYLE="background: url(http://
    style.com/marble.png)">
<BODY STYLE="background: red">
```

In the example above, the canvas will be covered with "marble." The background of the 'BODY' element (which may or may not fully cover the canvas) will be red.

Until other means of addressing the canvas become available, we recommend setting canvas properties on the 'BODY' element.

4.6 'BR' Elements

The current CSS1 properties and values cannot describe the behavior of the 'BR' element. In HTML, the 'BR' element specifies a line break between words. In effect, the element is replaced by a line break. We expect future versions of CSS to handle added and replaced content, but CSS1-based formatters must treat 'BR' in a special manner.

5. CSS1 Properties

Style sheets influence the presentation of documents by assigning values to style properties. This section lists the defined style properties, and their corresponding list of possible values, of CSS1. See section 7 for the conformance requirements.

5.1 Notation for Property Values

In the text below, the allowed values for each property are listed with the following syntax:

Value
    N | NW | NE

Value
    [<length> | thick | thin]{1,4}

Value
    [<family-name> ,]* <family-name>

Value
    <url>? <color> [/ <color>]?

Value
    <url> || <color>

The words between the open and close angle brackets (< and >) give a type of value. The most common types are <length>, <percentage>, <url>, <number>, and <color>; these are

described in the section on units. The more specialized types (e.g., <font-family> and <border-style>) are described following the property they appear under.

Other words are keywords that must appear literally, without quotes. The slash (/) and the comma (,) must also appear literally.

Several juxtaposed items mean that all of them must occur, in the given order. A bar (|) separates alternatives: one of them must occur. A double bar (A || B) means that either A or B or both must occur, in any order. Brackets ([]) are for grouping. Juxtaposition is stronger than the double bar, and the double bar is stronger than the bar. Thus a b | c || d e is equivalent to [a b] | [c || [d e]].

Every type, keyword, or bracketed group may be followed by one of the following modifiers:

- An asterisk (*) indicates that the preceding type, word, or group is repeated zero or more times.

- A plus sign (+) indicates that the preceding type, word, or group is repeated one or more times.

- A question mark (?) indicates that the preceding type, word, or group is optional.

- A pair of numbers in curly braces ({A,B}) indicates that the preceding type, word, or group is repeated at least A and at most B times.

5.2 Font Properties

Setting font properties will be among the most common uses of style sheets. Unfortunately, no well-defined and universally accepted taxonomy exists for classifying fonts, and terms that apply to one font family may not be appropriate for others. For example, *italic* is commonly used to label slanted text, but slanted text may also be labeled as being *oblique, slanted, incline, cursive,* or *kursiv.* Therefore, it is not a simple problem to map typical font selection properties to a specific font.

CSS1 defines the properties 'font-family', 'font-size', 'font-weight', 'font-style', 'font-variant', and 'font'. Additional font characteristics are being worked on in the W3C Fonts working group. These will complement the properties defined in CSS1.

5.2.1 Font matching

Because there is no accepted, universal taxonomy of font properties, matching properties to font faces must be done carefully. The properties are matched in a well-defined order to insure that the results of this matching process are as consistent as possible across UAs (assuming that the same library of font faces is presented to each of them).

1. The user agent makes (or accesses) a database of relevant CSS1 properties of all the fonts of which the UA is aware. The UA may be aware of a font because it has been installed locally or because it has been previously downloaded over the Web. If two fonts have exactly the same properties, one of them is ignored.

2. At a given element and for each character in that element, the UA assembles the font properties applicable to that element. Using the complete set of properties, the UA uses the 'font-family' property to choose a tentative font family. The remaining properties are tested against the family according to the matching criteria described with each property. If there are matches for all the remaining properties, that is the matching font face for the given element.

3. If no matching font face is within the 'font-family' being processed by step 2 and if a next alternative 'font-family' is in the font set, repeat step 2 with the next alternative 'font-family'.

4. If there is a matching font face, but it doesn't contain a glyph for the current character and if a next alternative 'font-family' is in the font sets, repeat step 2 with the next alternative 'font-family'. See Appendix C for a description of font and character encoding.

5. If there is no font within the family selected in step 2, use a UA-dependent default 'font-family' and repeat step 2, using the best match that can be obtained within the default font.

(The above algorithm can be optimized to avoid having to revisit the CSS1 properties for each character.)

The per-property matching rules from step 2 above are as follows:

1. 'font-style' is tried first. 'italic' will be satisfied if a face is in the UA's font database labeled with the CSS keyword 'italic' (preferred) or 'oblique'. Otherwise, the values must be matched exactly or 'font-style' will fail.

2. 'font-variant' is tried next. 'normal' matches a font not labeled as 'small-caps'; 'small-caps' matches one of the following
   1. A font labeled as 'small-caps'.
   2. A font in which the small caps are synthesized
   3. A font where all lowercase letters are replaced by uppercase letters.

   A small-caps font may be synthesized by electronically scaling uppercase letters from a normal font.

3. 'font-weight' is matched next; it will never fail. (See 'font-weight' below.)

4. 'font-size' must be matched within a UA-dependent margin of tolerance. (Typically, sizes for scalable fonts are rounded to the nearest whole pixel, while the tolerance for bitmapped fonts could be as large as 20 percent.) Further computations (e.g., by 'em' values in other properties) are based on the

'font-size' value that is used, not the one that is specified.

5.2.2 'font-family'

Value: [[<family-name> | <generic-family>],]* [<family-name> | <generic-family>]
Initial: UA specific
Applies to: all elements
Inherited: yes
Percentage values: N/A

The value is a prioritized list of font family names and/or generic family names. Unlike most other CSS1 properties, values are separated by a comma to indicate that they are alternatives:

```
BODY { font-family: gill,
    helvetica, sans-serif }
```

There are two types of list values:

<family-name>

The name of a font family of choice. In the previous example, `gill` and `helvetica` are font families.

<generic-family>

In the example above, the last value, `sans-serif`, is a generic family name. The following generic families are defined:

- 'serif' (e.g., Times)
- 'sans-serif' (e.g., Helvetica)
- 'cursive' (e.g., Zapf-Chancery)
- 'fantasy' (e.g., Western)
- 'monospace' (e.g., Courier)
  Style sheet designers are encouraged to offer a generic font family as a last alternative.

Font names containing whitespace should be quoted:

```
BODY { font-family: "new century
    schoolbook", serif }

<BODY STYLE="font-family:  My own
    font , fantasy">
```

If quoting is omitted, any whitespace characters before and after the font name are ignored, and any sequence of whitespace characters inside the font name is converted to a single space.

5.2.3 'font-style'

Value: normal | italic | oblique
Initial: normal
Applies to: all elements
Inherited: yes
Percentage values: N/A

The 'font-style' property selects between normal (sometimes referred to as *roman* or *upright*), italic, and oblique faces within a font family.

A value of 'normal' selects a font that is classified as 'normal' in the UA's font database, while 'oblique' selects a font that is labeled 'oblique'. A value of 'italic' selects a font that is labeled 'italic' or, if that is not available, one labeled 'oblique'.

The font that is labeled 'oblique' in the UA's font database may actually have been generated by electronically slanting a normal font.

Fonts with *oblique, slanted,* or *incline* in their names will typically be labeled 'oblique' in the UA's font database. Fonts with *italic, cursive,* or *kursiv* in their names will typically be labeled 'italic'.

```
H1, H2, H3 { font-style: italic }
H1 EM { font-style: normal }
```

In the example above, emphasized text within 'H1' will appear in a normal face.

5.2.4 'font-variant'

Value: normal | small-caps
Initial: normal
Applies to: all elements
Inherited: yes
Percentage values: N/A

Another type of variation within a font family is the small-caps. In a small caps font, the lowercase letters look similar to the uppercase ones, but in a smaller size and with slightly different proportions. The 'font-variant' property selects that font.

A value of 'normal' selects a font that is not a small-caps font; 'small-caps' selects a small-caps font. It is acceptable (but not required) in CSS1 if the small-caps font is a created by taking a normal font and replacing the lowercase letters by scaled uppercase characters. As a last resort, uppercase letters will be used as replacement for a small caps font.

The following example results in an 'H3' element in small caps, with emphasized words in oblique small caps:

```
H3 { font-variant: small-caps }
EM { font-style: oblique }
```

There may be other variants in the font family as well, such as fonts with old style numerals, small caps numerals, condensed, or expanded letters, etc. CSS1 has no properties that select those.

NOTE

> *CSS1 core:* insofar as this property causes text to be transformed to uppercase, the same considerations as for 'text-transform' apply.

5.2.5 'font-weight'

Value: normal | bold | bolder | lighter | 100 | 200 | 300 | 400 | 500 | 600 | 700 | 800 | 900
Initial: normal
Applies to: all elements
Inherited: yes
Percentage values: N/A

The 'font-weight' property selects the weight of the font. The values '100' to '900' form an ordered sequence, where each number indicates a weight that is at least as dark as its predecessor. The keyword 'normal' is synonymous with '400', and 'bold' is synonymous with '700'. Keywords other than 'normal' and 'bold' have been shown to be often confused with font names, and a numerical scale was therefore chosen for the 9-value list.

```
P { font-weight: normal }   /* 400
   */
```

```
H1 { font-weight: 700 }      /* bold
   */
```

The 'bolder' and 'lighter' values select font weights that are relative to the weight inherited from the parent:

```
STRONG { font-weight: bolder }
```

Child elements inherit the resultant weight, not the keyword value.

Fonts (the font data) typically have one or more properties whose values are names that are descriptive of the "weight" of a font. There is no accepted, universal meaning to these weight names. Their primary role is to distinguish faces of differing darkness within a single font family. Usage across font families is quite variant; for example, a font that you might think of as being bold might be described as being regular, roman, book, medium, semi-, or demibold, bold, or black, depending on how black the "normal" face of the font is within the design. Because there is no standard usage of names, the weight property values in CSS1 are given on a numerical scale in which the value '400' (or 'normal') corresponds to the "normal" text face for that family. The weight name associated with that face will typically be book, regular, roman, normal, or sometimes medium.

The association of other weights within a family to the numerical weight values is intended only to preserve the ordering of darkness within that family. However, the following heuristics tell how the assignment is done in typical cases:

- If the font family already uses a numerical scale with nine values (as OpenType does), the font weights should be mapped directly.

- If there is both a face labeled medium and one labeled book, regular, roman, or normal, the medium is normally assigned to the '500'.

- The font labeled bold will often correspond to the weight value '700'.

- If there are fewer than nine weights in the family, the default algorithm for filling the "holes" is as follows:
  - If '500' is unassigned, it will be assigned the same font as '400'.
  - If any of the values '600', '700', '800', or '900' remains unassigned, they are assigned to the same face as the next darker assigned keyword, if any, or the next lighter one, otherwise.
  - If any of '300', '200', or '100' remains unassigned, it is assigned to the next lighter assigned keyword, if any, or the next darker, otherwise.

The two examples in Table 1 illustrate the process. Assume four weights in the Example 1 family, from lightest to darkest: Regular, Medium, Bold, Heavy. Assume six weights in the Example 2 family: Book, Medium, Bold, Heavy, Black, ExtraBlack. Note how in the second example, "Example2 ExtraBlack" was *not* assigned to anything.

Since the intent of the relative keywords 'bolder' and 'lighter' is to darken or lighten the face *within the family* and because a family may not have faces aligned with all the symbolic weight values, the matching of 'bolder' is to the next darker face available on the client within the family, and the matching of 'lighter' is to the next lighter face within the family. To be precise, the meaning of the relative keywords 'bolder' and 'lighter' is as follows:

- 'bolder' selects the next weight that is assigned to a font that is darker than the inherited one. If there is no such weight, it simply results in the next darker numerical value (and the font remains unchanged), unless the inherited value was '900', in which case, the resulting weight is also '900'.

- 'lighter' is similar but works in the opposite direction. It selects the next lighter keyword with a different font from the inherited one, unless there is no such font, in which case, it selects the next lighter numerical value (and keeps the font unchanged).

There is no guarantee that there will be a darker face for each of the 'font-weight' values. For example, some fonts may have only a normal and a bold face, others may have eight different face weights. There is no guarantee on how a UA will map font faces within a family to weight values. The only guarantee is that a face of a given value will be no less dark than the faces of lighter values.

Table 1   Examples of font weights and numerical values

Available faces	Assignments	Filling the holes
"Example1 Regular"	400	100, 200, 300
"Example1 Medium"	500	
"Example1 Bold"	700	600
"Example1 Heavy"	800	

Available faces	Assignments	Filling the holes
"Example2 Book"	400	100, 200, 300
"Example2 Medium"	500	
"Example2 Bold"	700	600
"Example2 Heavy"	800	
"Example2 Black"	900	
"Example2 ExtraBlack"	(none)	

5.2.6 'font-size'

Value: <absolute-size> | <relative-size> | <length> | <percentage>
Initial: medium
Applies to: all elements
Inherited: yes
Percentage values: relative to parent element's font size

`<absolute-size>`

An <absolute-size> keyword is an index to a table of font sizes computed and kept by the UA. Possible values are: [**xx-small** | x-small | small | medium | large | x-large | xx-large]. On a computer screen, a scaling factor of 1.5 is suggested between adjacent indexes; if the 'medium' font is 10 points, the 'large' font could be 15 points. Different media may need different scaling factors. Also, the UA should take into account the quality and availability of fonts when computing the table. The table may be different from one font family to another.

`<relative-size>`

A <relative-size> keyword is interpreted relative to the table of font sizes and the font size of the parent element. Possible values are: [**larger** | **smaller**]. For example, if the parent element has a font size of 'medium', a value of 'larger' will make the font size of the current element 'large'. If the parent element's size is not close to a table entry, the UA is free to interpolate between table entries or round off to the closest one. The UA may have to extrapolate table values if the numerical value goes beyond the keywords.

Length and percentage values should not take the font size table into account when calculating the font size of the element.

On all other properties, 'em' and 'ex' length values refer to the font size of the current element. On the 'font-size' property, these length units refer to the font size of the parent element.

Note that an application may reinterpret an explicit size, depending on the context. For example, a font may get a different size inside a VR scene because of perspective distortion.

Examples:

```
P { font-size: 12pt; }
BLOCKQUOTE { font-size: larger }
EM { font-size: 150% }
EM { font-size: 1.5em }
```

If the suggested scaling factor of 1.5 is used, the last three rules are identical.

5.2.7 'font'

Value: [<font-style> || <font-variant> || <font-weight>]? <font-size> [/ <line-height>]? <font-family>
Initial: not defined
Applies to: all elements
Inherited: yes
Percentage values: allowed on <font-size> and <line-height>

This syntax of this property is based on a traditional typographical shorthand notation to set multiple properties related to fonts: 'font-style' 'font-variant' 'font-weight' 'font-size', 'line-height' and 'font-family'. For a definition of allowed and initial values, see the previously defined properties. Setting the 'font' property is equivalent to including separate declarations at the same point in the style sheet. Properties for which no values are given are set to their initial value.

```
P { font: 12pt/14pt sans-serif }
P { font: 80% sans-serif }
P { font: x-large/110% "new century
    schoolbook", serif }
P { font: bold italic large
    Palatino, serif }
P { font: normal small-caps 120%/
    120% fantasy }
```

In the second rule, the font size percentage value ('80%') refers to the font size of the parent element. In the third rule, the line height percentage refers to the font size of the element itself.

In the first three rules above, the 'font-style', 'font-variant', and 'font-weight' are not explicitly mentioned, which means they are all three set to their initial value ('normal'). The fourth rule sets the 'font-weight' to 'bold', the 'font-style' to 'italic', and implicitly sets 'font-variant' to 'normal'.

The fifth rule sets the 'font-variant' ('small-caps'), the 'font-size' (120% of the parent's font), the 'line-height' (120% times the font size), and the 'font-family' ('fantasy'). It follows that the keyword 'normal' applies to the two remaining properties, 'font-style' and 'font-weight'.

5.3 Color and Background Properties

5.3.1 'color'

> *Value:* <color>
> *Initial:* UA specific
> *Applies to:* all elements
> *Inherited:* yes
> *Percentage values:* N/A

This property describes the text color of an element—i.e., the "foreground" color. There are different ways to specify red:

```
EM { color: red }              /*
    natural language */
EM { color: rgb(255,0,0) }     /*
    RGB range 0-255  */
```

See section 6.3 for a complete description of possible color values.

5.3.2 'background', 'background-color', 'background-image', 'background-repeat', 'background-attachment', 'background-position'

> *Value:* see individual properties below
> *Initial:* see individual properties below
> *Applies to:* all elements, except 'background-position', which only applies to block-level and replaced elements
> *Inherited:* no
> *Percentage values:* allowed on 'background-position', refer to the size of the element itself

These properties describe the background of an element—i.e., the surface onto which the content is rendered. One can set a background color and/or a background image. The position of the image, if and/or how it is repeated, and whether it is fixed or scrolled relative to the canvas can also be set.

These properties do not inherit, but the parent element's background will shine through by default because of the initial transparent value.

'background'
> The 'background' property is a shorthand notation for setting the individual properties ('background-color', 'background-image', 'background-repeat', 'background-attachment', and 'background-position') at the same place in the style sheet.
>
> Possible values on the 'background' properties are the set of all possible values on the individual properties.
>
> ```
> BODY { background: red }
> P { background: url(chess.png)
>         gray 50% repeat fixed }
> ```
>
> The 'background' property always sets all the individual properties. In the first rule of the above example, only a value for 'background-color' has been given, and the other individual properties are set to their initial value. In the second rule, all individual properties have been specified.

'background-color'
> This property sets the background color of an element. Possible values are [<color> | transparent]. The initial value is 'transparent'.
>
> ```
> H1 { background-color: #F00 }
> ```

'background-image'
> This property sets the background image of an element. Possible values are [<url> | none]. The initial value is 'none'. When setting a background image, one should also set a background color that will be used when the image is unavailable. When the

image is available, it is overlaid on top of the background color.

```
BODY { background-image:
       url(marble.gif) }
P { background-image: none }
```

'background-repeat'

If a background image is specified, the value of 'background-repeat' determines how and/or if the image is repeated. Possible values are [repeat|repeat-x| repeat-y|no-repeat]. The initial value is 'repeat'.

A value of 'repeat' means that the image is repeated both horizontally and vertically. The 'repeat-x' ('repeat-y') value makes the image repeat horizontally (vertically) to create a single band of images from one side to the other. With a value of 'no-repeat', the image is not repeated.

```
BODY {
    background: red url(pendant.
       gif);
    background-repeat: repeat-y;
}
```

In the example above, the image will be repeated only vertically.

'background-attachment'

If a background image is specified, the value of 'background-attachment' determines if it is fixed with regard to the canvas or if it scrolls along with the content. Respectively, the possible values are [scroll | fixed]. The initial value is 'scroll'.

```
BODY {
    background: red url(pendant.
       gif);
    background-repeat: repeat-y;
    background-attachment: fixed;
}
```

NOTE

CSS1 core: UAs may treat 'fixed' as 'scroll'. However, it is recommended they interpret 'fixed' correctly, at least on the HTML and BODY elements,

since there is no way for an author to provide an image only for those browsers that support 'fixed'. (See section 7.)

'background-position'

If a background image has been specified, the value of 'background-position' specifies its initial position. Possible values are [[<percentage> | <length> [<percentage> | <length>]?] | [top | center | bottom] || [left | center | right]]. If no value is specified, '0% 0%' is assumed.

The 'background-position' property applies only to block-level and replaced elements.

With a value pair of '0% 0%', the upper left corner of the image is placed in the upper left corner of the box that surrounds the content of the element (i.e., not the box that surrounds the padding, border, or margin). A value pair of '100% 100%' places the lower right corner of the image in the lower right corner of the element. With a value pair of '14% 84%', the image is to be placed at the point 14% across and 84% down the element.

With a value pair of '2cm 2cm', the upper left corner of the image is placed 2 centimeters to the right and 2 centimeters below the upper left corner of the element.

If only one percentage or length value is given, it sets the horizontal position only, the vertical position will be 50 percent. If two values are given, the horizontal position comes first. Combinations of length and percentage values are allowed—e.g., '50% 2cm'. Negative positions are allowed.

One can also use keyword values to indicate the position of the background image. Keywords cannot be combined with percentage values or length values. The possible combinations of keywords and their interpretations are as follows:

- 'top left' and 'left top' both mean the same as '0% 0%'.
- 'top', 'top center', and 'center top' mean the same as '50% 0%'.
- 'right top' and 'top right' mean the same as '100% 0%'.
- 'left', 'left center' and 'center left' mean the same as '0% 50%'.
- 'center' and 'center center' mean the same as '50% 50%'.
- 'right', 'right center', and 'center right' mean the same as '100% 50%'
- 'bottom left' and 'left bottom' mean the same as '0% 100%'.
- 'bottom', 'bottom center', and 'center bottom' mean the same as '50% 100%'
- 'bottom right' and 'right bottom' mean the same as '100% 100%'.

Examples:

```
BODY { background: url(banner.
     jpeg) right top }
     /* 100%   0% */
BODY { background: url(banner.
     jpeg) top center }
     /* 50%   0% */
BODY { background: url(banner.
     jpeg) center }
     /* 50%  50% */
BODY { background: url(banner.
     jpeg) bottom }
     /* 50% 100% */
```

If the background image is fixed with regard to the canvas (see the 'background-attachment' property above), the image is placed relative to the canvas instead of the element. For example:

```
BODY {
    background-image: url(logo.png);
    background-attachment: fixed;
    background-position: 100% 100%;
}
```

In the example above, the image is placed in the lower right corner of the canvas.

5.4 Text Properties

5.4.1 'word-spacing'

Value: normal | <length>
Initial: normal
Applies to: all elements
Inherited: yes
Percentage values: N/A

The length unit indicates an addition to the default space between words. Values can be negative, but there may be implementation-specific limits. The UA is free to select the exact spacing algorithm. The word spacing may also be influenced by justification (which is a value of the 'align' property).

```
H1 { word-spacing: 0.4em }
```

Here, the word spacing between each word in 'H1' elements would be increased with '1em'.

NOTE

CSS1 core: UAs may interpret any value of 'word-spacing' as 'normal'. (See section 7.)

5.4.2 'letter-spacing'

Value: normal | <length>
Initial: normal
Applies to: all elements
Inherited: yes
Percentage values: N/A

The length unit indicates an addition to the default space between characters. Values can be negative, but there may be implementation-specific limits. The UA is free to select the exact spacing algorithm. The letter spacing may also be influenced by justification (which is a value of the 'align' property).

```
BLOCKQUOTE { letter-spacing: 0.1em }
```

Here, the letter spacing between each character in 'BLOCKQUOTE' elements would be increased with '0.1em'.

With a value of 'normal', the UAs may change the space between letters to justify text. This will not happen if 'letter-spacing' is explicitly set to a `<length>` value:

```
BLOCKQUOTE { letter-spacing: 0 }
BLOCKQUOTE { letter-spacing:
         0cm }
```

When the resultant space between two letters is not the same as the default space, UAs should not use ligatures.

NOTE

CSS1 core: UAs may interpret any value of 'letter-spacing' as 'normal'. (See section 7.)

5.4.3 'text-decoration'

Value: none | [underline || overline || line-through || blink]
Initial: none
Applies to: all elements
Inherited: no, but see clarification below
Percentage values: N/A

This property describes decorations that are added to the text of an element. If the element has no text (e.g., the IMG element in HTML) or is an empty element (e.g., `<EM></EM>`), this property has no effect. 'blink' causes the text to blink.

The color(s) required for the text decoration should be derived from the 'color' property value.

This property is not inherited, but elements should match their parent. For example, if an element is underlined, the line should span the child elements. The color of the underlining will remain the same even if descendant elements have different 'color' values.

```
A:link, A:visited, A:active
  { text-decoration: underline }
```

The example above would underline the text of all links (i.e., all 'A' elements with a 'HREF' attribute).

We expect UA vendors to propose several new values on this property.

UAs must recognize the keyword 'blink' but are not required to support the blink effect.

5.4.4 'vertical-align'

Value: baseline | sub | super | top | text-top | middle | bottom | text-bottom | `<percentage>`
Initial: baseline
Applies to: inline elements
Inherited: no
Percentage values: refer to the 'line-height' of the element itself

The property affects the vertical positioning of the element. One set of keywords is relative to the parent element:

'baseline'
> Align the baseline of the element (or the bottom, if the element doesn't have a baseline) with the baseline of the parent.

'middle'
> Align the vertical midpoint of the element (typically an image) with the baseline plus half the x-height of the parent.

'sub'
> Subscript the element.

'super'
> Superscript the element.

'text-top'
> Align the top of the element with the top of the parent element's font.

'text-bottom'
> Align the bottom of the element with the bottom of the parent element's font.

Another set of properties are relative to the formatted line that the element is a part of:

'top'
> Align the top of the element with the tallest element on the line.

'bottom'
> Align the bottom of the element with the lowest element on the line.

Using the 'top' and 'bottom' alignment, unsolvable situations can occur where element dependencies form a loop.

Percentage values refer to the value of the 'line-height' property of the element itself. They raise the baseline of the element (or the bottom, if it has no baseline) the specified amount above the baseline of the parent. Negative values are possible. For example, a value of '−100%' will lower the element so that the baseline of the element ends up where the baseline of the next line should have been.

NOTE

> This allows precise control over the vertical position of elements that don't have a baseline (such as images that are used in place of letters).

5.4.5 'text-transform'

> *Value:* `capitalize | uppercase | lowercase | none`
> *Initial:* none
> *Applies to:* all elements
> *Inherited:* yes
> *Percentage values:* N/A

'capitalize'
> Uppercases the first character of each word.

'uppercase'
> Uppercases all letters of the element.

'lowercase'
> Lowercases all letters of the element.

'none'
> Neutralizes inherited value.

The actual transformation in each case is human language dependent.

```
H1 { text-transform: uppercase }
```

The example above would capitalize 'H1' elements.

NOTE

> *CSS1 core:* UAs may ignore 'text-transform' (i.e., treat it as 'none') for characters that are not from the Latin-1 repertoire and for elements in languages for which the transformation is different from that specified by the case-conversion tables of Unicode.

NOTE

> See (15) for suggested ways to find the language of an element.

5.4.6 'text-align'

> *Value:* `left | right | center | justify`
> *Initial:* UA specific
> *Applies to:* block-level elements
> *Inherited:* yes
> *Percentage values:* N/A

This property describes how text is aligned within the element. The actual justification algorithm used is UA and human language dependent.

Example:

```
DIV.center { text-align: center }
```

Since 'text-align' inherits, all block-level elements inside the 'DIV' element with 'CLASS=center' will be centered. Note that alignments are relative to the width of the element, not the canvas. If 'justify' is not supported, the UA will supply a replacement. Typically, this will be 'left' for Western languages.

CSS1 core: UAs may treat 'justify' as 'left' or 'right', depending on whether the element's default writing direction is left to right or right to left, respectively.

5.4.7 'text-indent'

Value: `<length>` | `<percentage>`
Initial: 0
Applies to: block-level elements
Inherited: yes
Percentage values: refer to parent element's width

The property specifies the indentation that appears before the first formatted line. The value of 'text-indent' may be negative, but there may be implementation-specific limits. An indentation is not inserted in the middle of an element that was broken by another (such as 'BR' in HTML).

Example:

```
P { text-indent: 3em }
```

5.4.8 'line-height'

Value: normal | `<number>` | `<length>` | `<percentage>`
Initial: normal
Applies to: all elements except replaced elements
Inherited: yes
Percentage values: relative to the font size of the element itself

The property sets the distance between two adjacent lines' baselines.

When a numerical value is specified, the line height is given by the font size of the current element multiplied with the numerical value. This differs from a percentage value in the way it inherits; when a numerical value is specified, child elements will inherit the factor itself, not the resultant value (as is the case with percentage and other units).

Negative values are not allowed.

The three rules in the following example have the same resultant line height:

```
DIV { line-height: 1.2; font-size:
    10pt }       /* number */
DIV { line-height: 1.2em; font-
    size: 10pt }   /* length */
```

```
DIV { line-height: 120%; font-size:
    10pt }    /* percentage */
```

A value of 'normal' sets the 'line-height' to a reasonable value for the element's font. It is suggested that UAs set the 'normal' value to be a number in the range of 1.0 to 1.2.

See section 4.7 for a description on how 'line-height' influences the formatting of a block-level element.

5.5 Box Properties

See section 4, "Formatting Model," for examples on how to use the box properties.

5.5.1 'margin-top', 'margin-right', 'margin-bottom', 'margin-left', 'margin'

Value: [`<length>` | `<percentage>` | auto]{1,4} (for 'margin' property)
Initial: 0
Applies to: all elements
Inherited: no
Percentage values: refer to parent element's width

These properties set the margin of an element: the 'margin' property sets the border for all four sides while the other properties set only their respective sides.

The four lengths of the 'margin' property apply to top, right, bottom, and left, respectively. If there is only one value, it applies to all sides; if there are two or three, the missing values are taken from the opposite side.

```
BODY { margin: 2em } /* all margins
    set to 2em */
BODY { margin: 1em 2em } /* top &
    bottom = 1em, right & left =
    2em */
BODY { margin: 1em 2em 3em } /*
    top=1em, right=2em, bottom=3em,
    left=2em */
```

The 'margin' property is shorthand for setting 'margin-top', 'margin-right', 'margin-bottom', and 'margin-left' at the same place in the style sheet. These properties allow only one value. The last rule of the previous example is equivalent to the following example:

```
BODY {
    margin-top: 1em;
    margin-right: 2em;
    margin-bottom: 3em;
    margin-left: 2em;          /*
    copied from opposite side
    (right) */
}
```

For more examples on how these properties are used, see section 4, "Formatting Model."

Negative margin values are allowed, but there may be implementation-specific limits.

5.5.2 'padding-top', 'padding-right', 'padding-bottom', 'padding-left', 'padding'

Value: [`<length>` | `<percentage>`]`{1,4}` (for 'padding' only)
Initial: 0
Applies to: all elements
Inherited: no
Percentage values: refer to parent element's width

These properties describe how much space to insert between the border and the content (e.g., text or image). The 'padding' property sets the border for all four sides while the other properties only set their respective sides.

For the 'padding' property, the four lengths apply to top, right, bottom, and left, respectively. If there is only one value, it applies to all sides; if there are two or three, the missing values are taken from the opposite side.

The surface of the padding area is set with the 'background' property:

```
H1 {
    background: white;
    padding: 1em 2em;
}
```

The example above sets a '1em' padding vertically ('padding-top' and 'padding-bottom') and a '2em' padding horizontally ('padding-right' and 'padding-left'). The 'em' unit is relative to the element's font size: '1em' is equal to the size of the font in use.

Padding values cannot be negative.

See section 4, "Formatting Model," for more on these properties.

5.5.3 'border', 'border-top', 'border-right', 'border-bottom', 'border-left', 'border-color', 'border-width', 'border-style', 'border-top-width', 'border-right-width', 'border-bottom-width', 'border-left-width'

Value: see below
Initial: see below
Applies to: all elements
Inherited: no
Percentage values: N/A

These properties set the borders of an element. Each element has four borders, one on each side, that are defined by their width, color, and style. The initial value of the border widths is 'medium'; border styles are 'none', and border colors are taken from the 'color' property of the element. Using these properties, the initial values of the borders can be modified. The descriptions of width and style values are given after the description of the properties.

'border'. Possible values are [`<border-width>` || `<border-style>` || `<color>`].

The 'border' property is a shorthand for setting the same border width, color, and style on all four sides. For example, the first rule below is equivalent to the set of four rules shown after it:

```
P { border: solid red }
P {
    border-top: solid red;
    border-right: solid red;
    border-bottom: solid red;
    border-left: solid red
}
```

Unlike 'margin' and 'padding', the 'border' property cannot set different values on the four sides. To do so, one or more of the other border properties must be used.

'border-top', 'border-right', 'border-bottom', 'border-left'. Possible values are [<border-width> || <border-style> || <color>].

These properties set the width, style, and color on one of the four borders that surround an element.

```
H1 {border-bottom: thick solid red}
```

The above rule will set the width, style, and color of the border below the H1 element. Omitted values will be set to their initial values:

```
H1 {border-bottom: thick solid}
```

Since the color value is omitted in the example above, the border color will be the same as the 'color' value of the element itself.

'border-color'. Possible values for this property are [<color>{1,4}].

The 'border-color' property sets the color of the four borders. 'border-color' can have from one to four values, with the following interpretation:

- One value: all four sides are set to that value.

- Two values: top and bottom are set to the first value, right and left are set to the second.

- Three values: top is set to the first, right and left are set to the second, bottom is set to the third.

- Four values: top, right, bottom, and left, respectively.

If no color value is specified, the value of the 'color' property of the element itself will take its place:

```
P {
    color: black;
    background: white;
    border: solid;
}
```

In the above example, the border will be a solid black line.

'border-style'. Possible values are [<border-style>{1,4}].

The 'border-style' property sets the style of the four borders. It can have from one to four values, and the values are set on the different sides as for 'border-color' above.

```
#xy34 { border-style: solid dotted }
```

In the above example, the horizontal borders will be 'solid', and the vertical borders will be 'dotted'.

Since the initial value of the border styles is 'none', no borders will be visible unless the initial style is changed.

'border-width'. Possible values are [<border-width>{1,4}].

The 'border-width' property is a shorthand for the four properties 'border-top-width', 'border-right-width', 'border-bottom-width', and 'border-left-width'. It can have from one to four values, and the values are set on the different sides as for 'border-color' above.

'border-top-width', 'border-right-width', 'border-bottom-width', 'border-left-width'. Possible values are [<border-width>].

These properties set the width of a single border.

```
H1 { border-top-width: 0.2em }
```

Since the properties to some extent have overlapping functionality, the order in which the rules are specified becomes important. Consider this example:

```
BLOCKQUOTE {
    border-color: red;
    border-left: double
    color: black;
}
```

In the above example, the color of the left border will be black, while the other borders are red. This is due to 'border-left' setting the width, style, and color. Since the color value is not specified on the 'border-left' property, it will be taken from the 'color' property. The fact that the 'color' property is set after the 'border-left' property is not relevant.

Here is the list of values and their descriptions:

<border-width>

Possible values are [thin | medium | thick | <length>]. If not specified, 'medium' is assumed. The width of the keyword values are UA dependent, but the following holds: 'thin' <= 'medium' <= 'thick'.

The keyword widths are constant throughout a document:

```
H1 { border: solid thick red }
P  { border: solid thick blue }
```

In the example above, 'H1' and 'P' elements will have the same border width regardless of font size. To do relative width, the 'em' unit can be used:

```
H1 { border: solid 0.5em }
```

<border-style>

Possible values are [none | dotted | dashed | solid | double | groove | ridge | inset | outset]. If not specified, 'none' is assumed.

The border styles mean:

none

No border is drawn (regardless of any '<border-width>').

dotted

The border is a dotted line drawn on top of the background of the element.

dashed

The border is a dashed line drawn on top of the background of the element.

solid

The border is a solid line.

double

The border is a double line drawn on top of the background of the element. The sum of the two single and the space

between equals the '<border-width>' value.

groove

A 3D groove is drawn in colors based on the '<color>' value.

ridge

A 3D ridge is drawn in colors based on the '<color>' value.

inset

A 3D inset is drawn in colors based on the '<color>' value.

outset

A 3D outset is drawn in colors based on the '<color>' value.

NOTE

CSS1 core: UAs may interpret all of 'dotted', 'dashed', 'double', 'groove', 'ridge', 'inset', and 'outset' as 'solid'.

5.5.4 'width'

Value: <length> | <percentage> | auto
Initial: auto
Applies to: block-level and replaced elements
Inherited: no
Percentage values: refer to parent element's width

This property can be applied to text elements, but it is most useful with replaced elements such as images. The width is to be enforced by scaling the image if necessary. When scaling, the aspect ratio of the image is preserved if the 'height' property is 'auto'.

Example:

```
IMG.icon { width: 100px }
```

If the 'width' and 'height' of a replaced element are both 'auto', these properties will be set to the intrinsic dimensions of the element.

Negative values are not allowed.

See section 4, "Formatting Model," for a description of the relationship between this property and the margin and padding.

5.5.5 'height'

Value: `<length>` | `auto`
Initial: auto
Applies to: block-level and replaced elements
Inherited: no
Percentage values: N/A

This property can be applied to text, but it is most useful with replaced elements such as images. The height is to be enforced by scaling the image if necessary. When scaling, the aspect ratio of the image is preserved if the 'width' property is 'auto'.

Example:

```
IMG.icon { height: 100px }
```

If the 'width' and 'height' of a replaced element are both 'auto', these properties will be set to the intrinsic dimensions of the element.

If applied to a textual element, the height can be enforced with, for example, a scrollbar.

Negative values are not allowed.

NOTE

CSS1 core: UAs may ignore the 'height' property (i.e., treat it as 'auto') if the element is not a replaced element.

5.5.6 'float'

Value: `left` | `right` | `none`
Initial: none
Applies to: all elements
Inherited: no
Percentage values: N/A

With the value 'none', the element will be displayed where it appears in the text. With a value of 'left' (or 'right'), the element will be moved to the left (or 'right'), and the text will wrap on the right (or left) side of the element. With a value of 'left' or 'right', the element is treated as block

level (i.e., the 'display' property is ignored). See section 4.1.4 for a full specification.

```
IMG.icon {
    float: left;
    margin-left: 0;
}
```

The above example will place all IMG elements with 'CLASS=icon' along the left side of the parent element.

This property is most often used with inline images but also applies to text elements.

5.5.7 'clear'

Value: `none` | `left` | `right` | `both`
Initial: none
Applies to: all elements
Inherited: no
Percentage values: N/A

This property specifies if an element allows floating elements on its sides. More specifically, the value of this property lists the sides where floating elements are not accepted. With 'clear' set to 'left', an element will be moved below any floating element on the left side. With 'clear' set to 'none', floating elements are allowed on all sides. Example:

```
H1 { clear: left }
```

5.6 Classification Properties

These properties classify elements into categories more than they set specific visual parameters.

5.6.1 'display'

Value: `block` | `inline` | `list-item` | `none`
Initial: block
Applies to: all elements
Inherited: no
Percentage values: N/A

An element with a 'display' value of 'block' opens a new box. The box is positioned relative to adjacent boxes according to the CSS formatting model. Typically, elements like 'H1' and 'P' are of type 'block'. A value of 'list-item' is similar to 'block' except that a list item marker (determined by the 'list-item' property) is added. In HTML, 'LI' will typically have this value.

An element with a 'display' value of 'inline' results in a new inline box on the same line as the previous content. The box is dimensioned according to the formatted size of the content. If the content is text, it may span several lines, and a box will be on each line. The margin, border, and padding properties apply to 'inline' elements but will not have any effect at the line breaks.

A value of 'none' turns off the display of the element, including children elements and the surrounding box.

```
P { display: block }
EM { display: inline }
LI { display: list-item }
IMG { display: none }
```

The last rule turns off the display of images.

The initial value of 'display' is 'block', but a UA will typically have default values for all HTML elements according to the suggested rendering of elements in the HTML specification (9).

NOTE

CSS1 core: UAs may ignore 'display' and use only the UA's default values. (See section 7.)

5.6.2 'list-style', 'list-style-position', 'list-style-image', 'list-style-type'

Value: <keyword> || <position> || <url> (for 'list-style')
Initial: disc outside
Applies to: elements with 'display' property value 'list-item'
Inherited: yes
Percentage values: N/A

The 'list-style' property describes how list items (i.e., elements with a 'display' value of 'list-item') are formatted.

The 'list-style' property is a shorthand notation for setting the three properties 'list-style-image', 'list-style-type', and 'list-style-position'. The value of 'list-style-image' is [none | <url>], with initial value 'none'. The value of 'list-style-position' is [<position>], with initial value 'outside'. The value of 'list-style-type' is [<keyword>], with initial value 'disc'.

<keyword>

Possible values are [disc | circle | square | decimal | lower-roman | upper-roman | lower-alpha | upper-alpha | none]. If no value is specified, 'disc' is assumed. The keyword will be used to determine the appearance of the list marker if 'list-style-image' is 'none' or if the image pointed to by the URL cannot be displayed.

<position>

The value of <position> determines how the list item marker is drawn with regard to the content. Possible values are [inside | outside]. If no value is specified, 'outside' is assumed. For a formatting example, see section 4.1.3.

This property can be set on any element, and it will inherit normally down the tree. However, the 'list-style' will be displayed only on elements with a 'display' value of 'list-item'. In HTML this is typically the case for the 'LI' element.

```
UL { list-style: disc inside }
UL UL { list-style: circle outside }
LI.square { list-style: square }
OL { list-style: decimal }
    /* 1 2 3 4 5 etc. */
OL { list-style: lower-alpha }
    /* a b c d e etc. */
OL { list-style: lower-roman }
    /* i ii iii iv v etc. */
```

Setting 'list-style' directly on 'LI' elements can have unexpected results. Consider:

```
<STYLE TYPE="text/css">
    OL.alpha LI { list-style:
    lower-alpha }
```

```
    UL LI        { list-style:
      disc }
  </STYLE>
  <BODY>
     <OL CLASS=alpha>
       <LI>level 1
       <UL>
          <LI>level 2
       </UL>
     </OL>
  </BODY>
```

Since the specificity (as defined in the cascading order) is higher for the first rule in the style sheet in the example above, it will override the second rule on all 'LI' elements, and only 'lower-alpha' list styles will be used. It is therefore recommended to set 'list-style' only on the list type elements:

```
OL.alpha   { list-style: lower-alpha
     }
UL         { list-style: disc }
```

In the above example, inheritance will transfer the 'list-style' values from 'OL' and 'UL' elements to 'LI' elements.

A URL value can be combined with any other value:

```
UL { list-style: url(http://png.com/
   ellipse.png) disc }
```

In the example above, the 'disc' will be used when the image is unavailable.

5.6.3 'white-space'

> *Value:* normal | pre | nowrap
> *Initial:* normal
> *Applies to:* block-level elements
> *Inherited:* yes
> *Percentage values:* N/A

This property declares how whitespace inside the element is handled: the 'normal' way (in which whitespace is collapsed), as 'pre' (in which whitespace behaves like the 'PRE' element in HTML), or as 'nowrap' (in which wrapping is done only through BR elements):

```
PRE { white-space: pre }
P   { white-space: normal }
```

The initial value of 'white-space' is 'normal', but a UA will typically have default values for all HTML elements according to the suggested rendering of elements in the HTML specification (9).

NOTE

> *CSS1 core:* UAs may ignore the 'white-space' property in author's and reader's style sheets and use the UA's default values instead. (See section 7.)

6. Units

6.1 Length Units

The format of a length value is an optional sign character ('+' or '−', with '+' being the default) immediately followed by a number (with or without a decimal point) immediately followed by a unit identifier (a two-letter abbreviation). After a '0' number, the unit identifier is optional.

Some properties allow negative length units, but this may complicate the formatting model and there may be implementation-specific limits. If a negative length value cannot be supported, it should be clipped to the nearest value that can be supported.

The two types of length units are relative and absolute. Relative units specify a length relative to another length property. Style sheets that use relative units will more easily scale from one medium to another (e.g., from a computer display to a laser printer). Percentage units (described below) and keyword values (e.g., 'x-large') offer similar advantages.

These relative units are supported:

```
H1 { margin: 0.5em }
   /* ems, the height of the
      element s font */
H1 { margin: 1ex }
   /* x-height, ~ the height of
      the letter x */
P  { font-size: 12px }
   /* pixels, relative to canvas */
```

The relative units 'em' and 'ex' are relative to the font size of the element itself. The only exception to this rule in CSS1 is the 'font-size' property in which 'em' and 'ex' values refer to the font size of the parent element.

Pixel units, as used in the last rule, are relative to the resolution of the canvas—i.e., most often a computer display. If the pixel density of the output device is very different from that of a typical computer display, the UA should rescale pixel values. The suggested "reference pixel" is the visual angle of one pixel on a device with a pixel density of 90 dpi and a distance from the reader of an arm's length. For a nominal arm's length of 28 inches, the visual angle is about 0.0227 degrees.

Child elements inherit the computed value, not the relative value:

```
BODY {
    font-size: 12pt;
    text-indent: 3em;
    /* i.e. 36pt */
}
H1 { font-size: 15pt }
```

In the example above, the 'text-indent' value of 'H1' elements will be 36 points, not 45 points.

Absolute length units are useful only when the physical properties of the output medium are known. These absolute units are supported:

```
H1 { margin: 0.5in }
    /* inches, 1in = 2.54cm */
H2 { line-height: 3cm }
    /* centimeters */
H3 { word-spacing: 4mm }
    /* millimeters */
H4 { font-size: 12pt }
    /* points, 1pt = 1/72 in */
H4 { font-size: 1pc }
    /* picas, 1pc = 12pt */
```

In cases where the specified length cannot be supported, UAs should try to approximate. For all CSS1 properties, further computations and inheritance should be based on the approximated value.

6.2 Percentage Units

The format of a length value is a number (with or without a decimal point) immediately followed by '%'.

Percentage values are always relative to a length unit. Each property that allows percentage units also defines what length unit they refer to. Most often this is the font size of the element itself:

```
P { line-height: 120% }    /* 120%
    of the element s  font-size */
```

In all inherited CSS1 properties, if the value is specified as a percentage, child elements inherit the resultant value, not the percentage value.

6.3 Color Units

A color is a either a color name or a numerical RGB specification.

The suggested list of color names is: aqua, black, blue, fuchsia, gray, green, lime, maroon, navy, olive, purple, red, silver, teal, white, and yellow. These 16 colors are taken from the Windows VGA palette and will also be used in HTML 3.2. The RGB values for these color names are not defined in this specification.

```
BODY {color: black; background:
    white }
H1 { color: maroon }
H2 { color: olive }
```

The RGB color model is being used in numerical color specifications. These examples all specify the same color:

```
EM { color: #f00 }
    /* #rgb */
EM { color: #ff0000 }
    /* #rrggbb */
EM { color: rgb(255,0,0) }
    /* integer range 0 - 255 */
EM { color: rgb(100%, 0%, 0%) }
    /* float range 0.0% - 100.0% */
```

The three-digit RGB notation (#rgb) is converted into six-digit form (#rrggbb) by replicating digits, not by adding zeros. For example, #fb0 expands to #ffbb00. This makes sure that white

(#ffffff) can be specified with the short notation (#fff) and removes any dependencies on the color depth of the display.

These RGB colors are specified in the sRGB color space, see Part 1 of (1). UAs may vary in the fidelity with which they represent these colors, but use of sRGB provides an unambiguous and objectively measurable definition of what the color should be, which can be related to international standards (3).

UAs may limit their efforts in displaying colors to performing a gamma correction on them. sRGB specifies a display gamma of 2.2 under specified viewing conditions. UAs adjust the colors given in CSS such that, in combination with an output device's "natural" display gamma, an effective display gamma of 2.2 is produced. Appendix D gives further details of this. Note that only colors specified in CSS are affected; images are expected to carry their own color information.

Values outside the numerical ranges should be clipped. The three rules below are therefore equivalent:

```
EM { color: rgb(255,0,0) }
    /* integer range 0 - 255 */
EM { color: rgb(300,0,0) }
    /* clipped to 255 */
EM { color: rgb(110%, 0%, 0%) }
    /* clipped to 100% */
```

6.4 URL

A Uniform Resource Locator (URL) is identified with a functional notation:

```
BODY { background: url(http://www.
    bg.com/pinkish.gif) }
```

Partial URLs are interpreted relative to the source of the style sheet, not relative to the document:

```
BODY { background: url(yellow) }
```

Parentheses and commas appearing in a URL must be escaped with a backslash: '(', ')', ','.

7. CSS1 Conformance

A User Agent that uses CSS1 to display documents conforms to the CSS1 specification if it:

- Attempts to fetch all referenced style sheets and parse them according to this specification.

- Sorts the declarations according to the cascading order.

- Implements the CSS1 functionality within the constraints of the presentation medium (see the explanation below).

A User Agent that outputs CSS1 style sheets conforms to the CSS1 specification if it outputs valid CSS1 style sheets.

A User Agent that uses CSS1 to display documents *and* outputs CSS1 style sheets conforms to the CSS1 specification if it meets both sets of conformance requirements.

A UA does not have to implement all the functionality of CSS1; it can be conformant to CSS1 by implementing the core functionality. The core functionality consists of the whole CSS1 specification except those parts explicitly excluded. In the text, those parts are preceded by "CSS1 core" followed by an explanation of the functionality that is outside the core functionality. The set of features excluded from the core functionality is called "CSS1 advanced features."

This section only defines conformance to CSS1. Other levels of CSS in the future may require a UA to implement a different set of features in order to be compliant.

Examples of constraints of the presentation medium are limited resources (fonts, color) and limited resolution (so margins may not be accurate). In these cases, the UA should approximate the style sheet values. Also, different user interface paradigms may have their own constraints; a VR browser may rescale the document based on its "distance" from the user.

Example 3

```
stylesheet   : CDO? rules? CDC?
rules        : [ at-rule | rule ]+
rule         : selector decl-block
at-rule      : AT_KEYWORD token* [  ;  | decl-block | rule-block ]
selector     : token+
decl-block   : { declarations }
rule-block   : { rules }
declarations : declaration? [  ;  declaration? ]*
declaration  : IDENT : token+
token        : IDENT | [ token* ] | ( token* ) |
               SYMBOL | : | , | STRING | NUMBER | DIM
```

UAs may offer readers additional choices on presentation. For example, the UA may provide options for readers with visual impairments or may provide the choice to disable blinking.

Note that CSS1 does not specify all aspects of formatting. For example, the UA is free to select a letter spacing algorithm. This specification also recommends but doesn't require, that a UA allow:

- The reader to specify personal style sheets.
- Individual style sheets to be turned on and off.

The above conformance rules describe only functionality, not user interface.

7.1 Forward-Compatible Grammar

This section and the next describe a "meta-syntax," in the sense that they define the limits within which CSS1 and all future extensions will have to remain. In other words, the CSS1 language is a subset of the language described here, and all later versions of CSS are intended to be subsets of that language as well. Implementors must create parsers that are forward compatible; the text below tells the parser how much of the input can be safely skipped when unknown constructions are encountered.

Example 3 shows an EBNF-like grammar.

Note that this grammar is not LL(1); in practice, it will depend on the AT_KEYWORD whether an at-rule ends with a semicolon, a decl-block, or a rule-block.

In English, the grammar says a style sheet is a list of rules (normal rules or @-rules), and each rule ends either with a semicolon (;) or with a block ({...}). Blocks contain either declarations ('keyword-colon-value'), or they contain more rules, in which case they may be nested. Note that nested blocks are not used in CSS1.

The style sheet may be enclosed in <!-- and -->, which is useful when it is embedded in an HTML document.

Besides the nine punctuation characters (, : ; [ ] ( ) { }), the lexical tokens of CSS are shown in Example 4, using the auxiliary definitions provided in Example 5.

Example 4

```
IDENT      : namestart namechar*
AT_KEYWORD : @ IDENT
NUMBER     : [ - | + ]? decimal+
           | [ - | + ]? decimal* . decimal+
DIM        : NUMBER IDENT
STRING     : " [ stringchar | escape | sq ]* "
           | sq [ stringchar | escape | " ]* sq
WS         : whitespace+
CDO        : < ! - -
CDC        : - - >
SYMBOL     : symchar+
```

Example 5

```
symchar     :    |  ~  |  !  |  @  |  #  |  $  |  %  |  ^  |  &  |
                 *  |  -  |  _  |  +  |  =  |  |  |  <  |  >  |  .  |
                 /  |  ?
stringchar  : <I><any printable character except   and " including space></I>
decimal     : 0  |  ...  |  9
hex         : 0  |  ...  |  7  |  A  |  ...  |  F
sq          : <I><a single quote:   ></I>
namestart   : letter  |  latin1  |  escape
namechar    : letter  |  latin1  |  escape  |  decimal  |  -
letter      : A  |  ...  |  Z  |  a  |  ...  |  z
latin1      : <I><a Latin 1 character (codes 161-255)></I>
escape      : unicode  |  \xd5  printable
unicode     : \xd5  hex [ hex [ hex hex? ]? ]? ]?
printable   : <I><any printable character including space></I>
whitespace  : <tab>  |  <space>  |  <newline>  |  comment
comment     : /  *  any*  *  /
any         : <I><any character></I>
```

These definitions assume the Latin 1 character set. Future versions of CSS may widen some of them to allow Unicode characters.

Paraphrased in English:

IDENT

> A sequence of letters, digits, dashes, and backslash-escapes, not starting with a dash or a digit.

AT_KEYWORD

> An identifier preceded by an @ sign.

NUMBER

> A (possibly signed) sequence of digits, with at most one decimal point, which may not be at the start.

DIM

> A number with a unit.

STRING

> A sequence of printable characters, spaces, or backslash escapes, between double quotes, not containing double quotes (unless escaped). Or ditto between single quotes, not containing single quotes (unless escaped).

WS

> A sequence of whitespace characters (spaces, tabs, newlines)

CDO, CDC

> `<!--` and `-->`

punctuation

> `{ } ( ) [ ] , ; :`

SYMBOL

> Any sequence of other punctuation characters.

In case of ambiguity, take the longest match, except for comments.

7.2 Parsing Conventions

In order for CSS implementations to be interoperable, as well as being prepared for future extensions to CSS, a conforming UA must follow these parsing conventions:

- All selectors and property names are case-insensitive. Also, property values are case-insensitive unless they are outside the control of CSS; that is, in CSS1, font family names and URLs can be case-sensitive.

- All properties and values defined in CSS1 must be recognized.

- Unrecognized properties are ignored.

- Recognized but unsupported values on recognized properties can be replaced by appropriate fallback values of the UA's choice.

- Unrecognized values, *or values with unrecognized parts*, are treated as if the declaration weren't there at all:

```
IMG { float: left }       /* CSS1
   */
IMG { float: left top }   /* CSSx
   */
```

In the above example, a CSS1 parser would honor the first rule and ignore the second. A CSS*x* parser would accept both rules, but the last would override the first due to cascading.

- An unrecognized @-keyword is ignored together with everything following it, up to and including the next semicolon (;) or brace pair ({...}), whichever comes first.

- Braces, parentheses, brackets, and single and double quotes are always paired, except inside single or double quotes. Braces, parentheses, and brackets can be nested.

- In CSS1, selectors (element names, classes, and IDs) can contain only the characters A–Z, a–z, 0–9, and Unicode characters 161–255, plus dash (–); they cannot start with a dash or a digit. They can also contain escaped characters and any Unicode character as a numeric code (see next item).

- The backslash followed by at most four hexadecimal digits (0...9A...F) stands for the Unicode character with that number.

- Any character except a digit can be escaped to remove its special meaning, by putting a backslash in front. For example, "\"" is a string consisting of one double quote.

Example A

```
BODY {
    margin: 1em;
```

- The two preceding items define backslash-escapes. Backslash-escapes are always considered to be part of an identifier, except inside strings (i.e., 7B is not punctuation, even though { is, and 32 is allowed at the start of a class name, even though 2 is not).

NOTE

The CLASS attribute of HTML allows more characters in a class name than the set allowed for selectors above. In CSS1, these characters have to be escaped or written as Unicode numbers: B&W? can be written as B&W? or B26W3F, κουρος (Greek "kouros") has to be written as 3BA3BF3C53C13BF3C2. It is expected that in later versions of CSS more characters can be entered directly.

As a help to implementers, a more detailed grammar for CSS1 is included in Appendix B.

8. References

See page 122 for the "References" section.

9. Acknowledgments

See page 122 for the "Acknowledgments" section.

Appendix A: Sample Style Sheet for HTML 2.0

(This appendix is informative, not normative.)

The style sheet in Example A is written according to the suggested rendering in the HTML 2.0 specification. Some styles—e.g., colors—have been added for completeness. It is suggested that a style sheet similar to the one in Example A is used as a UA default.

Advancing HTML: Style and Substance

Example A *(continued)*

```
        font-family: serif;
        line-height: 1.1;
        background: white;
        color: black;
}


H1, H2, H3, H4, H5, H6, P, UL, OL, DIR, MENU, DIV,
DT, DD, ADDRESS, BLOCKQUOTE, PRE, BR, HR { display: block }


B, STRONG, I, EM, CITE, VAR, TT, CODE, KBD, SAMP,
IMG, SPAN { display: inline }


LI { display: list-item }


H1, H2, H3, H4 { margin-top: 1em; margin-bottom: 1em }
H5, H6 { margin-top: 1em }
H1 { text-align: center }
H1, H2, H4, H6 { font-weight: bold }
H3, H5 { font-style: italic }


H1 { font-size: xx-large }
H2 { font-size: x-large }
H3 { font-size: large }


B, STRONG { font-weight: bolder }  /* relative to the parent */
I, CITE, EM, VAR, ADDRESS, BLOCKQUOTE { font-style: italic }
PRE, TT, CODE, KBD, SAMP { font-family: monospace }


PRE { white-space: pre }


ADDRESS { margin-left: 3em }
BLOCKQUOTE { margin-left: 3em; margin-right: 3em }


UL, DIR { list-style: disc }
OL { list-style: decimal }
MENU { margin: 0 }                /* tight formatting */
LI { margin-left: 3em }


DT { margin-bottom: 0 }
DD { margin-top: 0; margin-left: 3em }


HR { border-top: solid }          /* border-bottom could also have been used */

A:link { color: blue }            /* unvisited link */
A:visited { color: red }          /* visited links */
A:active { color: lime }          /* active links */


/* setting the anchor border around IMG elements
   requires contextual selectors */


A:link IMG { border: 2px solid blue }
A:visited IMG { border: 2px solid red }
A:active IMG { border: 2px solid lime }
```

Appendix B: A Sample lex/yacc Grammar

(This appendix is informative, not normative.)

The minimal CSS grammar that all implementations need to support is defined in section 7. However, that grammar is not very helpful when implementing CSS1. Hopefully, the yacc/lex grammar given in Example B-1 better serves that purpose.

The format of the productions is optimized for human consumption and some shorthand notation beyond yacc is used.

```
*  : 0 or more
+  : 1 or more
?  : 0 or 1
|  : separates alternatives
[] : grouping
```

The productions are shown in Example B-1.

Example B-1

```
stylesheet
  : CDO? import* ruleset* CDC?
  ;
import
  : IMPORT_SYM [STRING|URL]  ; /* E.g., @import url(fun.css); */
  ;
unary_operator
  : -  |  +
  ;
          /*
           * The only operators in CSS1 are slash, space and comma.
           * An expression  a b c, d e f  stands for a list
           * [[a,b,c],[d,e,f]]. Note that  a,b,c  is the list
           * [a,b,c], *not* [[a],[b],[c]].
           */
operator
  : /  |  ,  | /* empty */
  ;
property
  : IDENT
  ;
ruleset
  : selector [  ,  selector ]*
    { declaration [ ; declaration ]*  }
  ;
selector
  : simple_selector+ [  :  pseudo_element ]?
  ;
          /*
           * A simple_selector is something like H1, PRE.FOO,
           * .FOO, etc., or it is an ID: #p004
           *
           * DOT_WO_WS is a  .  without preceding whitespace.
           * DOT_W_WS is a  .  with preceding whitespace.
           */
simple_selector
  : element_name [ DOT_WO_WS class ]? pseudo_class?
  | DOT_W_WS class
  | id_selector
```

```
  ;
element_name
  : IDENT
  ;
pseudo_class
  : LINK_PSCLASS
  | VISITED_PSCLASS
  | ACTIVE_PSCLASS
  ;
class
  : IDENT
  ;
pseudo_element
  : IDENT
  ;
id_selector
  :  #  IDENT
  ;
declaration
  : property  :  expr prio?
  | /* empty *//* Prevents syntax errors... */
  ;
prio
  : IMPORTANT_SYM /* !important" */
  ;
expr
  : term [ operator term ]*
  ;
term
  : unary_operator?
    [ NUMBER | STRING | PERCENTAGE | LENGTH | EMS | EXS
    | IDENT | HEXCOLOR | URL | RGB ]
  ;
```

Example B-2 is the input to a lex/flex scanner.

Note that this assumes an 8-bit implementation of
(f)lex.

Example B-2

```
%{
#include "constants.h"
/*
    The constants include definitions similar to the following:
    #define INCH (25.4 * MM)
    #define CM (10 * MM)
    #define MM 1
    #define PICA (12 * INCH/72 * MM)
    #define POINT (INCH/72 * MM)
*/
%}
```

Example B-2 *(continued)*

```
%a 3000
%o 4000
unicode         \[0-7A-Z]{1,6}
latin1          [¡- ]
escape          {unicode}|\[ -~¡- ]
stringchar      {escape}|{latin1}|[ !#$%&(-~]
nmstrt          [a-zA-Z]|{latin1}|{escape}
nmchar          [-a-zA-Z0-9]|{latin1}|{escape}
ident           {nmstrt}{nmchar}*
d               [0-9]
notnm           [^-a-zA-Z0-9\]|{latin1}
w               [ \t\n]
num             {d}+|{d}*.{d}+
h               [0-9a-fA-F]
h3              {h}{h}{h}
h6              {h3}{h3}
h9              {h3}{h3}{h3}

%x COMMENT
%%
"/*"                            {BEGIN(COMMENT);}
<COMMENT>"*/"                   {BEGIN(INITIAL);}
<COMMENT>\n                     {/* ignore */}
<COMMENT>.                      {/* ignore */}
@import                         return IMPORT_SYM;
"!"{w}important                 return IMPORTANT_SYM;
{ident}                         {yylval.sym = str2Symbol(yytext); return IDENT;}
\"({stringchar}|\xd5 )*\"       |
\xd5 ({stringchar}|\")*\        {yylval.str = noquotes(yytext); return STRING;}
{num}                           {yylval.num = atof(yytext); return NUMBER;}
{num}"%"                        {yylval.num = atof(yytext); return PERCENTAGE;}
{num}pt/{notnm}                 {yylval.num = atof(yytext) * POINT; return LENGTH;}
{num}mm/{notnm}                 {yylval.num = atof(yytext); return LENGTH;}
{num}cm/{notnm}                 {yylval.num = atof(yytext) * CM; return LENGTH;}
{num}pc/{notnm}                 {yylval.num = atof(yytext) * PICA; return LENGTH;}
{num}in/{notnm}                 {yylval.num = atof(yytext) * INCH; return LENGTH;}
{num}px/{notnm}                 {yylval.num = atof(yytext) * pixelwd; return LENGTH;}
{num}em/{notnm}                 {yylval.num = atof(yytext); return EMS;}
{num}ex/{notnm}                 {yylval.num = atof(yytext); return EXS;}
":"link                         {return LINK_PSCLASS;}
":"visited                      {return VISITED_PSCLASS;}
":"active                       {return ACTIVE_PSCLASS;}
"#"{h9}                         |
"#"{h6}                         |
"#"{h3}                         {yylval.str = yytext; return HEXCOLOR;}
"url("[^\n)]+")"                {yylval.str = noquotes (yytext+3); return URL;}
"rgb("{w}{num}%?{w},{w}{num}%?{w},{w}{num}%?"{w})"     {yylval.str = yytext;
                                                       return RGB;}
":"                             return : ;
^"."                            |
[ \t]+"."                       return DOT_W_WS;
"."                             return DOT_WO_WS;
"/"                             return / ;
```

Example B-2 *(continued)*

```
"+"                          return + ;
"-"                          return - ;
"{"                          return { ;
"}"                          return } ;
";"                          return ; ;
","                          return , ;
"#"                          return # ;
[ \t]+                       {/* ignore whitespace */}
\n                           {/* ignore whitespace */}
\x3c !--                     return CDO;
--\x3e                       return CDC;
.                            {yyerror("Illegal character");}
```

Appendix C: Encoding

(This appendix is informative, not normative.)

HTML documents may contain any of approximately 30,000 different characters defined by Unicode. Many documents need only a few hundred. Many fonts also contain just a few hundred glyphs. In combination with section 5.2, this appendix explains how the characters in the document and the glyphs in a font are matched.

Character Encoding

The content of an HTML document is a sequence of characters and markup. To send it "over the wire," it is encoded as a sequence of bytes, using one of several possible encodings. The HTML document has to be decoded to find the characters. For example, in western Europe it is customary to use the byte 224 for an a-with-grave-accent (à), but in Hebrew, it is more common to use 224 for an aleph. In Japanese, the meaning of a byte usually depends on the bytes that preceded it. In some encodings, one character is encoded as two (or more) bytes.

The UA knows how to decode the bytes by looking at the **charset** parameter in the HTTP header. Typical encodings (charset values) are ASCII (for English), ISO-8859-1 (for western Europe), ISO-8859-8 (for Hebrew), Shift-JIS (for Japanese).

HTML (assuming the HTML-i18n document [15] is adopted) allows some 30,000 different characters, namely those defined by Unicode. Not many documents will use that many different characters, and choosing the right encoding will usually ensure that the document only needs one byte per character. Occasional characters outside the encoded range can still be entered as numerical character references: 'Π' will always mean the Greek uppercase Pi, no matter what encoding was used. Note that this entails that UAs have to be prepared for any Unicode character, even if they only handle a few encodings.

Font Encoding

A font doesn't contain *characters*, it contains pictures of characters, known as *glyphs*. The glyphs, in the form of outlines or bitmaps, constitute a particular representation of a character. Either explicitly or implicitly, each font has a table associated with it, the *font encoding table*, that tells for each glyph what character it is a representation for. In Type 1 fonts, the table is referred to as an *encoding vector*.

In fact, many fonts contain several glyphs for the same character. Which of those glyphs should be used depends either on the rules of the language, or on the preference of the designer.

In Arabic, for example, all letters have four different shapes, depending on whether the letter is used at the start of a word, in the middle, at the end, or in isolation. It is the same character in all cases, and thus there is only one character in the HTML document, but when printed, it looks differently each time.

There are also fonts that leave it to the graphic designer to choose from among various alternative shapes provided. Unfortunately, CSS1 doesn't yet provide the means to select those alternatives. Currently, it is always the default shape that is chosen from such fonts.

Font Sets

To deal with the problem that a single font may not be enough to display all the characters in a document, or even a single element, CSS1 allows the use of *font sets*.

A font set in CSS1 is a list of fonts, all of the same style and size, that are tried in sequence to see if they contain a glyph for a certain character. An element that contains English text mixed with mathematical symbols may need a font set of two fonts, one containing letters and digits, the other containing mathematical symbols. See section 5.2 for a detailed description of the selection mechanism for font sets.

Here is an example of a font set suitable for a text that is expected to contain text with Latin characters, Japanese characters, and mathematical symbols:

```
BODY { font-family: Baskerville,
   Mincho, Symbol, serif }
```

The characters available in the Baskerville font (a font with only Latin characters) will be taken from that font, Japanese will be taken from Mincho, and the mathematical symbols will come from Symbol. Any other characters will (hopefully) come from the generic font family 'serif'. The 'serif' font family will also be used if one or more of the other fonts is unavailable.

Appendix D: Gamma Correction

(This appendix is informative, not normative.)

See the Gamma Tutorial (6) in the PNG specification (12) if you aren't already familiar with gamma issues.

In the computation, UAs displaying on a CRT may assume an ideal CRT and ignore any effects on apparent gamma caused by dithering. That means the minimal handling they need to do on current platforms is provided in the table below.

"Applying gamma" means that each of the three R, G, and B must be converted to $R =R^{gamma}$, $G =G^{gamma}$, $G =B^{gamma}$ before handing to the OS.

This may be done rapidly by building a 256-element lookup table once per browser invocation thus:

```
for i := 0 to 255 do
   raw := i / 255;
   corr := pow (raw, gamma);
   table[i] := trunc (0.5 + corr *
   255.0)
end
```

which then avoids any need to do transcendental math per color attribute, far less per pixel.

PC using MS-Windows	None
Unix using X11	None
Mac using QuickDraw	Apply gamma 1.39 (2). (ColorSync-savvy applications may simply pass the sRGB ICC profile [10] to ColorSync to perform correct color correction.)
SGI using X	Apply the gamma value from */etc/config/system.glGammaVal* (the default value being 1.70; applications running on Irix 6.2 or above may simply pass the sRGB ICC profile to the color management system).
NeXT using NeXTStep	Apply gamma 2.22.

Appendix E: The Applicability and Extensibility of CSS1

(This appendix is informative, not normative.)

The goal of the work on CSS1 has been to create a simple style sheet mechanism for HTML documents. The current specification is a balance between the simplicity needed to realize style sheets on the Web and pressure from authors for richer visual control. CSS1 offers:

- *Visual markup replacement.* HTML extensions—e.g., CENTER, FONT, and SPACER—are easily replaced with CSS1 style sheets.

- *Nicer markup.* Instead of using FONT elements to achieve the popular small caps style, one declaration in the style sheet is sufficient. Compare the visual markup:

```
<H1>H<FONT SIZE=-1>EADLINE
    </FONT></H1>
```

with the style sheet:

```
H1 { font-style: small-caps }

<H1>Headline</H1>
```

- *Various integration levels.* CSS1 style rules can be fetched from external style sheets, included in the 'STYLE' element or put into 'STYLE' attributes. The latter option offers easy transition from HTML extensions.

- *New effects.* Some new visual effects have been added to offer users new toys. The typographical pseudo-elements and the extra values on the background property fall into this category.

- *Scalability.* CSS1 will be useful on equipment ranging from text terminals to high-resolution color workstations. Authors can write one style sheet and be reasonably sure that the intended style will come across in the best possible manner.

CSS1 does not offer:

- *Per pixel control.* CSS1 values simplicity over level of control, and although the combination of background images and styled HTML is powerful, control to the pixel level is not possible.

- *Author control.* The author cannot enforce the use of a certain sheet, only suggest one.

- *A layout language.* CSS1 does not offer multiple columns with text-flow, overlapping frames, etc. However, see (5) for a proposal.

- *A rich query language on the parse tree.* CSS1 can only look for ancestor elements in the parse tree, while other style sheet languages (e.g., DSSSL [4]) offer full query languages.

We expect to see extensions of CSS in several directions:

- *Paper.* Better support for printing HTML documents.

- *Support for nonvisual media.* Work is in process to add a list of properties and corresponding values to support speech and braille output.

- *Color names.* The currently supported list may be extended. CNS (2) is one possible option.

- *Fonts.* More precise font specification systems are expected to complement existing CSS1 font properties.

- *Values, properties.* We expect vendors to propose extensions to the CSS1 set of values and properties. Extending in this direction is trivial for the specification, but interoperability between different UAs is a concern.

- *Layout language.* Support for two-dimensional layout in the tradition of desktop publishing packages. See (5) for a proposal based on CSS.

- *Other DTDs.* CSS1 has some HTML-specific parts (e.g., the special status of the 'CLASS' and 'ID' attributes) but should easily be extended to apply to other DTDs as well.

We do not expect CSS to evolve into a programming language. ∎

References

1. Anderson, M., R. Motta, S. Chandrasekar, M. Stokes. Proposal for a Standard Color Space for the Internet—sRGB, *http://www.hpl.hp.com/personal/Michael_Stokes/srgb.htm*

2. Berk, T., L. Brownston, A. Kaufman, "A New Color-Naming System for Graphics Languages," IEEE CG&A, May 1982.

3. CIE Publication 15.2–1986, "Colorimetry, Second Edition," ISBN 3-900-734-00-3, *http://www.hike.te.chiba-u.ac.jp/ikeda/CIE/publ/abst/15-2-86.html*

4. DSSSL (*http://occam.sjf.novell.com:8080/dsssl/dsssl96*) is a tree transformation and style language from the SGML community. Bert Bos has written some notes, "Translating CSS to DSSSL," *http://www.w3.org/pub/WWW/Style/css/css2dsssl.html*

5. "Frame-based layout via Style Sheets," *http://www.w3.org/pub/WWW/TR/WD-layout.html*

6. Gamma Appendix of PNG Specification, *http://www.w3.org/pub/WWW/TR/PNG-GammaAppendix.html*

7. Gamma correction on the Macintosh Platform, *ftp://ftp.inforamp.net/pub/users/poynton/doc/Mac/Mac_gamma.pdf*

8. HTML 3 and Style Sheets, *http://www.w3.org/pub/WWW/TR/WD-style.html*

9. HyperText Markup Language Specification Version 3.0 *http://www.w3.org/pub/WWW/MarkUp/html3/CoverPage.html* (the draft has now expired).

10. International Color Consortium Profile, version 3.2, *ftp://sgigate.sgi.com/pub/icc/ICC32.pdf*

11. ISO 8879, Information Processing—Text and Office Systems—Standard Generalized Markup Language (SGML), 1986.

12. PNG specification, *http://www.w3.org/pub/WWW/TR/REC-png-multi.html*

13. RFC 1866: Hypertext Markup Language 2.0, *ftp://ds.internic.net/rfc/rfc1866.txt*. The specification is also available in hypertext form at *http://www.w3.org/pub/WWW/MarkUp/html-spec/html-spec_toc.html*

14. W3C, Resource page on Web style sheets, *http://www.w3.org/pub/WWW/Style*

15. Yergeau, F., G. Nicol, G. Adams, M. Dürst, "Internationalization of the Hypertext Markup Language," *ftp://ietf.org/internet-drafts/draft-ietf-html-i18n-05.txt*

Acknowledgments

During the short life of HTML, there have been several style sheet proposals to which this proposal is indebted. The proposals from Robert Raisch, Joe English, and Pei Wei were especially influential.

A number of people have contributed to the development of CSS1. We would especially like to thank Terry Allen, Murray Altheim, Glenn Adams, Tim Berners-Lee, Yves Bertot, Scott Bigham, Steve Byrne, Robert Cailliau, James Clark, Daniel Connolly, Donna Converse, Adam Costello, Todd Fahrner, Todd Freter, Roy Fielding, Neil Galarneau, Wayne Gramlich, Phil Hallam-Baker, Philipp Hoschka, Kevin Hughes, Scott Isaacs, Tony Jebson, Gilles Kahn, Philippe Kaplan, Phil Karlton. Evan Kirshenbaum, Yves Lafon, Murray Maloney, Lou Montulli, Colas Nahaboo, Henrik Frystyk Nielsen, David Perrell, William Perry, Scott Preece, Paul Prescod, Liam Quin, Vincent Quint, Jenny Raggett, Thomas Reardon, Cécile Roisin, Michael Seaton, David Seibert, David Siegel, David Singer, Benjamin Sittler, Jon Smirl, Charles Peyton Taylor, IrÈne Vatton, Daniel Veillard, Mandira Virmani, Greg Watkins, Mike Wexler, Lydja Williams, Brian Wilson, Chris Wilson, Lauren Wood and Stephen Zilles.

Three people deserve special mention: Dave Raggett (for his encouragement and work on HTML 3), Chris Lilley (for his continued contributions, especially in the area of colors and fonts), and Steven Pemberton (for his organizational as well as creative skills).

About the Authors

Håkon W. Lie
W3C/INRIA
2004, route des Lucioles—B.P. 93
06902 Sophia Antipolis Cedex
France
howcome@w3.org

Håkon is working for W3C at INRIA/Sophia-Antipolis in southern France. As the first W3C employee at INRIA, he coordinated the growing development team in addition to working on style sheets and HTML.

He came to W3C in July 1995 from CERN where he was a research associate in the WWW project. He is a graduate of the MIT Media Lab where he worked in the Electronic Publishing group.

Bert Bos
W3C/INRIA
2004, route des Lucioles—B.P. 93
06902 Sophia Antipolis Cedex
France
bert@w3.org

Bert has a degree in Mathematics from the University of Groningen, The Netherlands (1987), and a Ph.D. from the Faculty of Arts of that same university, on a thesis about a rapid-prototyping language for Graphical User Interfaces (1993). Afterwards, he lead a project called PROSA, aimed at helping scholars in the humanities make better use of the Internet and the World Wide Web in particular. He joined W3C in France in October 1995, as coordinator for internationalization.

Better Web user interfaces aren't built from technical specs alone. Users and designers learn together about what works and what doesn't, to guide the intelligent application of new "whiz-bang" features. The World Wide Web Journal *is uniquely positioned to showcase both halves of the equation because of its joint sponsorship by the Web Consortium and O'Reilly & Associates.*

The most tangible result of this partnership is the Journal's ability to release late-breaking specs and *developer's guides. We are proud to present Chuck Musciano's expert introduction to "What's New in HTML 3.2" and Norman Walsh's "Introduction to Cascading Style Sheets." Both writers succeed at presenting the concepts and context of each specification and concrete how-to tips you can start using today.*

This section also includes papers on graphic animation, interactive scripting, Web usage measurement, and guidelines on usability, multimedia deployment, and accessibility. Richard Koman introduces "GIF Animation," based on his recent book of the same title. From the PNG community, the successor to the lossless GIF format comes Glenn Randers-Pehrson's proposal for "MNG: A Multiple-Image Format in the PNG Family." JavaScript is another popular tool site designers use to enliven their pages: David Flanagan surveys "User Interfaces with HTML and JavaScript," which is also based on his own recent book on the subject. The end goal for designers using these technologies is ultimately to build a more popular and compelling user experience, which demands measured results. Novak and Hoffman's "New Metrics for New Media" offers much-needed guidance on terms and models of Web usage measurement, a field first surveyed a few months ago in Issue 2, Volume 1, The Web After Five Years.

Designers should use these technologies with care, though. "Popular" and "compelling" are not synonyms for "universally accessible" and "usable." Keith Instone investigates that distinction in "Usability Engineering for the Web," which brings computer systems usability literature to bear on the Web's "new-fangled" problems. Jakob Nielsen offers a similarly motivated set of "Guidelines for Multimedia on the Web." Finally, as a matter of self interest and social justice, designers should heed Mike Paciello's manifesto, "People with Disabilities Can't Access the Web!" Mr. Paciello is working with W3C as it ramps up its own efforts in this area.

WHAT'S NEW IN HTML 3.2
FORMALIZING ENHANCEMENTS TO HTML 2.0

Chuck Musciano

Abstract

The collapse of the HTML 3.0 standard and the broad acceptance of vendor-devised HTML enhancements has threatened to render the standards process irrelevant, at least with respect to HTML. In an effort to formalize the most recent extensions to the language, the World Wide Web Consortium released a new draft standard defining HTML 3.2. In contrast to the expansive HTML 3.0 proposal, the 3.2 standard addresses a much smaller set of extensions to the original HTML 2.0 standard.

This article will focus on the differences between HTML 2.0 and HTML 3.2, assuming that the reader has a basic knowledge of the HTML 2.0 standard.

In some ways, the explosive success of the World Wide Web has been one of the worst things to happen to it. As more users connect to the Web, the demand for better documents and greater control over document appearance has driven browser vendors to extend HTML to meet user needs. These extensions are often in conflict with other vendor extensions and deviate from proposed HTML standards. Nonetheless, the Web authoring community usually adopts these new features almost overnight, making them part of the "street version" of HTML used on most Web sites. Market competition forces other browser vendors to comply, and users are left wondering which features of HTML can be reliably used to create widely available documents.

Into this fray comes the latest HTML draft standard from the World Wide Web Consortium: HTML 3.2. Unlike its predecessor, 3.0, this standard treads no new ground. Instead, it makes a concerted effort to capture and define a large number of popular enhancements that have been made to HTML since the HTML 2.0 standard was first defined some three years ago.

In this article, we'll begin with a bit of historical background, defining HTML 3.2's place in history. We'll then cover, feature by feature, the new items in HTML 3.2 versus HTML 2.0. We'll close with a brief look at the next HTML standard and

what can be reasonably expected to emerge from the W3C in the next few months.

Historical Perspective

In general, the next version of some product is typically more feature laden and advanced than its predecessor. When comparing HTML 3.0 to HTML 2.0, this is certainly the case. HTML 3.0 was an attempt to define a vastly more complex and richer version of HTML than the simple one described by HTML 2.0. As an ever-increasing group of people tried to define exactly what HTML 3.0 would be, the standards process collapsed under its own weight, making it almost impossible for the standard to converge.

HTML 3.0 died a quiet death in June of 1995. While browser vendors continued to innovate and introduce new, nonstandard extensions to HTML, the HTML standards process had little to offer the Web authoring community. Finally, in May of 1996, the first draft standard for HTML 3.2 emerged.

Contrary to what its number might indicate, HTML 3.2 offers much less than HTML 3.0. Far from breaking new ground, this version of HTML instead formalizes a number of popular extensions to HTML that have come into common use in the past two years. It is much more of an incremental improvement to HTML 2.0, instead of a complete overhaul of the HTML language.

The new features in HTML 3.2 should be received with a sigh of relief by Web authors everywhere. No longer must you feel guilty putting a table in your documents or changing the background color of your documents. By significantly improving the baseline set of features every browser will now be expected to support, HTML 3.2 makes it much easier to create attractive documents that will look good on a broad range of browsers.

In the following sections, we'll examine the new features in HTML 3.2. Some are minor, such as allowing headings to be center and right aligned. Others are major, such as finally formalizing a table model for HTML. As a convenience, all the new features in HTML 3.2 are summarized in Table 1.

Table 1   Summary of New Features in HTML 3.2[1]

Tag	Attribute	Description
`<applet>`	`align`	Invoke a Java applet, with the display area aligned like an `<img>`
	`alt`	. . . with this alternative text for Java-challenged browsers
	`code, codebase`	. . . loaded from this file based on this URL
	`height, width`	. . . in a display area this high and wide
	`hspace, vspace`	. . . with a specific horizontal and vertical margin
	`name`	. . . with this instance name
`<area>`	`alt`	Define an area in a client-side image map, with this alternative text string
	`coords`	. . . and these coordinates
	`href`	. . . referencing this URL
	`nohref`	. . . or no URL at all
	`shape`	. . . having this geometric shape
`<basefont>`	`size`	Define the base font size for the document
`<big>`		Render text one size bigger
`<body>`	`background`	Define the document body with a tiled background image
	`bgcolor`	. . . with a specific background color
	`text`	. . . with a specific text color
	`alink, vlink, link`	. . . with specific colors for active, visited, and unvisited links
` `	`clear`	Break the current flow, optionally resuming when the left or right margin is clear of floating elements
`<caption>`	`align`	Create a table caption aligned to the top or bottom of the table
`<center>`		Create a centered text flow
`<dfn>`		Render text as a term definition
`<div>`	`align`	Create a document division, aligned to left, center, or right
`<font>`	`color`	Change the font of the enclosed text to this color
	`size`	. . . and this size
`<hn>`	`align`	Define headers aligned to the left, center, or right

Table 1 *(continued)* Summary of New Features in HTML 3.2[1]

Tag	Attribute	Description
`<hr>`	`align`	Create a horizontal rule, aligned left, center, or right
	`noshade`	. . . without 3D shading
	`size`	. . . with a specific thickness
	`width`	. . . with a specific width
`<img>`	`align`	Now supports **left** and **right** for text flow around images
	`border`	. . . with borders at a specified width
	`height, width`	. . . scaled to a specific width and height
	`hspace, vspace`	. . . with a specific horizontal and vertical margin
	`usemap`	. . . used as a client-side image map
`<input>`	`align`	Now supports **left** and **right** for image alignment in forms
	`type`	Now supports **file** for client file upload
`<isindex>`	`prompt`	Define a searchable document with a custom prompt string
`<li>`	`type`	Change the bullet or numbering style of a list element
	`value`	Change the number of a list item in an ordered list
`<map>`	`name`	Create a map for use in a client-side image map
`<ol>`	`start`	Change the starting value of an ordered list
	`type`	Change the numbering style of an ordered list
`<p>`	`align`	Define a paragraph aligned to the left, center, or right
`<param>`	`name`	Pass a parameter to an applet with this name
	`value`	. . . and this value
`<small>`		Render text one size smaller
`<script>`		Reserved for future use
`<strike>`		Strikethrough text
`<style>`		Reserved for future use
`<sub>`		Render text as a subscript
`<sup>`		Render text as a superscript
`<table>`	`align`	Create a table, aligned left, center, or right
	`border`	. . . with a specific border thickness
	`cellpadding`	. . . with a specific number of pixels around each cell's content
	`cellspacing`	. . . with a specific number of pixels between cells
	`width`	. . . with a specific width
`<th>,<td>`	`colspan`	Create a table header or data cell, spanning one or more columns
	`halign`	. . . horizontally alignment left, center, or right
	`height`	. . . with a specific height

Table 1 *(continued)* Summary of New Features in HTML 3.2[1]

Tag	Attribute	Description
	nowrap	. . . with word wrapping suppressed
	rowspan	. . . spanning one or more rows
	valign	. . . vertically aligned top, middle, or bottom
	width	. . . with a specific width
`<tr>`	align	Create a table row, with cell content aligned left, center, or right
	valign	. . . with cell content vertically aligned top, middle, or bottom
`<u>`		Underline text
`<ul>`	**type**	Change the bullet style of an unordered list

[1] New tags and attributes are shown in boldface; existing tags with new attributes or values only are shown in plain text.

Document Structure

The overall structure of an HTML 3.2 document is no different than that of an HTML 2.0 document. The entire document is contained within the `<html>` and `</html>` tags and consists of a document head (delimited by `<head>` and `</head>`) and a body (delimited by `<body>` and `</body>`). To be absolutely correct, your HTML 3.2 document should begin with this DOCTYPE declaration:

```
<!DOCTYPE HTML PUBLIC -//W3C/DTD
    HTML 3.2 Draft//EN >
```

When the draft proposal is fully ratified by the W3C member organizations, the word "Draft" will be replaced by "Final."

A few minor changes to some of the tags affect document structure, including several additional attributes for the `<body>` tag, the ability to supply a custom prompt for the `<isindex>` tag, and the ability to include applets in your documents via the `<applet>` tag.

`<body>` Tag Enhancements

In HTML 2.0, the `<body>` tag accepted no attributes. HTML 3.2 defines several new attributes for the `<body>` tag, all but one concerned with document, text, and link colors. These new attributes are:

bgcolor

This attribute controls the background color of the document. Like all other attributes that support color, it accepts either a hexadecimal triple defining the red, green, and blue components of the color, or one of 16 predefined color names. These colors are shown in Table 2.

If a hexadecimal triple is used, it has the format `#rrggbb`, where `rr`, `gg`, and `bb` are hexadecimal values in the range 00 to FF corresponding to the brightness of the red, green, and blue components of the color.

text

This attribute determines the color used to render the text of the document. Its value is either a hexadecimal triple or one of the color names defined in Table 1. This attribute is usually used in conjunction with the `bgcolor` or `background` attributes to ensure that the text is readable against the document background.

link, vlink, and alink

These three attributes define the colors used to render unvisited links, visited links, and active links, respectively. They may be used together or separately and are commonly used to ensure that textual links are appro-

Table 2 HTML 3.2 Predefined Colors

Color Name	RGB Equivalent	Color Name	RGB Equivalent
Black	#000000	Green	#008000
Silver	#C0C0C0	Lime	#00FF00
Gray	#808080	Olive	#808000
White	#FFFFFF	Yellow	#FFFF00
Maroon	#800000	Navy	#000080
Red	#FF0000	Blue	#0000FF
Purple	#800080	Teal	#008080
Fuchsia	#FF00FF	Aqua	#00FFFF

priately visible in the document. Again, these attributes accept either a hexadecimal triple or a color name defined in Table 1.

background

This attribute defines an image to be used to fill the background of the document. Its value is the URL of the desired image. If the image is smaller than the actual document window, it will be tiled to fill the document window.

This attribute overrides the `bgcolor` attribute if both are specified. Using both makes sense, however. If a user has disabled image loading for bandwidth reasons, the specified background color will be used in lieu of the background image.

Custom <isindex> Prompts

In HTML 2.0, the `<isindex>` tag provided a standard way to create a searchable document. Placing this tag in the `<head>` of your document created a text entry field in your document that would accept parameters to be passed to the server. The server would, presumably, use these parameters to search for and display an appropriate document to the user.

Unfortunately, the `<isindex>` tag uses a generic prompt for the text field. Although browser-dependent, it is usually something along the lines of "This is a searchable document. Enter keywords:". Although use of the `<isindex>` tag has declined in favor of more sophisticated forms-

based search front ends, HTML 3.2 nonetheless provides the ability to supply a custom prompt string for your `<isindex>` tags.

To define a custom prompt, add the `prompt` attribute to the `<isindex>` tag. The value of the attribute is any arbitrary string. HTML markup inside the string is not allowed.

The <applet> Tag

Recognizing the popularity of Java, HTML 3.2 supports the `<applet>` tag, used to embed a Java applet in your document. The ending `</applet>` tag must always be supplied; the content within the `<applet>` and `</applet>` tags is ignored by Java-enabled browsers and presented to the user by Java-challenged browsers. This allows the document author to provide to users without Java some alternative content, ranging from a simple text description of the applet, to an image of the running applet, to an admonishment to upgrade to a better browser.

Parameters are passed to an applet using the `<param>` tag within the `<applet>` and `</applet>` tags. The attributes to the `<applet>` tag define the applet to be executed and how that applet should be placed in the document. These attributes are:

align

Like the equivalent attribute for the `<img>` tag, this attribute controls how the applet display area is aligned with respect to the surrounding text. Values include top, middle, and bottom, which align the applet vertically with respect to the surrounding text, and left and right, which shift the applet to the corresponding margin and allow subsequent text to flow around the applet display area.

alt

This attribute supplies a text string that can be displayed to the user in lieu of the actual applet. If there is also content within the <applet> and </applet> tags, the use of the <alt> tag is left up to the browser.

code

This attribute supplies the name of the file containing the compiled applet. This attribute cannot supply an absolute URL; the value is always assumed to be relative to the applet's base URL, as defined by the codebase attribute.

codebase

This attribute defines the base URL used to retrieve the applet specified in the code attribute. Typically, the codebase attribute specifies a directory of Java applets, one of which is explicitly selected by the code attribute. If this attribute is not supplied, the base URL for the applet is assumed to be the document URL.

height and width

These attributes define the size of the display area to be used for the applet. This area is flowed into the surrounding text exactly like an inline image.

hspace and vspace

These attributes define the horizontal and vertical margins, in pixels, to be placed around the applet display area. This lets you create some white space between your applet and the surrounding text.

name

This attribute defines a name for this instance of the applet. This name is needed only if multiple applets on the same page need to communicate with each other.

To see how the <applet> and <param> tags might be used to insert an applet in a document, consider this HTML fragment:

```
<applet>
    name=my_clock
    code=Clock
    codebase= http://www.com/java
    height=150
    width=150>
    <param name=style value=analog>
</applet>
```

In this example, a class named "clock" is instanced and passed a parameter indicating how the time is to be displayed. The clock itself will be displayed in an area of the document 150 pixels square.

Text Layout and Flow

Some of the best new features in HTML 3.2 involve text alignment, better unordered and ordered lists, and fancier horizontal rules.

Aligned Headings and Paragraphs

Both the heading tags (<h1> through <h6>) and the <p> tag now accept the align attribute. This attribute can be set to either left, center, or right and controls the margin alignment of the text within the tag.

If omitted, the default alignment is, of course, against the left margin. Using center centers each line within the text flow; using right places the right end of each line flush against the right margin of the page.

Unfortunately, since this attribute does not yet accept justify as a value, justified text is still not possible using standard HTML.

Altering Bullet Styles

HTML 2.0 specified that nested unordered lists may use different bullets for different levels of nested lists but gave no control as to which bullets could be used at a specific level. HTML 3.2

rectifies this situation, allowing the `type` attribute to be applied to the `<ul>` tag to specify the bullet to be used for the list.

This attribute accepts one of three values. If `disc` is used, the bullet is a solid circle. Using `square` renders list elements with a solid square bullet. Specifying `circle` uses a hollow circle. All of the items in the list, denoted by `<li>` tags, will be given the same bullet.

If you need to override the type of bullet used on a specific list element, you can use the `type` attribute within the `<li>` to change the bullet for that item. Unfortunately, some browsers continue to use that bullet type for subsequent list items, so you may have to switch back to the original bullet type on the next item.

As an example, placing this piece of HTML into any document will create a bullet sampler for you to peruse:

```
<ul>
    <li type=disc>Disc bullet!
    <li type=circle>Circle bullet!
    <li type=square>Square bullet!
</ul>
```

Controlling Ordered Lists

Like unordered lists, ordered lists have been extended in HTML 3.2 to allow you to control the numbering style and starting value of the list.

In HTML 2.0, lists were numbered using Arabic numbers. In HTML 3.2, you can use one of five numbering formats by adding the `type` attribute and the appropriate numbering code, shown in Table 3, to the `<ol>` tag. For example, to create a numbered list using lowercase Roman numerals, you would say

```
<ol type=i>
```

Note that the value of the `type` attribute in the `<ol>` tag may be the only case-sensitive value in the HTML 3.2 standard.

If you would like your list to start at some value other than 1, you can add the `start` attribute to the `<ol>` tag and supply it with an appropriate integer value. To start our Roman numeral list at 6 (actually, `vi`), you would use

```
<ol type=i start=6>
```

Note that starting values are always supplied as Arabic numerals, without regard to the format specified by the `type` attribute.

There is no way to adjust the amount by which each element is incremented. Ordered lists always count by one.

It is possible, however, to use the `type` and `value` attributes with the `<li>` tags within an ordered list to control the style and value used for that element, along with any subsequent elements in the list. Thus, if you were so inclined, you could have different items in your list use different numbering styles and values.

Like our bullet sampler, above, you can create a numbering style sampler:

```
<ol start=6>
    <li type=1>The number 6
    <li type=A>The letter  G
    <li type=a>The letter  h
    <li type=I>Roman numeral IX
    <li type=i>Roman numeral x
</ol>
```

Table 3   Display Codes Used with the type Attribute Within the `<ol>` Tag

Code	Style
1	Arabic numbers (`1, 2, 3, . . .`)
a	Lowercase letters (`a, b, c, . . .`)
A	Uppercase letters (`A, B, C, . . .`)
i	Lowercase Roman (`i, ii, iii, . . .`)
I	Uppercase Roman (`I, II, III, . . .`)

The <div> Tag

The <div> tag did not exist in HTML 2.0. In HTML 3.0, <div> provided all sorts of capabilities, from document organization to simple layout control to applying class and style definitions to sections of a document. In HTML 3.2, <div> assumes a lesser role, but there are high hopes for the <div> tag in the future.

The <div> tag is used as a container, holding any HTML content that would normally appear within the <body> tag. The <div> tag accepts a single parameter, align, which can be used to align the text in the tag to the left, center, or right of the document window.

Because <div> is a block-like element, it will terminate a paragraph and render paragraph spacing between a previous paragraph and the text within the <div>. Other than this, the <div> tag should not render paragraph breaks before or after the tag.

The <center> Tag

The <center> tag is functionally equivalent to using <div align=center>. It is included in the HTML 3.2 standard because of its widespread usage. The <center> tag was introduced by Netscape before they supported the <div> tag, and for a long time was the only way to get centered text in your documents.

In general, you should not use <center>, opting for the more standard <div> tag with the appropriate attribute. It is expected that the usage of <center> will decline as more HTML 3.2-compliant browsers become available.

Improved Horizontal Rules

The original horizontal rule in HTML 2.0 was a simple as possible: a single rule, stretched across the page, rendered with a standard thickness. In HTML 3.2, several attributes have been added to the <hr> tag to provide all sorts of rendering options. These attributes are:

align
> This attribute may be set to either left, center, or right to align the rule to left, center, or right edge of the page. This attribute has an effect only if the rule is less than the width of the full page. If not specified, the rule will be centered on the page.

noshade
> Normally, a rule is rendered with a pseudo-3D effect, making the rule look either incised or embossed upon the page. Specifying noshade in an <hr> tag creates the rule as a flat, filled rectangle, with no gratuitous shading effects.

size
> This attribute determines the thickness, in pixels, of the rule. If not specified, the rule is usually two or three pixels thick, depending on the browser.

width
> This determines the length of the rule. You can use a numeric value to indicate a specific number of pixels or provide a percentage, indicating a percentage of the document window size.

These attributes are pretty straightforward, but some examples never hurt:

```
<hr width= 50%  align=center>
<hr size=10>
<hr size=4 width=50 noshade>
```

The first example creates a rule that is half as wide as the document window and is centered within the window. The second creates a rule that is the width of the document window and is 10 pixels thick. The last creates a flat rectangle, centered in the window, that is 4 pixels high and 50 pixels wide.

Improved Break Handling

With the advent of floating images and tables in HTML 3.2, a mechanism has been provided to suspend the current text flow and resume after any floating elements have been rendered. To achieve this affect, add the clear attribute to the `<br>` tag.

When the `<br>` tag is encountered, the text flow is broken. The `clear` attribute accepts a value of `left`, `right`, or `both`, indicating that the flow should resume when the specified margin, or both margins, are free from any floating elements.

This is especially helpful when flowing text around an image or table at the end of a document section. Use the `<br>` tag with the `clear` attribute to push the start of the next section down until the margins are clear, preventing the section from starting adjacent to an image related to the previous section of your document.

For example, consider this code:

```
<img src= picture.gif  align=left>
In the picture to the left, you can
see blah, blah, blah
<br clear=left>
<h3>The Next Section</h3>
```

In this example, the text following the `<img>` tag will flow along the right edge of the picture. If the picture is taller than the space occupied by the text, the `<br clear=left>` tag forces the following `<h3>` tag to be displayed below the picture, not immediately following the text adjacent to the picture.

Text Formatting

HTML 3.2 retains all of the physical text styles and content-based text styles of HTML 2.0 and adds a few new styles. HTML 3.2 also provides a way to control text size and color.

Additional Text Styles

There are six new physical text style tags in HTML 3.2. These tags change the appearance of the contained text in some way without associating any semantic information with the enclosed text. These new tags are:

`<big>`
This tag renders the enclosed text one size larger than the current text size. The effect of nested `<big>` tags is cumulative. This tag has no effect on text that is already the largest size supported by the browser.

`<small>`
This tag renders the enclosed text one size smaller that the current text size. The effect of nested `<small>` tags is cumulative. This tag has no effect on text that is already the smallest size supported by the browser.

`<strike>`
This tag renders the enclosed text with a single line struck through the middle of the text. Some browsers also accept the abbreviated form, `<s>`, for this tag.

`<sub>`
The enclosed text in this tag is rendered as a subscript to the surrounding text. Multiple subscripts can be created using nested `<sub>` tags.

`<sup>`
The enclosed text in this tag is rendered as a superscript to the surrounding text. Multiple superscripts can be created using nested `<sup>` tags.

`<u>`
This tag underlines the enclosed text.

In addition, there is one new tag that changes the text appearance based upon the meaning of the contained text:

`<dfn>`
This tag defines the enclosed text to be the defining instance of a word or phrase. Browsers may choose to place such a term in italics or some other distinctive text. In additional, it might be useful for the browser to collect such terms and create a dynamic glossary, with hyperlinks, of all the terms defined in a document.

Font Sizes and Colors

Sorely missing in HTML 2.0 was the ability to control the size of a font, resulting in all sorts of creative applications of the various heading tags. To remedy this, HTML 3.2 provides the `<basefont>` and `<font>` tags.

The `<basefont>` tag

The `<basefont>` tag is used to define the base font size used in the document. Within HTML, fonts are provided in seven sizes, ranging from 1 (the smallest) to 7 (the largest). The exact implementation of these sizes is left to the browser, but in general, each font size is about 20 percent larger than its predecessor.

The `<basefont>` tag has a single attribute, `size`, which specifies the base font size used throughout the document. By default, the base font size is 3. This tag is not a container and has no closing tag. Instead, all text following the `<basefont>` tag is rendered in the new size, until the end of the document is reached or a differing `<basefont>` tag is encountered.

The `<font>` tag

The `<font>` tag affects the appearance of the enclosed text like any other physical text style. It accepts two parameters:

`color`
> This changes the color of the enclosed text to the specified hexadecimal value or the predefined color name listed in Table 2.

`size`
> This changes the size of the enclosed text to either an absolute size or a size relative to the document base font size. Relative values are expressed with a leading plus or minus sign.
>
> Relative values are not cumulative. Nested `<font>` tags are always relative to the current base font size, not the current size set by a containing `<font>` tag.

Images

HTML 3.2 adds a number of extensions to the `<img>` tag, improving image positioning, spacing, and scaling. These new attributes are:

`border`
> This attribute is used to control the border around an image. Normally, images contained within an `<a>` tag are rendered with a border; images outside of an `<a>` tag are shown without borders. To force a border to always be drawn, use the `border` attribute with a value equal to the thickness of the border in pixels. To always suppress borders, use the `border` attribute with a value of zero.

`height` and `width`
> These two attributes define the size of the area within the document that will hold the image. If the image is smaller than the defined area, it will be stretched to fill the area. Similarly, if the image is larger than the area, it will be scaled down (not cropped) to fit in the area.
>
> Even if your images do not need scaling, these attributes are still useful. By informing the browser of the area needed to hold the image, the browser can preallocate the space and continue rendering the documents as the image downloads. This lets users see more of the document sooner as it is downloaded by the browser.

`hspace` and `vspace`
> These attributes let you specify an amount of space, in pixels, to be placed around the image. Using these attributes, you can create margins between your images and the surrounding text. By default, browsers usually place one or two pixels of space between an image and any surrounding text.

`usemap`
> This attribute indicates that the image is to be used as a client-side image map. The value of the attribute is the URL of an image

map contained in some HTML document. The map name is appended to the URL as if it were a document fragment identifier. Thus, *http://server.com/maps.html#my_map* might be a reference to a map named *my_map* in a document named *http://server.com/maps. html*.

Since most maps are defined in the same document in which they are used, a more abbreviated form of this attribute is usually used, with only the map name specified. In this case, the value of this attribute might be something simpler like *#my_map*.

The referenced map contains "hot spot" definitions for the image and is described in "Client-Side Image Maps," below.

In addition to these new attributes, the `<img>` tag also accepts two new values for the previously supported `align` attribute. In HTML 2.0, the `align` attribute concerned itself only with vertical alignment of the image with respect to the surrounding text. In HTML 3.2, this attribute can also be used to flow text around an image.

To create a so-called "floating" image, use the value `left` or `right` with the `align` attribute. The image will be rendered against the specified margin, and subsequent text will flow up and around the image. When the end of the image is reached, text is once again rendered against the previous left margin.

Client-Side Image Maps

HTML 2.0 supported the idea of an *image map*, a mouse-sensitive image that hyperlinked to different documents depending on where the user clicked within the image. Such images are extremely useful for creating graphical navigation aids within HTML documents. Unfortunately, their implementation in HTML 2.0 requires server-side support, making life much more difficult for the HTML author.

HTML 3.2 fixes many of the problems with the original image maps by allowing authors to cre-

ate image maps entirely within their HTML documents without intervention on the server side. In this section we'll explore the differences between the two kinds of maps and show how to create a client-side image map in HTML 3.2.

Client-Side and Server-Side Image Maps

In any image map, three activities must occur as the user interacts with the image map. The mouse position must be tracked as the user clicks on the image. This position must be translated to a specific document. Finally, the document is retrieved and presented to the user.

In both client-side and server-side image maps, the browser tracks the mouse position as the user clicks on the image. At this point, the similarities end. In the server-side image map, this position is transmitted to the server, where a special program is invoked to translate the mouse position to a specific document to be loaded. The location of this document is then passed back to the browser, who then loads the document and presents it to the user.

In the client-side image map, the client has enough information to translate the mouse position to a document URL. It loads the document and presents it to the user, without having to first interact with a server. The efficiencies are obvious. In addition, because the browser has more knowledge about the document, it may choose to display the image maps in some special way, perhaps by highlighting the hot spots in the image as the mouse passes over them.

Defining a Client-Side Image Map

Defining a client-side image map is easy. HTML 3.2 provides two new tags, `<map>` and `<area>`, to perform this task.

The `<map>` tag

The `<map>` tag performs two functions: it associates a name with this particular map, and it serves as a container for the various `<area>` tags that define the hot spots in the image. The ending `</map>` tag is always required, and no content other than `<area>` tags is allowed within the `<map>` tag.

The only attribute for the `<map>` tag is the required name attribute. Its value is the name of this map. This name is used with the usemap attribute of an `<img>` tag to associate this particular map with that image. Several maps may be defined in one document, as long as they each have a different name.

The `<area>` tag

The `<area>` tag defines an area within a map and associates a URL with that area. The `<area>` tag may only appear within a `<map>` tag and is ignored if it appears elsewhere in an HTML document.

The `<area>` tag accepts several attributes. These attributes are:

alt

This tag provides alternative text that describes this hot spot in the image. It might be used to create an alternative selection mechanism for nongraphical browsers or as an informative prompt as users pass their mouse over this particular area.

coords

This attribute accepts a list of comma-separated values representing points in the image that define the shape of this area. All coordinates are positive integers. The upper left corner of the image is at position (0,0).

The exact number of values provided to this attribute is dependent on the shape attribute, discussed below. For circles, three values are required: the x and y coordinates of the center and the radius of the circle. For rectangles, four values, representing the x and y coordinates of the upper left and lower right corners of the rectangle, are required. For polygons, a list of x and y coordinate pairs, corresponding to the vertices of the polygon, are required. The last

pair need not match the first pair; the browser will automatically close the polygon by connecting the last point to the first point.

href

This attribute defines the URL associated with this area. If the user clicks within this area, this URL will be loaded by the browser.

nohref

This attribute indicates that there is no URL for this area, making it a "dead spot" in the image. This attribute is handy for defining holes in other shapes in your images.

shape

This attribute defines the shape of the image and controls how the values supplied with the coords attribute are interpreted. There are four values for this attribute: rect (for "rectangle"), circle, poly (for "polygon"), and default.

The first three values are obvious, but the last warrants some explanation. If the value default is used, it matches against the entire image. This is useful for defining a URL to be loaded if the user clicks in the background of the image. However, since most browsers check for matches between your mouse position and the map areas in the order the areas were defined, placing the default area first in your image map may have dire consequences. Since the default image matches any mouse click, any areas defined after the default area will be ignored. As a result, play it safe, and put your default image definition last in your list of areas in your `<map>` tag.

An Example

While this may all sound complicated, it is actually quite simple. In Example 1, an `<img>` tag places an image into the document and indicates that this image is to be a mouse-sensitive client-side image map with the usemap attribute. This attribute uses a relative URL to reference a map named map1 in the current document.

Example 1

```
<img src="pics/map.gif" usemap="#map1">
...
<map name="map1">
  <area shape=rect coords="0,0,49,49"
      href="link1.html" alt="The rectangle">
  <area shape=poly coords="50,0,99,0,99,49"
      href="link2.html" alt="The polygon">
  <area shape=circle coords="50,50,25"
      href="link3.html" alt="The circle">
  <area shape=default
      href="link4.html" alt="The rest of the image">
</map>
```

Later in the document, the map is defined. The `<map>` tag denotes the start of the map and supplies the map name. Within the map are four `<area>` tags, each defining one hot spot in the image and its corresponding URL. Assuming that the image is 100 x 100 pixels, the `<area>` tags define a rectangle over the upper left corner of the image, a triangle over the upper right corner of the image, and a circle with a radius of 25 pixels in the center of the image. Finally, the last `<area>` defines a URL for the remaining areas of the image by using the `default` value for the `shape` attribute.

Form Enhancements

HTML 3.2 offers two enhancements to elements within forms: image button alignment and client file uploads.

Image Button Alignment

Within HTML, a form button can be created using an image as the button's representation. This is accomplished with the `<input type=image>` tag. You must include the `src` attribute, specifying the URL of the image to be used for the button and can optionally include the `align` attribute to control the position of the image in the document.

In HTML 2.0, image buttons, like regular images created with the `<img>` tag, could only be vertically aligned with respect to the surrounding text. In HTML 3.2, the `align` attribute now accepts the `left` and `right` values, meaning that the image button is moved to the corresponding margin of the document and any subsequent text is flowed around the image.

Client File Upload

One of the more esoteric new features in HTML 3.2 is the ability for the client to upload a file to the server. This is accomplished with a new form input element, created by specifying `type=file` in the `<input>` tag.

From the user's perspective, the file upload element is nothing more than another text entry field with an associated browsing capability. Like a regular text entry field, the `size` and `maxlength` attributes can be used with the file input element to specify the size of the text entry field and the maximum number of characters the field may accept.

The user may type a pathname into the field or use the browsing feature to select the file to be uploaded. The browsing capability differs between browsers and may not be provided at all in some low-end browsers.

If you choose to place a file upload element in your form, you must change the form's data encoding to ensure that the file is correctly transmitted to the server. The default form encoding, *application/x-www-form-urlencoded*, will transmit the file's pathname, not its contents. To send the contents to the server, you must use the enctype attribute in the `<form>` tag to request *multipart/form-data* encoding instead.

Finally, your server-side form processing application will have to be written to accept this particular encoding format. It is significantly different from the conventional format and will require completely different form parameter handling routines within your server-side applications.

Tables

HTML 3.2 standardizes the table model that was first introduced in Netscape 1.1 and has since been enhanced by Internet Explorer and later releases of Netscape. HTML 2.0 had no support for tables, so this addition marks the first formal introduction of tables to HTML.

The HTML Table Model

In HTML 3.2, a table is a collection of rows, which in turn are collections of cells. Cells may be designated as data or heading cells, with their format adjusted appropriately by the browser. Various attributes control the alignment of cell contents and the spacing and size of cells in the table.

Tables are considered standalone objects and always cause a break in the containing text flow. The text flow normally resumes after the table but can be made to flow around the table if desired.

Any HTML content is allowed, within a table cell, including other tables. While the basic table model does not support a number of more complex layout options, many complex layouts can be achieved by nesting tables within tables.

Tables provide primitive border capabilities and also support captioning. Because they are the only HTML element that can place elements on the page in a controlled manner, tables are often used as a layout management tool within an HTML document, instead of a traditional data presentation tool.

The `<table>` Tag

A table is defined using the `<table>` tag. This tag accepts these attributes:

align

This attribute controls the horizontal placement of the table within the document window. Values of `left` or `right` place the table against the desired margin, with subsequent text flowing around the table. Using `center` centers the table on the page, with the text flow resuming after the table has been displayed. The default is to place the table according to the containing text flow's alignment, without text wrapping enabled.

border

This attribute determines the width of the border surrounding the table and each cell within the table. By default, no borders are drawn around the table. If specified, the value of this attribute defines the border width in pixels. Using `border=0` explicitly turns borders off.

It is not possible, using a single table, to display only cell borders or only the table border. Judicious use of nested tables, though, makes some of these combinations possible.

cellpadding

This attribute defines the space, in pixels, between the edge of a cell and its contents. Normally, a browser might place one or two pixels of space between a cell's contents and its surrounding cell border. To reduce or enlarge this space, use the `cellpadding` attribute accordingly.

cellspacing

This attribute defines the amount of space between adjacent cells in the table. Cells are normally rendered a few pixels apart; this attribute lets you place more or less space between the cells in your table.

width

This attribute defines the overall width of the table. The cells within the table will be sized so that the contents fit within the desired width, if possible. You can specify the width as an absolute number of pixels or as a percentage of the width of the document window. By default, a table is only wide enough to contain the cells within it.

The `<table>` tag is a container for `<tr>` and `<caption>` tags that further define the table content. Placing any other content within a `<table>` tag may cause unexpected results.

The <tr> Tag

Within the `<table>` tag, the table content is defined as a series of one or more rows. Each row is defined by the `<tr>` tag, which accepts these attributes:

align

This attribute defines the default horizontal alignment of the cell contents in this row. It can be set to `left`, `center`, or `right`. Individual cells can override this setting, if desired.

valign

This attribute controls the default vertical alignment of the cell contents in this row. The cell contents are align to either the `top`, `middle`, or `bottom` of the cell, depending on the value assigned to this attribute. Individual cells can override this value, if desired.

The `<tr>` tag does not hold table content directly. Instead, it is a container for `<th>` and `<td>` tags that hold the actual cell contents.

The <th> and <td> Tags

The `<th>` and `<td>` tags define individual cells within a table row. They differ only in how they are formatted by the browser, with the content of `<th>` tags assumed to be heading cells and `<td>` tags to be data cells. Some browsers, for exam-

ple, render `<th>` tags as bold, centered text, while `<td>` tags are set in Roman, left justified text.

Both tags accept the same set of attributes, which are:

align

This attribute specifies the horizontal alignment of the cell's contents within the cell. Valid values include `left`, `center`, and `right`. If no `align` attribute is specified, the cell uses the alignment set by the containing table row's `align` attribute. If that has not been set, heading cells are typically centered while data cells are typically left aligned.

colspan

This attribute defines the number of table columns occupied by this cell. If not specified, the cell occupies one column in the table. If `colspan` is greater than one, the cell will span (or straddle) multiple columns in the table, beginning with the current column. This attribute is used to create spanning column headers or to create unusual cell alignments within a table.

height

By default, all the cells in a single row are as tall as the tallest cell in the row, whose height is determined by its contents. This attribute may be used to set the height of cell, in pixels. If that height is the largest among all the cells in the current row, the entire row will be set to that height. If some cell is taller, the specified height will be ignored.

In short, this attribute need only be specified on one cell in a row to define the minimum height for that row.

nowrap

This attribute disables automatic word wrapping within a cell. By default, the contents of each cell are treated as a separate HTML text flow with normal HTML line filling rules.

rowspan

Similar to `colspan`, this attribute defines the number of rows this cell will occupy. If not specified, the cell occupies the current row only. If `rowspan` is greater than 1, the cell will span multiple rows starting with the current row. This attribute is used to create spanning row headers or unusual cell alignments within a table.

valign

This attribute controls the vertical alignment of the cell's contents. Valid values include `top`, `middle`, or `bottom`. If `valign` is not specified, the cell uses the value of the containing row's `valign` attribute. If that is not specified, the default is `middle`.

width

This attribute defines the width of the cell, either as an absolute number of pixels or as a percentage of the table width. If not specified, the cell will be as wide as the widest cell in its column. If specified, it defines a minimum width for the cell, which will be stretched if its contents cannot be placed within the desired width, or if some cell in the column is wider than the specified width.

In short, like the `height` attribute, this attribute need only be specified on one cell in a column to define the minimum width for that column. Commonly, this attribute is used on the cells in the first row of a table to define the width of each column of the table.

The <caption> Tag

The table caption is defined using the `<caption>` tag, which accepts a single attribute, `align`. The value of align can be set to either `top` or `bottom`, and the caption will be placed accordingly. Most browsers default to placing the caption above the table.

The caption tag may appear anywhere within the `<table>` tag. The ending `</caption>` tag is required, and everything within the tag is rendered as the table's caption.

A Simple Example

Tables are actually much simpler than their tags would imply. An example goes a long way in showing how to construct a table. Consider the HTML table in Example 2 and its resulting table in Figure 1.

The example begins by creating a table with borders set to a single pixel, the spacing between cells set to zero, and the spacing around each cell's contents set to 5 pixels. Since no width is supplied, the table will be just large enough to hold its contents.

The `<caption>` tag adds the caption at the bottom of the table.

This table has four rows, two containing headers and two containing data. Each row has four cells, two containing headers and two containing data. The headers in the first row and column are spanned over the cells containing the individual column and row headers.

To ensure that the various cells line up, the first cell of the first row spans the first two rows and columns and has no content. The second cell in the first row spans the remaining two columns and supplies the heading in the first row.

In the second row, the first two cells are already occupied by the first cell of the row above, which was set to span two rows. The only cells needed in this row are the two column headers.

The third row has four distinct cells. The first creates the "Gender" heading, which spans both rows of data in the table. The next defines the "Male" heading, and the last two actually place data into the table.

In the last row, the first cell is occupied by the first cell of the third row, which is set to span the first cell of the row below it. The only cells in this row are the cell defining the "Female" heading, along with the two data cells for this row.

While the HTML is somewhat lengthy, the results are fairly elegant. A bit of experimentation with

Example 2

```
<table border=1 cellspacing=0 cellpadding=5>
    <caption align=bottom>Kumquat versus a poked eye, by gender</caption>
    <tr>
        <td colspan=2 rowspan=2></td>
        <th colspan=2 align=center>Preference</th>
    </tr>
    <tr>
        <th>Eating Kumquats</th>
        <th>Poke In The Eye</th>
    </tr>
    <tr align=center>
        <th rowspan=2>Gender</th>
        <th>Male</th>
        <td>73%</td>
        <td>27%</td>
    </tr>
    <tr align=center>
        <th>Female</th>
        <td>16%</td>
        <td>84%</td>
    </tr>
</table>
```

column and row spanning is usually all it takes to get up to speed with HTML tables.

Future Use

The HTML 3.2 standard defines two additional tags that are reserved for future use. These are the <script> and <style> tags.

The <script> Tag

The <script> tag provides a way to insert scripts and programmatic code into an HTML document. These scripts are executed by the browser, presumably enhancing the document being presented to the user. Currently, the most common scripting language used in this manner is JavaScript.

		Preference	
Gender	Male	Eating Kumquats	Poke In The Eye
		73%	27%
	Female	16%	84%

Kumquat versus a poked eye, by gender

Figure 1

Common uses for these kinds of scripts include animated advertising, form parameter validation, and dynamic document links.

The <style> Tag

The <style> tag appears in the <head> of a document and defines one or more styles to be used to render the document. The contents of the <style> tag are defined by the draft standard on Cascading Style Sheets, Level 1. Presumably, as this standard matures, this tag will be fully included in a future version of HTML.

Styles, used properly, can transform a document into dozens of different formats. They make life much easier for the document author and simplify the management of large Web sites.

What's Missing?

When HTML 3.2 was announced in May 1996, it was already obsolete. That is to say, it did not include features that were already in wide use at the time of its release.

HTML 3.2 was never intended to be a catch-all standard for the current state of HTML at the time. Instead, it strives to capture common elements of HTML in use. These elements had become fairly standardized across several browsers and their usage was well understood.

Still, one might wonder what was omitted from HTML 3.2, since the answer would shed some light on the next version of HTML.

Frames

The most widely deployed HTML feature that missed inclusion in HTML 3.2 is frames. Work is underway on a formal frames standard, so a future version of HTML may include this popular feature.

Frames were introduced by Netscape as a way to divide a single browser window into multiple panes, each containing a separate HTML document. Extension to the <a> tag allows links in one frame to affect the document displayed in one frame to affect the document displayed in another frame. In this way, authors can create navigation aids in one frame that drive the content of another frame.

Used correctly, frames can enhance a set of Web pages with an elegant look and feel. Used improperly, frames impede a reader's access to a set of pages. Sadly, most sites using frames tend to fall into the latter category. Within the Web authoring community, emotions run high when the topic of using frames is broached.

Whether you love them or hate them, it is clear that frames are not going away. With that in mind, standardizing frames in a future version of HTML would be useful.

Style Sheets

Although only available in test form when HTML 3.2 was announced, style sheets are becoming increasingly popular on the Web. With the release of Internet Explorer 3.0 and its limited support of style sheets, authors can finally begin experimenting with different document styles. As support for style sheets extends to other browsers, we can expect the popularity of style sheets to increase rapidly in the next six months.

Style sheets, simply put, allow an author to capture a set of document rendering styles and apply them to one or more documents. The look and feel of an entire web of documents can be controlled from one style sheet, making management of large document collections much easier.

Miscellany

As always, browser vendors are constantly enhancing the HTML they support. Some of the more common extensions currently in wide deployment but missing in HTML 3.2 include:

Font face specification
> The majority of browsers now support the ability to specify a font to be used to render text. While this flies in the face of the fundamental rule of HTML (content matters, not presentation), it makes life much easier for

Table 4	Documents Related to the HTML 3.2 Standard and Their URLs
Document	**URL**
HTML 2.0 materials	*http://www.w3.org/pub/WWW/MarkUp/html-spec/*
HTML 3.2 Reference Specification	*http://www.w3.org/pub/WWW/TR/PR-html32-961105*
HTML 3.2 features at a glance	*http://www.w3.org/pub/WWW/MarkUp/Wilbur/features.html*
Cascading Style Sheets	*http://www.w3.org/pub/WWW/Style/*

the myriad professional designers who are now designing thousands of pages for the Web.

Colored table cells

Color support has been extended from document backgrounds and text colors to allow entire tables or individual cells to be colored separately. This results in some extremely pleasing and elegant documents.

Better image alignment

Most browsers provide additional image alignment features, allowing images to be aligned to various baselines in the surrounding text. In addition, some browser support text alignment across cells in a table, allowing baselines to be synchronized in multiple cells.

For More Information

This article has only touched on the HTML 3.2 standard and related documents. For further information, consult any of the URLs listed in Table 4, and see the corresponding specifications printed in this issue. ∎

About the Author

Chuck Musciano
8445 Antelope Avenue
Palm Bay, FL 32909
CMusciano@aol.com

Chuck Musciano received a B.S. in computer science from Georgia Tech in 1982. He works at Harris Corporation in Melbourne, Florida, where he is currently the Manager of Unix Systems at Harris' Corporate Data Center. Chuck has contributed to a number of publicly available tools for the Internet, and started the still-running "Internet Movie Ratings Report." He has written on Unix-related topics for the past decade, most visably as the "Webmaster" columnist for *Sunworld Online* (*http://www.sun.com/sunworldonline*). He is also the coauthor of *HTML: The Definitive Guide*, published by O'Reilly & Associates.

AN INTRODUCTION TO CASCADING STYLE SHEETS

Norman Walsh

Abstract

Style sheets offer a new and powerful mechanism for supplying presentational information to a user agent displaying structured documents. The author begins by discussing the issues of structure and presentation, then follows with a discussion of style sheets on the Web. The focus of this article is Cascading Style Sheets from the W3C. The author discusses the mechanisms available for incorporating style sheets into Web documents and the general nature of cascading style sheets, and provides an overview of the display properties that may be modified with style sheets and the syntax for doing so. Finally, the author concludes with a short list of other style sheet resources on the Web.

In the Beginning . . .

Since its inception, HTML has been primarily concerned with representing the structure of documents online. By this, I mean that it allows the author to identify headings, paragraphs, lists, etc., but it does not provide (very many) facilities for specifying how the information can be presented (fonts, colors, spacing, text flow, etc.).

In the early days, this was fine; the Web was used mostly by technical people to publish articles and documents without much emphasis on how the documents looked. With the explosion of interest in the Web, both the audience and the authors have changed. Many people writing and designing for the Web want to exert much more control over the presentation of their documents. This brings the issue of structure versus presentation into sharp relief.

Structure versus Presentation

Look at this page. What do you see? There are two ways to answer that question. One is structural and one is presentational:

Structural

This is an article in a journal. It has a title, an author, and an abstract. The body of the article is divided into sections. Each section has a title and may include subsections. Most of the article is comprised of paragraphs, but lists, figures, and other elements are interspersed.

The most fundamental question in structural markup is, "what *is* it?" What structural significance does it have? Is it a filename, or a paragraph, or a list item? Is it a chapter title, or a person, place, or thing?

Presentational

This is a typeset page. The page begins with a centered title in 18 point ITC Garamond small caps. The author's name appears below the title in italics, also centered. Following the author's name is 40 points of white space followed by the abstract, also set in italics and with the bold, centered title "Abstract." The body of the article appears in two columns below the abstract. It is introduced by a heading in 15 point Franklin Gothic Book Compressed. Most of the article is comprised of paragraphs set in 9/12 ITC Garamond Light. The main text wraps around other elements that appear interspersed in the text.

The most fundamental question in presentation markup is, "what does it look like?" Is it green, or bold, or does it blink? Does it move, is it in a box, does it stand out, or is it hard to see?

Both of these answers are correct and useful.

The structural view of a document is useful because it provides us with context. Using the structural view, you can answer questions like "where is the section on font styles?" or build a table of contents with first- and second-level section headings, or identify the list of authors in a journal.

The presentation view is useful because we have expectations about how information will be presented. We expect books, journals, marketing information, advertisements, annual reports, and technical bulletins to *look different* (even when they have similar structure). In addition, many institutions have a distinctive look and feel that they expect to appear in all their published documents.

Ideally we want to be able to express both views of our documents whenever we publish them.

HTML is the Structure

The problem is that HTML, the primary markup language used to code documents on the World Wide Web, is really only useful for expressing the structure of a document.

It is possible to exert some control over the presentation, by employing tables and a variety of other tricks, but doing so blurs the structural view of the document. Adding new presentational tags to HTML isn't going to help, either. Presentational tags further blur the underlying structure of the document and could lead rapidly to multiple, incompatible HTML variants.

Style Sheets are the Presentation

Style sheets, which should become commonplace on the Web over the next few months, provide a means of associating presentational information with the structural elements of a document in a way that does not corrupt the underlying structure of the document.

A style sheet is a set of guidelines for the browser indicating how the various elements of a docu-

ment should be presented. For example, the following set of instructions constitute a style sheet for web documents:

- The document background should be blue.

- Top-level headings should be in 20 point Bold Arial (or Helvetica, or at least a sans-serif face).

- Body text should be 10 point Times Roman. Body text should be white; links should be light red; visited links should be yellow.

- Block quotations should be set in 8 point Times Italic. The body text should be black and the background white.

- Warnings should be indented on both sides and set in yellow.

- Itemized lists should use a fancy bullet.

A sample document of this style is shown in Figure 1. I'm not convinced that that is a very attractive document style, but it's a style nonetheless.

For comparison, the same document is shown in Figure 2 using the presentational information for HTML hardcoded into Microsoft's Internet Explorer.

Style Sheets on the Web

At present, there are basically two style sheet proposals on the Web: Cascading Style Sheets, level 1 (CSS1) from the W3C (included in this issue of the *Web Journal*) and DSSSL from the ISO. This paper describes CSS1, a style sheet mechanism for Web documents in HTML. DSSSL is more complex than CSS1 but also more powerful. When fully implemented, DSSSL will be rich enough to support print as well as online publishing from any SGML DTD. The online subset of DSSSL is available now in Jade (*http://jclark.com/jade*) but is not yet available in any commercial browsers.

Historically, there have been a number of proposals for style sheets on the Web. The W3C accepts that several may be adopted by different

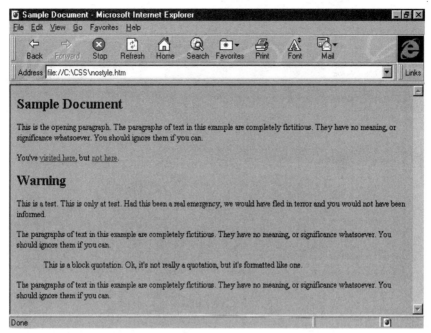

Figure 1   A sample document with a style sheet

browser vendors over time, but they have focused their present efforts on Cascading Style Sheets as a simple, easy-to-learn mechanism for adding style information to HTML documents. The W3C Web Style Sheets page (*http://www.w3. org/pub/WWW/Style/*) provides more background information and pointers to a number of alternative proposals.

In using style sheets in your HTML documents, you will face three common problems: availability, support, and compatibility:

Availability

Style sheets are not supported by all browsers. At the time of this writing, support for CSS1 is limited to Microsoft's Internet Explorer 3.0, Emacs w3 mode (the Gnuscape Navigator), and two experimental products from the W3C: Arena and Amaya.

If you code a document in such a way that your style sheet is essentially required in order to meaningfully read the document,

you will be limiting your audience. In the case of style sheets, this problem should be less severe than the current availability problem of browser-specific HTML extensions because the underlying HTML should be recognizable by any browser. As a further warning against this sort of coding, see the section "Conflicting Style Sheets: The Cascade."

Support

Until style sheets are widely used, corners and holes will remain where the browser developers either will fail to implement a feature described in the specification or will interpret it in such a way that it behaves differently than you think it should. The only remedy for this problem is test, test, test.

Compatibility

The compatibility problem will occur as soon as Netscape supports style sheets; it's really a generalization of the support problem. Netscape and Microsoft are bound to interpret parts of the specification in subtly

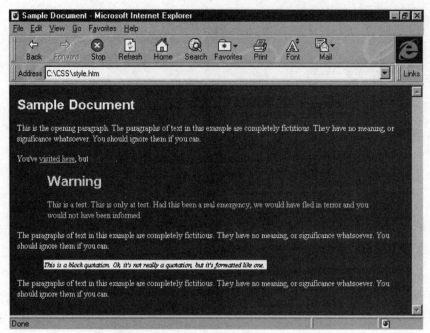

Figure 2   A sample document without a style sheet

different ways or implement different over-lapping subsets of the specification.

This means that for a time, your documents may not appear to have the same style when viewed with different browsers. C'est la vie.

From the perspective of providing structurally meaningful documents for publishing content on the Web, and this is my perspective, style sheets are still an immediate win. They allow you to provide a meaningful document that looks better some of the time but is always viewable. If you are looking for cross-platform, pixel-level control of your display, CSS1 isn't the answer.

What Can You Do?

A CSS1 style sheet contains five basic types of presentational information, called *properties*:

- Foreground and background colors and background images.

- Fonts properties.

- Text properties (word spacing, letter spacing, etc.).

- Boxes (margins and borders around block elements, floating elements, etc.).

- Classifications (control over list styles and the formatting of elements—whether they should be presented inline or displayed as a block, for example).

Beyond the question of what you can specify is the question of what effect will it have. The answer will depend largely on the capabilities of the program that is interpreting the style sheet. In the CSS1 specification, the authors carefully use the term "user agent" rather than "browser" to describe the program that is interpreting the document. The presentation (and meaningfulness) of style elements will be very different if a document is processed by a text-only browser or a braille reader or a speech synthesis tool than when it is processed by a full color, graphical browser.[*]

Within a given browser, you may encounter other limitations. Most of the properties that expect a size or length accept both positive and negative values as well as percentages. Each browser is free to impose implementation-specific limits on the acceptable range of values. Different browsers are also likely to do slightly different things when they encounter conflicting or illogical property values. Browsers may even implement different behaviors depending on the language used by the document or local user settings.

The bottom line is that styles are suggestions, hints if you will, to the browser. There is no provision for enforcing any aspect of the presentation. You can no more guarantee that another user viewing your document with a style sheet will see precisely the same thing you see than you can currently guarantee if they are viewing your document without a style sheet on different browser or platform.

How Do You Include Your Style Sheet?

Style information can be included in a document in several ways:

- With a style sheet `<LINK>` in the `<HEAD>` of the document:
  ```
  <LINK REL=STYLESHEET TYPE="text/
      css" HREF="http://...">
  ```

- In the `<STYLE>` element in the `<HEAD>` of the document.

- Directly in the STYLE attribute of individual elements of the document. This method is discouraged since it mixes presentation information directly into the document. Note that style information can be provided for a individual element, regardless of its context, through its ID.

- The `@import` command in a style sheet allows one CSS1 style sheet to explicitly import another.

How Do You Assign Styles to Elements?

However the style sheet is imported, the content of the style sheet itself is a text document containing rules and possibly comments (in the C language style `/* comment */` notation).

Simple Style Rules

A simple style rule has the following form:

```
element-name { property: list }
```

where the element name is the name of an HTML tag (H1, P, DIV, etc.) and the property list is the associated style commands. (We'll cover the specific properties in more detail a little later.)

Inheritance

Many of the property values applied to an element are inherited by elements placed inside it. For example, if you specify that text in headings should be red, emphasized text in the headings will also be red.

Elements In Context

Although there is no general mechanism for identifying elements in context (parents, children, siblings, etc.), a simple scheme is provided for specifying presentation based upon parent elements (you can specify formatting for EM inside of H1, for example, as distinct from EM elsewhere).

If you list a series of element names, instead of a single name, in a formatting rule, that rule

---

[*] This article is not a specification, and I've chosen to use the term "browser" rather than "user agent" because it is reasonable to be less formal in this context. For the record, I'm committed to supporting every effort to make Web documents accessible by everyone, and I really mean "user agent" when I say "browser."

applies only to elements that have all of the parents listed. For example,

```
DIV H1 EM { properties }
```

assigns the specified properties to **EM** only if it occurs inside of an **H1** inside of a **DIV**. Note that other intervening elements are possible; this rule would apply to an EM inside of an H1 inside of a TABLE inside of a DIV as well. If multiple nestings apply, the longest nesting wins.

Subclassing Elements

Sometimes it is desirable to treat specific instances of an element differently. For example, you might want to present warnings in a distinct way or have special formatting for links to URLs that are on another server.

Since HTML does not provide a great richness of structure for this purpose, CSS1 has hooks to the CLASS attribute, which can be placed on any element to assign a specific role to an element. For example, the preceding cases might be coded like this:

```
<P CLASS=warning>
<A CLASS=offsite HREF="http://...">.
..</A>
```

To specify the styles for elements of a particular class, add the class name to the element name with a period in the style sheet:

```
P.warning { properties }
A.offsite { properties }
```

Subclasses and nesting are independent operations. You can mix them freely in your style sheet.

Subclassing by ID

Another form of subclassing is by ID. This is the mechanism that allows you to avoid embedding specific style information in your document even for a unique element. If you have a specific element that must be uniquely treated, you can give it an ID:

```
<P ID="special-case">
```

and then assign style information to that element with a #:

```
#special-case { properties }
```

Note that IDs are *required* to be unique within a document. This requirement may not be enforced by current browsers, but it is a requirement for a truly conforming document. If you have several elements that need special treatment, that's a CLASS.

Pseudo-Classes

Some aspects of the presentation are not dependent strictly on the structure of your document but are rather a function of the browser or of user interaction. You may wish to control the formatting of the first line of a paragraph, for example, or the display of visited links.

In CSS1, these aspects of presentation are controlled by pseudo-classes. Like classes, they are specified with the element in the style sheet. Pseudo-classes use : as the separator character. Classes and pseudo-classes may be mixed:

```
A:visited { properties }
P.initial:first-letter
    { properties }
```

The first example here changes the properties of visited HTML links, the second changes the properties of the first letter of paragraphs with the CLASS "initial".

Conflicting Style Sheets: The Cascade

One fact that cannot be overlooked when considering style sheets is that both the publisher and the reader may wish to specify a style. Publishers frequently have a distinctive look that they wish to be reflected in all of their publications, and readers may have expectations as well, motivated by limitations of their environment or simple matters of artistic taste. (Personally, for example, I wish to specify that the background of all Web documents be white. I have a grayscale monitor at home, and most colored or graphical backgrounds on Web pages result in black-on-black text on my display.)

In addition, using modular style sheets is bound to result in occasional conflicts. It is necessary to know how these conflicts will be resolved (and frequently desirable to be able to specify how they should be resolved).

This raises the question of who gets control and this is where the word "cascade" comes from in *Cascading Style Sheets*. CSS1 includes a scheme for assigning priority to each style element. In every case, the style with the highest priority wins.

CSS1 is biased toward the publisher's styles. There is a single level of negotiation between the publisher and the reader; styles may be identified as "normal" or "important." If two styles have the same priority, the publisher's style sheet wins; otherwise, the higher priority style wins. Note, however, that browsers should provide a mechanism for disabling style sheets altogether so, in fact, the reader has final control.

Whether or not you agree with the philosophy that CSS1 uses, it's important to realize that this is a difficult problem, and there is no perfect solution. In some cases, the publisher may feel that absolute control is required (for example, if there is a legal obligation that warnings not be presented in a font smaller than 8 point), and in some cases, the reader must have control (for example, I simply cannot read dark red on black text).

A Closer Look at Properties

A property in CSS1 consists of a property name followed by a property value. The property name and value are separated by a colon. Some properties may have more than one value, in which case the value selected is dependent on some local condition (the accessibility of a particular font or image, for example).

Multiple properties may be specified by including multiple property name, value pairs separated by semicolons. The following example selects yellow on blue text for top-level headings and an italic font for paragraphs in block quotes:

```
H1 { background: blue;
     color: yellow }
BLOCKQUOTE P { font-style: italic }
```

The following sections describe some of the properties that are available.

Foreground and Background Colors and Background Images

There are two properties for specifying colors: `color` and `background`.

The `color` property controls the foreground color of an element. Usually this is the color of the text of an element. Colors may be identified either by name or by RGB value.

The `background` property controls the background color or texture of an element. When an image is specified for use as a texture, its position, scrolling aspect, and repeatability can be controlled.

Fonts Properties

There are five properties that control which fonts are used:

`font-family`
> Identifies the font family, or typeface, to use. A series of names may be requested; the first available font will be used. There are five classes of "generic" fonts that may be specified as a last resort, `serif` for serifed faces like Times Roman; `sans-serif` for sanserif faces like Helvetica; `monospace` for fixed-width fonts like Courier; `cursive` for swash faces like Zapf Chancery, and `fantasy` for other hard-to-classify faces like Grunge or Western.

`font-style`
> Identifies the style of the face, `normal`, `italic`, or `oblique`.

font-variant

> Identifies another variation on the face—either **normal** or **small-caps** in CSS1.

font-size

> The size of the face. Font size may be specified in absolute units or relative to the "current" size.

font-weight

> The weight or boldness of the font, specified with either a keyword (**bold** or **bolder**, for example) or as a member of the ordered series 100, 200, 300, . . . , 900, where higher numbers are correspondingly darker.

Text Properties

Several text properties are available:

word-spacing

> Modifies the default inter-word spacing.

letter-spacing

> Modifies the default inter-letter spacing.

text-decoration

> Selects underlining, overlining, link-through, or blink attributes (with additional, unspecified decorations anticipated from vendors).

vertical-align

> Adjusts the vertical alignment of an element.

text-transform

> Shifts text to uppercase or lowercase.

text-align

> Specifies left, right, center, or justified alignment.

text-indent

> Determines the amount of indentation on the first line of a block of text.

line-height

> Specifies the distance between the baselines of consecutive lines of text.

Boxes

The formatting model suggested by CSS1 is one of concentric rectangles. Each element has a margin, inside the margin is an optional border, inside the border is optional padding, and inside the padding is the actual formatted content of the element. The box properties allow you to specify the nature of the rectangles and determine how the content of the element is formatted to fit in the space provided.

margin margin-bottom, margin-left margin-right

> Determine the size of the top, bottom, left, and right margins. Setting **margin** adjusts all of the margins simultaneously.

padding padding-bottom, padding-left padding-right

> Adjusts the amount of padding on the top, bottom, left, and right sides of the element. Setting **padding** adjusts all of them simultaneously.

border border-bottom, border-left border-right

> Selects the nature of the border on the top, bottom, left, and right sides of the element. Setting **border** adjusts all of borders simultaneously. You can specify the size, color, and style of the border.

width height

> Identifies the width and height of the rectangle that contains the formatted content. Images should be scaled to the specified size, if necessary.

float

> Identifies an element that should float to the left or right of a flow of text, allowing the text to flow around it.

clear

> Specifies where floating elements may occur with respect to the element. For example, specifying **clear: left** indicates that there may be no floating elements to the left of the

element; this will force the element to start below an image floating on the left side of the display, for example.

Classifications

There are three classification properties, display, list-style, and white-space:

display
> Allows you to specify what category of object an element belongs to: is it a block element, like a heading or paragraph; an inline element, like emphasis or anchors; or a list-item block element, like LI. An additional category is none, which indicates that the content of the element should not be displayed at all.

list-style
> Influences the selection of numbers or bullets for lists. In addition to selecting one of the built-in enumeration or bullet styles, you can specify an image for use as the bullet character. You can also influence the posi-tion of the list mark with respect to the flow of the text. An outside list mark occurs to the left of the entire list item, whereas text wraps under an inside mark.

white-space
> Identifies how the line breaking of an element is to be accomplished. Possible values are normal, where white space serves merely to delimit elements that are formatted according to the alignment of the surrounding element; pre, where all white space is significant; and nowrap where white space serves primarily as a delimiter, but no wrapping is done except where <BR> elements occur.

A Sample Style Sheet

Finally, Example 1 shows how we might code a CSS1 style sheet for the style I specified in the section "Style Sheets are the Presentation."

Does it work? Sort of.

Example 1

```
BODY           { background: blue;
                 color: white;
                 font-family: times, serif;
                 font-size: 10pt }
A:link         { color: red }
A:visited      { color: yellow }
H1             { font-family: arial, helvetica, sans-serif;
                 font-size: 20pt;
                 font-style: bold }
DIV.warning    { margin-left: 0.5in;
                 margin-right: 0.5in;
                 color: yellow;
                 background: red }
BLOCKQUOTE     { background: white;
                 color: black;
                 font-style: italic;
                 font-size: 8pt }
/* Background color isn t inherited, so we repeat it
   on paras inside block quotes.
*/
BLOCKQUOTE P { background: white }
UL             { list-style: url(fancybullet.gif) disc }
```

Support for style sheets in Internet Explorer 3.0 is disappointingly thin. Microsoft seems not to have supported style attributes on all elements (setting colors on block quotations has no effect, selecting a graphical bullet for lists does not work, etc.). I can find no documentation of what they do support, so it's a sometimes tedious process of trial-and-error to build a style sheet that works, and there is no warning when a style is syntactically incorrect although that error may have a wide-reaching effect on the style sheet.

Gnuscape Navigator does the best it can, but the text-only environment of GNU Emacs is fairly limiting (better support may be available in XEmacs, I haven't tried).

Conclusion

Despite these difficulties, I'm still a fan. It will get better, and the time to start experimenting is now. The examples that I presented here are fairly plain. For some examples of much more dramatic effects, see the Microsoft Style Gallery (*http://www.microsoft.com/truetype/css/gallery/ entrance.htm*).

In this article, I've tried to give an overview of CSS1, but I haven't tried to supply all of the details. For more information, start at the aforementioned W3C Web Style Sheets page (*http://www. w3.org/pub/WWW/Style/*); it contains numerous links to information about CSS1 and style sheets in general. ∎

About the Author

Norman Walsh
O'Reilly & Associates
90 Sherman Street
Cambridge, MA 02140
norm@ora.com

Norman Walsh is the author of *Making TeX Work* as well as Technical Director of Online Publishing at O'Reilly & Associates. Before Norm joined O'Reilly, he was a research assistant at UMass, Amherst, where he earned his master's degree in computer science. Norm has been programming and working with computers for more than a decade.

Besides maintaining a number of TeX and font-related resources on the Net, Norm enjoys bicycling, herpetology, rowing, and browsing record and book stores. Norm lives in Amherst with his wife Deborah, two cats, and a small menagerie of turtles, toads, frogs, and newts.

When he's not working, Norm dreams of buying a house so that he can build a pond in the backyard, construct an elaborate garden, and find other ways to spend most of his time outdoors.

Guidelines for Multimedia on the Web[*]

Jakob Nielsen

Abstract

Multimedia is gaining popularity on the Web with several technologies that support the use of animation, video, and audio, which supplement the traditional media of text and images. These new media provide more design options but also require design discipline. Unconstrained use of multimedia results in user interfaces, which are harder to understand. Not every Web page needs to bombard the user with the equivalent of Times Square in impressions and movement.

Animation

Moving images have an overpowering effect on the human peripheral vision. This is a survival instinct from a time when it was of supreme importance to be aware of saber-toothed tigers before they could sneak up on you. These days, tiger-avoidance is less of an issue, but anything that moves in your peripheral vision still dominates your awareness. For example, it is very hard to concentrate on reading text in the middle of a page that has a spinning logo up in the corner. Never include a permanently moving animation on a Web page since it will make it very hard for your users to concentrate on reading the text.

Animation is good for:

- *Attracting attention.* Advertisements are an area where the ability of animation to dominate the user's visual awareness can be turned to an advantage in the interface. If the goal is to draw the user's attention to a single element out of several or to alert the user to updated information, an animated headline will do the trick. Animated text should be drawn by a one-time animation (for example, text sliding in from the right, growing from the first character, or smoothly becoming larger) and never by a continuous animation since moving text is much harder to read than static text. The user should be drawn to the new text by the initial animation and then left in peace to read the text without further distraction.

- *Showing continuity in transitions.* When something has two or more states, changes between states will be much easier for users to understand if the transitions are animated instead of being instantaneous. An animated transition allows the user to track the mapping between different subparts through the perceptual system instead of having to involve the cognitive system to deduce the mappings. A great example is the winner of the first Java programming Pythagorean theorem by animating the movement of various squares and triangles as they move around to demonstrate that two areas are the same size. (Unfortunately, this otherwise good page uses animated text inappropriately: the text moves constantly and is hard to relate to the events in the main animation.)

- *Indicating dimensionality in transitions.* Sometimes opposite animated transitions can be used to indicate movement back and forth along some navigational dimension.

---

[*] This article, which is part of the Alertbox columns for Sun Microsystems (see *http://www.sun.com/columns/alertbox.html*), was reprinted by permission from the author.

For example, paging through a series of objects can be shown by an animated sweep from the right to the left for turning the page forward (if using a language in which readers start on the left). Turning back to a previous page can then be shown by the opposite animation (sweeping from the left to the right). If users move orthogonally through the sequence of pages, other animated effects can be used to visualize the transition. For example, following a hypertext link to a footnote might be shown by a "down" animation, and tunneling through hyperspace to a different set of objects might be shown by an "iris open" animation.

One example used in several user interfaces is zooming to indicate that a new object is "grown" from a previous one (for example, a detailed view or property list opened by clicking on an icon) or that an object is closed or minimized to a smaller representation. Zooming out from the small object to the enlargement is a navigational dimension, and zooming in again as the enlargement is closed down is the opposite direction along that dimension.

- *Illustrating change over time.* Since an animation is a time-varying display, it provides a one-to-one mapping to phenomena that change over time. For example, deforestation of the rain forest can be illustrated by showing a map with an animation of the covered area changing over time.

- *Multiplexing the display.* Animation can be used to show multiple information objects in the same space. A typical example is client-side imagemaps with explanations that pop up as the user moves the cursor over the various hypertext anchors. It is also possible to indicate the active areas by having them shimmer or by surrounding them with a mar-

quee of "marching ants." As always, objects should move only when appropriate (for example, when the cursor is over the image).

- *Enriching graphical representations.* Some types of information are easier to visualize with movement than with still pictures. Consider, for example, how to visualize the tool used to remove pixels in a graphics application. The canonical icon is an eraser as shown on the left in Figure 1, but in user testing I have found that sometimes people think the icon is a tool for drawing three-dimensional boxes. Instead, one can use an animated icon as shown on the right:[*] when the icon animates, the eraser is moved over the background, and pixels are removed, clearly showing the functionality of the tool. In icon design, it is always easier to illustrate objects (a box) than operations (removing pixels), but animation provides the perfect support for illustrating any kind of change operation. In an experiment reported at the CHI'91 conference, Baecker, Small, and Mander[†] increased the comprehension of a set of icons from 62 percent to 100 percent by animating them. Of course, an icon should animate only when the user indicates a special interest in it (for example, by placing the mouse cursor over it or by looking at it for more than a second if eye-tracking is available). Especially considering the preponderance of toolbars in current applications, it would be highly distracting if all icons were to animate at all times.

- *Visualizing three-dimensional structures.* Since the computer screen is two-dimensional, users can never get a full understanding of a three-dimensional structure by a single illustration, no matter how well designed. Animation can be used to emphasize the

---

[*] To see the animation, go to *http://www.sun.com/951201/columns/alertbox/*
[†] Baecker, Ronald, Ian Small, and Richard Mander. *Proceedings of ACM CHI'91 Conference on Human Factors in Completing Systems*, "Bringing Icons to Life." See *http://www.fu-graz.ac.at/ox81160205_Ox0005cfOf* for abstract.

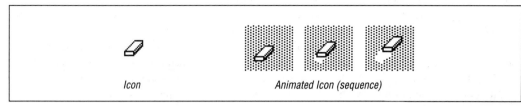

Icon   Animated Icon (sequence)

Figure 1

three-dimensional nature of objects and make it easier for users to visualize their spatial structure. The animation need not necessarily spin the object in a full circle: just slowly turning it back and forth a little will often be sufficient. The movement should be slow to allow the user to focus on the structure of the object. Three-dimensional objects may be moved under user control, but often it is better if the designer determines in advance how to best animate a movement that provides optimal understanding of the object: this pre-determined animation can then be activated by the user by simply placing the cursor over the object, whereas user-controlled movements require the user to understand how to manipulate the object (which is inherently difficult with a two-dimensional control device like the mouse used with most computers). (To be honest, 3D is never going to make it big time in user interfaces until we get a true 3D control device.)

Video

Due to bandwidth constraints, use of video should currently be minimized on the Web. Eventually, video will be used more widely, but for the next few years most videos will be short and will use very small viewing areas. Under these constraints, video has to serve as a supplement to text and images more often than it will provide the main content of a Web site.

Currently, video is good for:

- Promoting television shows, films, or other noncomputer media that traditionally have used trailers in their advertising.

- Giving users an impression of a speaker's personality. Unfortunately, most corporate executives project a lot less personality than, say, Captain Janeway from *Star Trek*, so it is not necessarily a good idea to show a talking head unless the video clip truly adds to the user's experience.

- Showing things that move—for example, a clip from a ballet. Product demos of physical products (for example, a coin counter) are also well suited for video, whereas software demos are often better presented as a series of full-sized screen dumps where the potential customer can study the features at length.

A major problem with most videos on the Web right now is that their production values are much too low. User studies of CD-ROM productions have found that users expect broadcast-quality production values and get very impatient with low quality video.

A special consideration for video (and spoken audio) is that any narration may lead to difficulty for international users as well as for users with a hearing disability. People may be able to understand written text in a foreign language because they have time to read it at their own speed and because they can look up any unknown words in a dictionary. Spoken words are sometimes harder to understand, especially if the speaker is sloppy, has a dialect, speaks over a distracting soundtrack, or simply speaks very fast. Poor audio quality may contribute to the difficulty of under-standing spoken text: it is recommended to use professional quality audio equipment and/or lavaliere microphones when recording a narrator. The classic solution to these problems is to use subtitles, but as shown in Figure 2, subtitles require special attention on the Web.

Figure 2 shows a subtitled frame from Sun's Star-fire video. The small subtitles (left image) look good on the original video tape (JPEG, 197K) but are virtually unreadable on the smaller image size currently used for computerized videos. Using bigger subtitles that have been anti-aliased for computer viewing (middle image) significantly improves readability, but the best results are achieved by the letterbox format (right image). In this example, the subtitles in the letterbox are constructed by enlarging the video area for the movie file with a 24-pixel-high black area. Doing so does not proportionally increase the file size since the black area compresses very nicely. Even so, it would be better to transmit the subtitles as ASCII (or Unicode) and have them rendered in the letterbox on the client machine—a perfect job for an applet. It would even be possible to have the user select the language for the subtitles through a preference setting or a pop-up menu (JPEG, 206K).

Audio

The main benefit of audio is that it provides a channel that is separate from that of the display.

Speech can be used to offer commentary or help without obscuring information on the screen. Audio can also be used to provide a sense of place or mood as done to perfection in the game "Myst." Mood-setting audio should employ very quiet background sounds in order not to compete for the user's attention with the main information.

Music is probably the most obvious use of sound. Whenever you need to inform the user about a certain work of music, it makes much more sense to simply play it than to show the notes or to try to describe it in words. For example, if you are out to sell seats to the La Scala opera house in Milan, Italy, it is an obvious ploy to allow users to hear a snippet of the featured opera: yes, Verdi really *could* write a good tune (AU file, 1.4MB), so maybe I will go and hear the opera next time I am over there. In fact, the audio clip is superior to the video clip from the same opera, which is too fidgety to impress the user and yet takes much too long to download (QuickTime, 3.6MB).

Voice recordings can be used instead of video to provide a sense of the speaker's personality (AU file, 1.4MB); the benefits are smaller files, easier production, and the fact that people often sound good even if they would look dull on television. Speech is also perfect for teaching users the pro-nounciation of words as done by the French wine site. It used to be the case that you could buy good wine cheaply by going for chateaus that were hard to pronounce (because nobody dared

Figure 2

ask for them in shops or restaurants)—no more in the webbed world.

Non-speech sound effects can be used as an extra dimension in the user interface to inform users about background events: for example, the arrival of new information could be signaled by the sound of a newspaper dropping on the floor and the progress of a file download could be indicated by the sound of water pouring into a glass that gradually fills up. These kinds of background sounds have to be very quiet and nonintrusive. Also there must be a user preference setting to turn them off.

Good quality sound is known to substantially enhance the user experience so it is well worth investing in professional quality sound production. The classic example is the video game study where users claimed that the graphics were better when the sound was improved, even though the exact same graphics were used for both the poor quality sound and the good quality sound experiments. Simple examples from Web user interfaces are the use of a low-key clicking sound to indicate when users click a button and the use of opposing sounds (cheeeek chooook) when moving in different directions through a navigational space.

Response Time

Many multimedia elements are big and take a long time to download with the horribly low bandwidth available to most users. It is recommended that the file format and size be indicated in parentheses after the link whenever you point to a file that would take more than 15 seconds to download with the bandwidth available to most users. If you don't know what bandwidth your users are using, you should do a survey to find out since this information is important for many other page design issues. At this time, most home users have at most 28.8KB, meaning that files longer than 50KB need a size warning. Business users often have higher bandwidth, but you should probably still mark files larger than about 200KB.

The 15-second guideline in the previous paragraph was derived from the basic set of response time values that have been known since around 1968. System response needs to happen within about 10 seconds to keep the user's attention, so users should be warned before slower operations. On the Web, current users have been trained to endure so much suffering that it may be acceptable to increase the limit value to 15 seconds. If we ever want the general population to start treating the Web as more than a novelty, we will have to provide response times within the acceptable ranges, though.

Design of client-side multimedia effects has to consider the other two response time limits also:

- The feeling of directly manipulating objects on the screen requires **0.1 second** response times. Thus, the time from when the user presses a key on the keyboard or moves the mouse until the desired effect happens has to be faster than 0.1 second if the goal is to let the user control a screen object (for example, rotate a 3D figure or get pop-ups while moving over an imagemap).

- If users do not need to feel a direct physical connection between their actions and the changes on the screen, response times of about **1.0 second** become acceptable. Any slower response and the user will start feeling that he or she is waiting for the computer instead of operating freely on the data. So, for example, jumping to a new page or recalculating a spreadsheet should happen within a second. When response times surpass a second, users start changing their behavior to a more restricted use of the system (for example, they won't try out as many options or go to as many pages). ■

About the Author

Jakob Nielsen
Sun Microsystems
2550 Garcia Avenue
MPK 17-105
Mountain View, CA 94043-1100
jakob.nielsen@sun.com
http://www.useit.com/

Dr. Jakob Nielsen is a Sun Microsystems Distinguished Engineer currently leading SunSoft's Advanced Web Technology project, working to improve the usability of the Web user experience and enhance the future of Web service creation. He has been usability lead for several design and redesign rounds of Sun's Web site and intranet (SunWeb), including the original SunWeb design in 1994.

Jakob Nielsen's recent books include *Multimedia and Hypertext: The Internet and Beyond*, *Usability Engineering*, *Usability Inspection Methods* (with Bob Mack), and *International User Interfaces* (with Elisa del Galdo). He also writes the monthly Alertbox column on Internet user interface issues at *http://www.sun.com/columns/alertbox*.

Dr. Nielsen's previous affiliations include Bell Communications Research (Bellcore), the Technical University of Denmark, and the IBM User Interface Institute at the T.J. Watson Research Center.

Usability Engineering
for the Web

Keith Instone

Abstract

As ease of use becomes more important than being "cool" on the World Wide Web, usability engineering techniques will let developers create more usable Web sites by helping them know their audience, valuating their user interfaces, and redesigning their sites based on user feedback. Understanding the tradeoffs between standards and new Web technologies is essential in creating usable sites.

Introduction

The ability to be "cool" on the World Wide Web —that is, taking advantage of the latest and greatest features—has been an important factor for those who want to stand out from the crowd. Lately, however, users have made it clear that it's not enough to simply use the newest technologies, such as frames, JavaScript, animated GIFs, or Shockwave. Many sites have been forced to provide alternatives to their frame designs because visitors have found them too hard to use [1].

Usability engineering techniques can create more usable Web sites by helping developers focus on the users rather than the technology. Understanding users' needs and the tasks they are trying to accomplish is steadily becoming more important than adopting the latest whiz-bang feature. Of course, if the latest technology fulfills a need, it should be used; but incorporating this technology just to be cool is becoming less and less acceptable.

In the very competitive world of the Web, usability will become crucial to the survival of sites (and their corresponding businesses). The value of usability engineering was put in perspective when Robert Hertzberg, *WebWeek* editor, advised that the observation of users "may be more valuable than what most businesses get from a $10,000-a-day consultant" [2].

Improving usability is not a black art: it can be accomplished by heeding common sense advice and applying techniques that help us understand and meet the needs of users. A good introduction to this topic is Jakob Nielsen's *Usability Engineering* [5]. Applying usability engineering to the Web is not that difficult, although the Web does introduce a few interesting problems—and solutions. Darrell Sano's *Designing Large-Scale Web Sites* [10] discusses many Web usability issues, such as limitations and constraints for Web publishing and structuring the information space.

What follows is a review of usability techniques and methods, seen in light of the constraints and tradeoffs of the World Wide Web. The best place to see usability engineering applied to the Web is the Sun-on-Net project [6], where usability testing, iterative design, and other activities improve the usability of Sun's Web site.

Web Usability Engineering Life Cycle

The usability engineering life cycle (see the following list [5]) represents a menu of choices that can be worked into the broader development context in order to increase usability. The techniques focus on understanding users, promoting usable designs, finding usability problems, and understanding other constraints in development.

1. Know the user
   a. Individual user characteristics
   b. The user's current and desired tasks

c. Functional analysis

d. The evolution of the user and the job

2. Competitive analysis

3. Setting usability goals

a. Financial impact analysis

4. Parallel design

5. Participatory design

6. Coordinated design of the total interface

7. Applying guidelines and heuristic analysis

8. Prototyping

9. Empirical testing

10. Iterative design

a. Capturing design rationale

11. Collecting feedback from field use

Steps 1, 7, 10, and 11 (Know the user, Applying guidelines and heuristic analysis, Iterative design, and Collecting feedback from field use) are most pertinent to Web usability and are elaborated upon in the sections that follow.

Know the User

The most basic of usability guidelines, "know the user," can be very difficult on the Web, where international access, exponential growth, and wide-ranging demographics (from school-age children to elderly citizens) are the norm. It is also difficult to understand what people really want from this new medium, in which so much is possible. The many surveys of general Internet demographics will provide some information on "who is out there," but talking to users is still the best way to get a handle on user-specific usability problems.

On the Web, "know the user" also means knowing the speed of their Internet connection, which browser version they are using, what plug-ins they have, and so on. Understanding these factors plays a big part in choosing advanced Web technologies and determining when they can be safely introduced.

Applying Guidelines and Heuristic Analysis

Many usability problems can be avoided by following the published guidelines [6] and by adhering to some general rules of thumb (see the Heuristics section below). Since the guidelines and heuristics are very general, additional usability techniques, such as empirical testing, are needed to determine the best solution for each particular problem.

Iterative Design

Iterative design involves a four-step process:

- Creating something.

- Testing it out with users.

- Understand the strengths and weaknesses.

- Designing a better version.

This fits very well into the Web "culture," in which a site does not have to be perfect the first time and the technology is constantly changing. Iterative design works best if it is part of the overall Web management process rather than an extra chore performed every year or so. Between iterations, one should be gathering user feedback, analyzing log data, creating rapid prototypes, and testing users.

Part of the iterative design should also be an evaluation of new technologies for the next version. Such a technology should not drive the change but rather be seen as a solution to known usability problems.

Collecting Feedback from Field Use

One of the easiest and most effective ways to improve the usability of a Web site is to see what real users do with it.

A strength of the Internet is the ease with which the users can provide feedback. A common practice is to place *mailtos* and feedback buttons on every page, encouraging users to take a moment to send the developers a note if they have a problem, a complaint, or some praise. The best user feedback can be designed into the site transparently.

Good logging of Web site usage is important for those who have to justify the cost of developing and supporting a site. As far as improving usability, logs can also indicate how people access the site, what problems they are having, and how a redesign affects usage.

Heuristics

Heuristic evaluation is one of the most important aspects of usability engineering: it is easy, fast, and inexpensive. It involves study of a user interface by a small set of evaluators for violations of common usability principles (rules of thumb, heuristics) so that the next iterative design can try to solve the usability problems. See the list that follows for some of the common usability heuristics [5].

- Simple and natural dialog

- Speak the users' language

- Minimize the users' memory load

- Consistency

- Feedback

- Clearly marked exits

- Shortcuts

- Good error messages

- Prevent errors

- Help and documentation

Heuristic evaluation is well suited to the Web, where everyone is in a hurry and the site can be evaluated from half-way around the world. When doing a heuristic evaluation for the Web, the common heuristics of consistency, feedback, and so on apply. But a few other rules of thumb are also useful when evaluating a Web user interface.

User Control

Because of the Web's architecture, in which browsers are responsible for interpreting HTML, developers never really know who—or what—will be processing their pages. Forcing users into particular fonts, sizes, colors, screen widths, or browser versions will generally reduce usability. Of course, designers need to have some control. But the more general the implementations and designs, the more likely we will reach satisfactory levels of usability for the widest range of users and over the longest periods of time.

Emerging Web technologies should often be avoided because they fail on this user control heuristic early in their life spans. One example is animation. To accommodate a diverse set of situations, users should be allowed to start and stop animation on their own. On one hand, animations that repeat forever are distracting; on the other, those that cannot be repeated lose their value. Until users gain adequate control over this technology on the Web, animations should be used very carefully. (Even once user control is in place, animation should be used only when appropriate [7]).

A new Web feature that will enable greater user control is cascading style sheets.* Style sheets force the developer to separate the presentation aspects of the page from the content, making it easier for a user to "intercept" the presentation information and insert his or her own requirements for display. Beyond selecting link color, for example, style sheets will extend the amount of control users have to include many other items of personal taste. The largest gain, however, will be that users can specify style attributes in a standard way to ensure their own personal requirements for usable access. For example, users with poor eyesight could specify large font sizes for headers and text, overriding the font sizes specified by the authors.

* This issue of the *World Wide Web Journal* features the latest CSS1 (Cascading Style Sheets) spec from the W3C, as well as an introduction to Cascading Style Sheets by Norman Walsh.

When evaluating a site for user control, the following questions can be asked to determine what usability problem might arise:

- Can users override this feature?

- Can they customize to suit their tastes or needs?

- Will giving users control of this feature reduce the usability of the site?

Structure

In all hypermedia systems, some underlying structure is important to help users figure out where they are and where they can go next. On the Web, where search engines and links from other places can throw users into the middle of any site, showing this structure is even more important. Since Web browsers lack substantial navigation aids to help users discover this structure, Web authors have to do a lot of this work themselves. To evaluate structure, one can look at every major page of a site and ask the following questions:

- If a user were taken directly to this page from an outside site, what could they figure out about the rest of the site from this one page?

- Is the site "brand" present?

- Is it clear which part of the site they are in?

- Is it clear how to navigate to other parts of the site?

Figure 1 provides an example of a page that indicates its position within the overall site structure.

Design for Change

The Web is about change, so a user interface had better be able to deal with both continually changing content and design. The evaluator can ask the following questions:

- How is old content archived?

- How is new content added?

- Can this design withstand the addition of 20 times the current content?

If everything has to be introduced through a "What's new" page, the site was not properly designed for changing content. If iterative design is going to work well, the design has to be flexible enough to withstand small changes without having to be thrown away. For example, if user feedback indicates a need for an additional major section to a Web site, can the design handle it, or would the site have to be redone from scratch? Figure 2 shows the design of a page on the Netscape Web site. How easy would it be to add an eighth section to this page? If improving the usability is too difficult, it simply will not happen.

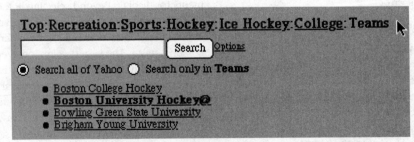

Figure 1   The location of the current page is indicated within the overall structure of the Yahoo Web site (November 26, 1996, http://www.yahoo.com/Recreation/Sports/Hockey/Ice_Hockey/ College/Teams/)

Advancing HTML: Style and Substance

Figure 2   How easy would it be to add an eighth section to this page? (November 25, 1996, http:/
home.netscape.com/)

Usability Tradeoffs

Usable interface design involves tradeoffs: weighing the costs and benefits to develop the best solution under the current conditions. The Web requires some very serious tradeoff decisions because of its low bandwidth, the role of browsers, and the existence of standards.

It is important to note that these tradeoffs are not meant to mandate one decision over another. What is important is to understand the pros and cons in order to make an informed decision.

Sometimes usability has to be sacrificed because of cost, time, or management issues, but blindly adopting a new Web technology rather than studying the usability tradeoffs is not appropriate.

For example, third generation site design [4] improves usability by providing better page layout: paragraphs are indented, headers are close to their associated paragraphs, and there are left margins. (This is done with such "tricks" as single-bit GIFs, as shown in Figures 3 and 4, to place the text in certain places.) One of the costs, however, is that access with graphic loading

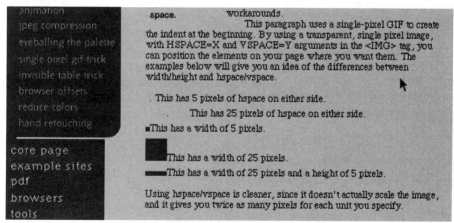

Figure 3   Single-pixel GIF trick at a third-generation site with graphics loaded (November 26, 1996, http:/
/www.killersites.com/1-design/signle_pixel.html)

turned off (to speed the process) presents a significantly less usable site; the precisely aligned text is no more, and "unloaded graphics" icons litter the screen. So if one is willing to eliminate use by one segment of the Internet population, a third-generation site might be appropriate. (Note also that several other populations of users are disenfranchised by third-generation site design such as those who have disabilities [8]). Part of the tradeoff is found in the answers to the following questions: is this a very usable site for a few users, a fairly usable site for the majority of users, or a "good enough" site for all users?

Bandwidth

Access speed is currently one of the major constraints on design. The best design, no matter how good, will not be seen if it takes too long to download. Until access speed is no longer a major problem, tradeoffs involving the quality of the graphics, the complexity of the design, and the use of higher bandwidth advanced technologies will be important to understand in creating usable Web sites. In addition, developers would benefit from observing users at very slow speeds.

Browsers

Another tradeoff occurs because of the crucial role that browsers play on the Web. The browser does certain things that are out of the author's control—history, bookmarks, and exact page layout, for example. The fact that the developer has to rely on the browser to provide certain functionality may limit the creation of usable sites. One need only look at the sophisticated and easy-to-use interface on CD-ROMs today to realize the limits that browsers impose on the Web. Browsers often have bugs that make certain features unusable. Netscape Navigator's early implementation of frames had serious problems with Back and bookmarking, which made frames quite unusable. (Now those bugs are fixed and frames are more usable—but not necessarily usable enough for certain applications.) Since not

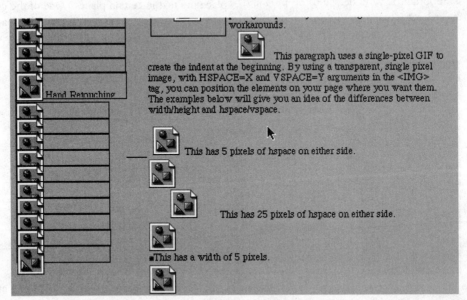

Figure 4   Single-pixel GIF trick at a third-generation site without graphics loaded (November 26, 1996, http://www.killersites.com/1-design/signle_pixel.html)

everyone has the most current version of browsers, these bugs are still an issue when designing a site today. Finally, there are a lot of browsers, each acting slightly different. Developers need to test their sites on as many platforms as possible in order to ensure usability for the widest range of visitors.

Standards

Standards make the World Wide Web interoperable. The most important standard for developers is HTML (even though other standards, such as HTTP, affect usability). The latest version of HTML is 3.2 [9].[*] While HTML 3.2 is not a great technological leap from 2.0 (several new features that were planned for 3.0 never made it into the oddly numbered 3.2), this latest version does represent a very important political advance for the Web. HTML 3.2 has brought the major Web vendors together for the time being, making the Web more interoperable and slowing the "tag wars" that were impeding the creation of usable Web sites across the different platforms. Knowing the HTML standard and following it when appropriate are crucial in making informed design and implementation decisions.

In general, the more meticulous we are in following the standards, the more usable a site is for the largest audience. Any variation from the standard, even if it follows "Netscape's standard," will have an effect on some part of the user population. It would help to consider the following questions:

- Is that new tag useful enough for those who can take advantage of it?

- Does it significantly affect those who cannot take advantage of it?

The best extensions are those that give added functionality for the "haves" while having no negative effect on the "have nots." A good example of this is the BGCOLOR attribute for table cells.

Because they are not part of the HTML 3.2 specification, table cell background colors are ignored by those browsers that follow the standard and have not implemented this extension. Developers need to be aware that this is indeed not part of the standard and should ensure that their sites are still usable for those who do not have access to this added feature.

Developers should also be aware of cases in which browsers are "forgiving"—i.e., those that create usable layouts of nonstandard HTML. For example, images are not allowed in PRE sections according to the HTML specification, but most browsers will generate reasonable interpretations of such markup. Designs that rely on such nonstandard use of HTML should be carefully considered.

"Following the standards" also means adhering to the spirit of the standards. For example, because it gives the desired appearance, an H6 header or other formatting is often used to "sign" a page. However, the ADDRESS tag was specifically created for this purpose ("specifies information such as authorship and contact details for the current document" [9]). More sophisticated search engines and other indexers might focus on the ADDRESS tag to improve searching. (See Figure 5.) Being able to search for pages authored by a certain person or group could be a very useful way to find information on the Web; if developers do not follow the standard as it was intended to be used, such advances cannot be made.

Designers of a corporate Intranet have it much easier than those with an Internet audience. If all users are known to have a particular browser and version, one can more safely take advantage of nonstandard aspects. Still, any nonstandard usage could tie that corporation to one particular vendor, so some intelligent decisions need to be made.

---

[*] See the HTML 3.2 specification in this issue of the *World Wide Web Journal.*

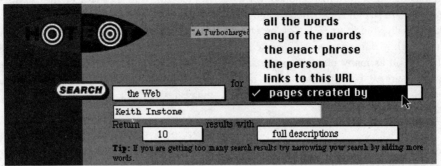

Figure 5 Search engines could key on address information in pages if the ADDRESS tag was used as intended by the HTML standard (November 26, 1996, adapted from http://www.hotbot.com/)

Conclusion

Usability engineering techniques, such as user testing, iterative design, heuristic evaluation, and user feedback, can make Web sites easier to use. Usability evaluations of new and emerging Web technologies, such as frames, JavaScript, Java and animated GIFs, are particularly important so that the tradeoffs of incorporating them into a site can be understood. Web standards, such as HTML 3.2, provide the basis of interoperability and help to ensure that designs will remain usable over time. Although excitement about the Web is still motivating users to play with new technologies, the rapidly expanding base of noncomputer-expert users, along with the increased use of the Web for "everyday" tasks and not just for fun, indicates a trend in which "what's useful" will become more important than "what's cool." Those sites that incorporate usability engineering into their development process will find that they are better able to survive in the highly competitive marketplace of the World Wide Web. ■

References

1. Andrews, Whit. "The Frame Tag: A Bit of a Bust, for Now," *Web Week* 2, 7, June 3, 1996. *http://www.webweek.com/96Jun03/news/frame.html*

2. Hertzberg, Robert. "Jumpin' Jehoshaphat," *Web Week* 2, 13, September 9, 1996. *http://www.webweek.com/96Sep09/opinion/editor.html*

3. Instone, Keith. "WebHCI: Design, design design." *http://www.acm.org/sigchi/webhci/design.html*

4. Lie, Håkon, and Bert Bos. "Cascading Style Sheets, Level 1," in this issue of the *World Wide Web Journal* and at *http://www.w3.org/pub/WWW/TR/PR-CSS1-961112*

5. Nielsen, Jakob. *Usability Engineering*, Boston: Academic Press, 1993. (Table of contents at *http://www.sun.com/columns/jakob/useengbook.html*)

6. Nielsen, Jakob. "Interface Design for Sun's WWW Site," *http://www.sun.com/sun-on-net/uidesign/*

7. Nielsen, Jakob. "Guidelines for Multimedia on the Web," Sun Microsystem's Alert Box for December 1995, included in this issue of the *World Wide Web Journal* and at *http://www.sun.com/951201/columns/alertbox/*

8. Paciello, Michael. "People with Disabilities Can't Access the Web!" in this issue of the *World Wide Web Journal.*

9. Raggett, Dave. "HTML 3.2 Reference Specification," in this issue of the *World Wide Web Journal* and at *http://www.w3.org/pub/WWW/TR/PR-html32-961105*

10. Sano, Darrell. *Designing Large-Scale Web Sites: A Visual Design Methodology*, New York: John Wiley & Sons, 1996. *http://www.wiley.com/compbooks/catalog/07/14276-X.html*

11. Siegel, David. *Creating Killer Web Sites*, Hayden Books, 1996. *http://www.killersites.com/*

About the Author

Keith Instone
Research Associate
Computer Science Department
Bowling Green State University
Bowling Green, OH 43403
instone@cs.bgsu.edu
http://web.cs.bgsu.edu/instone/

Keith Instone is the Research Associate for the Computer Science Department at Bowling Green State University. His research currently focuses on usability aspects of the World Wide Web. He maintains the Human-Computer Interaction Virtual Library and WebHCI, ACM SIGCHI's forum on user interface aspects of the Web. His volunteer efforts include Information Director for SIGCHI and Newsletter Editor for SIGLINK.

People with Disabilities Can't Access the Web!

Mike Paciello

Abstract

Information access for people with disabilities is creating numerous opportunities and challenges in the Information Highway community. In addition, as a result of the increasing paradigm shift by the publishing industry toward Internet and WWW-based document delivery systems, the importance of producing accessible information using electronic document mechanisms has increased immeasurably.

This paper is focused on the production of electronic documents for people with disabilities. However, the key principals involved in the design, production, and delivery of information apply regardless of the document medium. The paper will attempt to identify major problems in information and software design that deny access; cite successful products that can be used by people with disabilities to access publications; and point to resources that assist developers in creating accessible products in the future.

Introduction

The publishing paradigm shift is nearly complete: we have moved from a paper-based, typewriter-generated, hand-edited, printing press produced publication to a paperless, intelligent, WYSIWYG, software generated, WWW-published hyperdocument. Not only has the shift changed the way information is produced, it has changed the way individuals read that information.

For temporarily able bodied persons (TABs), the shift has resulted in increased availability to a global information set never before achieved. Because of this apparent increased availability of information the publishing industry has wrongly assumed that "what is good for the goose, is good for the gander."

The sad truth is that the proliferation of information does not guarantee its accessibility. Availability does not equate to accessibility. Where people with disabilities (particularly those with print disabilities) are concerned, thoughtless barriers to information are being constructed by electronic publishers. The barrier factor is increased by the magnitude of inexperienced online businesses and organizations who have correctly assessed the inexpensive cost of delivering information on the Internet but have inaccurately assumed that because it's on the Web, it must be easy to read—or access.

What are the key issues involving information accessibility for people with disabilities? Do solutions exist to assist publishers in the design, production, and delivery of accessible publications? Can publishers increase the accessibility and availability of their documents without sacrificing additional time, creativity, quality, personnel, and money?

The answers to these questions and available resources are discussed in the sections that follow.

Access Systems for People with Disabilities

Generally speaking, people with disabilities require assistive or adaptive devices to assist them in rendering or viewing a document. Those in the disability technology field refer to these as "access systems." For example:

- The blind may require a document output of braille or synthetic voice.

- Those with low vision or dyslexia may need large text or spatial adjustments.

- Individuals who are deaf or the hearing impaired may require visual cues for electronic documents that include sound or audio events.

- The physically or mobility challenged may require the ability to use the document viewer or browser without being able to use a keyboard, mouse, or input device that requires a part of their body other than just their eyes or mouth.

Access systems for people with disabilities include (but are not limited to): screen magnifiers, refreshable braille displays, screen readers, synthetic speech, caption-ready monitors, or alternative keyboards. The important point here is that the designer of the information need not worry about producing several versions of specialized documents. Rather, the focus should be on designing the source document with a rich set of characteristics that can be subsequently rendered or viewed by a wider audience.

To emphasize, this is not a new technology. Those involved in online publishing know that a source document can be coded using, for example, symbolic reference tags that are recognized by the document processor and then rendered to plain text, PostScript, or browser-compatible output. The same pre- and post-processing capabilities can be refined to produce braille, large text, and synthetic-voice output documents. No doubt, with the advent of publishing mechanisms like HyTime and Digital Audio, natural language voice documents (NLVDs) are possible. Therefore, access is not only achieved for people with disabilities, but language barriers are also diminished. Indeed with W3C and SGML consortium support for style sheets and link process definitions, the ability to produce accessible information for all people, disabled or not, has never been greater. This is the essence of universal design.

Identifying Key Issues in Information Accessibility

To identify the key issues related to information accessibility it is necessary to break down the publishing process into its natural phases: design, production, and delivery.

Design

In the design phase, the most common issues related to document inaccessibility involve the following:

- Complex notation

- Image rendering

- Multimedia features

- Navigation

Complex notation, including math and science, is extremely difficult to render in an acceptable format, especially for the blind. Most blind persons require an alternative format of the information, either ASCII text, Grade II Braille, or synthetic speech. Therefore, the proper rendition of the notation is critical to the reader. However, the challenge of rendering complex notation that tends to be graphical often requires a transformation process in which few information publishers are interested in investing.

Image rendering provides similar problems. Because the blind or low vision user is likely to be using alternative output (access systems), certain design considerations should be implemented—for example, using meaningful descriptive text in conjunction with figures, images, or other graphical entities within a document. Descriptive or alternative text has become a standard for Web-based documents. In fact, some authoring tools like HotMeTaL Pro, HotDog Pro, and Corel Web.Designer have built-in prompts for alternate text. Ideally, browser providers should then be able to properly display alternative text. The best implementation of alternate text display (are you listening Bill?) is Microsoft's

Internet Explorer, which automatically displays alternative text using bubble-help type notes as the user passes over the image with the mouse cursor. What will it take to get Netscape into the picture?

Electronic documents that contain *multimedia features*, including sound or video clips, require additional attention. Keep in mind that anything that emits sound cannot be heard by the deaf. It may not be heard by the hard of hearing or, for that matter, anyone viewing the document in a noisy environment. If you believe this to be an impractical example, consider the current industry move to WebTV and public kiosks. While a specific solution for providing Web captioning does not exist today, this should be considered an important feature of the document. Logic dictates that if consumer electronic manufacturers can produce televisions and monitors that support internal captioning controls, browser manufacturers and server protocol developers can design the means for delivering captioning through browsers.

Descriptive video provides a blind or low vision user with additional narrative that is useful, sometimes critical, to their comprehension of an electronic document. The process simply requires the interjection of descriptive narration during the spots within the video that are not otherwise filled with sound effects or dialog. As a result, the blind or visually impaired viewer achieves increased comprehension of the video event.

The National Center for Accessible Media (NCAM) in Boston, Massachusetts, currently provides a service that implements descriptive video for the motion picture industry. Descriptive video and captioning are perfect examples of how the power of markup should be used to enhance the richness and accessibility of a document. NCAM have recently been awarded grants to assist them in the research, design, and delivery of Web-based information for public television.

Navigating an electronic document, particularly a hypertext document, is a challenge for anyone.

Keeping track of where you've been, where you want to go, and then getting there can be a cybernightmare. Still, being able to visually navigate through a document has obvious advantages the blind or low vision user cannot easily imitate. A navigational cue as simple as providing colored text provides meaning and definition that the non-visual user cannot see. Therefore, there is a need to design solutions that implement audio cues in concert with visual cues.

Remember too that navigation is often closely tied with memory and consistent design. People with cognitive limitations simply require visual memory aids and simplified page design. An example of this can be found at the WebABLE! Web site (*http://www.yuri.org/webable/*). The designer, Colin Moock, implemented a system of visual cues consisting of opened and closed doors. The concept is basic to most people and is simple to learn and remember.

Navigational difficulties clearly present challenges to every user. Consider the difficulty a visual user has today and then imagine doing the same with your computer monitor turned off! Or try navigating through a multicolumn table or an online newspaper that contains multiple columns on a single page.

Without a doubt, navigation requires acute sensory awareness. Navigation is not just a document road map; it is not a linear link. Rather, good navigational design includes a combination of seeing, hearing, and "feeling" your way to a specific destination in a comprehensible way.

Design guidelines for Web pages

Creating Web pages has never been easier. Authoring tools have removed much of the associated complexity of the language. Additionally, where markup languages are concerned, HTML is about as easy as they come. Therein lies the dichotomy: while creating pages is simple, *designing* pages is not—particularly, designing accessible Web pages. Following is a brief list of guidelines for designing accessible Web pages:

1. *Use short, functional, descriptive text* for text links within a page. Avoid using one- to two-word text links. Using functional text descriptions provides better navigation and coherent feedback to blind users who rely on synthetic speech to render a page.

2. *Always provide text descriptions* for images. This guideline benefits visually impaired users, people who use text-based browsers, and individuals who turn off the ability to display inline graphics within GUI-based browsers. To accomplish this, use the `ALT="text"` attribute. The negative effect of not including alternative text is highlighted in Figure 1, which shows the Windham Hill Record company Web page.

In Figure 1, the seven image icons that border the left side of the page are menu-related icons that provide the user with navigational aids throughout the rest of the Web site. Note the use of `ALT` text for some images and not for others. How will a blind person comprehend or navigate this site?

3. *ALT text should be included for bulleted lists,* horizontal rules, or thumbnail links to larger images.

Where images require lengthy text descriptions in order to convey proper definition, some Web masters have created a *text anchor* to a page. In this case, the preferred method has been to use the uppercase letter "D" to signify "descriptive text." Users then

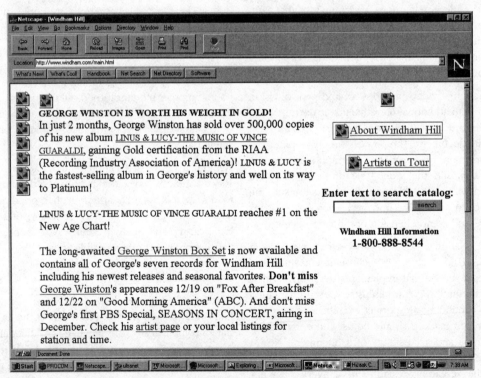

Figure 1   How could a blind person comprehend or navigate this site?

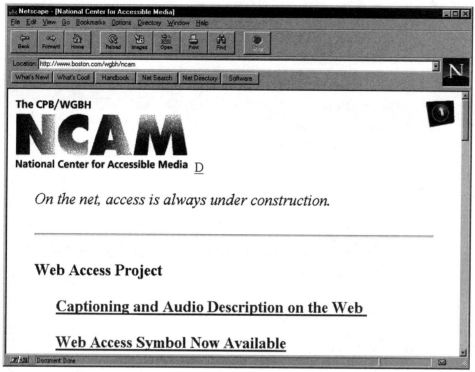

Figure 2 The uppercase letter "D" signifies descriptive text, indicating that users can click on a text anchor to access a full text version of the page

click on a text anchor, and a full text version of the page is rendered. The WGBH National Center for Accessible Media accomplishes this nicely as noted in the examples in Figure 2.

Figure 3 shows the text anchor page that results once the user clicks on the "D" text anchor link.

4. *Consider using a text anchor page for tables.* Synthetic voice software is capable only of reading left to right, one line at a time. The use of complex table constructs are very difficult for the blind reader to interpret.

5. *Use text anchors for image maps* as logical connections to their associated links. This generally is done by placing the links directly below the image map. Designers

may also consider providing users with a choice between viewing the image map or a text rendition (anchor page).

6. *Provide text transcriptions of audio clips* or video clips that contain audio. This benefits deaf and hearing impaired users. Again, text anchors are the preferred method.

7. *Test your pages for color contrasts.* Samu Mielonen recommends that you test your pages by adjusting your monitor to 256 shades of gray and then look for the following:
   – Can you distinguish the different colors on the basis of their lightness values?
   – Can somebody else who has not designed your screen discern the differences?
   – Is the text pleasant to read or does it tire you?

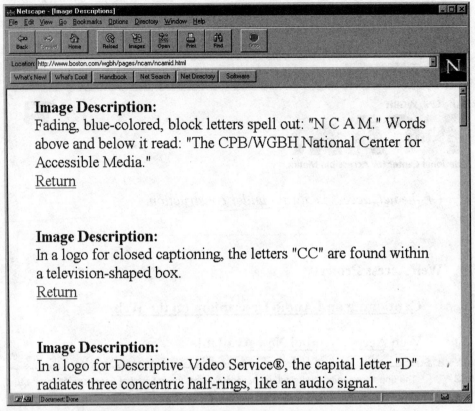

Image Description:
Fading, blue-colored, block letters spell out: "N C A M." Words above and below it read: "The CPB/WGBH National Center for Accessible Media."
Return

Image Description:
In a logo for closed captioning, the letters "CC" are found within a television-shaped box.
Return

Image Description:
In a logo for Descriptive Video Service®, the capital letter "D" radiates three concentric half-rings, like an audio signal.

Figure 3   A full text version of the page shown in Figure 2

- Are you using too many different colors (lightness values) that just confuse the reader without adding information to your design?
- Check for blue/yellow and red/green combinations—these color pairs are difficult or impossible to distinguish for those who have dichromatism (a form of color-blindness in which only two of the three fundamental colors can be distinguished due to a lack of one of the cone pigments).

8. *Avoid using frames.* Frames cannot be easily read by the blind or visually impaired. Jakob Nielson also notes, "Splitting a page into frames is very confusing for users since frames break the fundamental user model of the Web page. All of a sudden, you cannot bookmark the current page and return to it (the bookmark points to another version of the frameset), URLs stop working, and print-outs become difficult. Even worse, the predictability of user actions goes out the door: who knows what information will appear where when you click on a link?" [4]*

9. *Do not use blinking text,* scrolling text, marquees, or continuous animation.

10. *Provide forms* that can be downloaded, then mailed, or emailed. Forms cannot be easily

---

* See also Jakob Nielsen's article, "Guidelines for Multimedia on the Web," in this issue.

processed by the blind and visually impaired.

11. *Do not use browser-specific tags.*

12. *Always test your pages* with a variety of browsers.

Document Production

The accessibility issues related to the production of a document primarily involve the following:

- Authoring tools that are themselves accessible and also enforce accessible design tags, semantics, and protocols.

- The ability of the processor to receive a single source document and build accessible or alternative outputs.

For example, the IBM Bookmanager can build documents for the blind to use with their screen readers and voice synthesizers. This is because IBM Bookmanager supports the ICADD (International Committee for Accessible Document Design) DTD, which was designed to produce accessible documents for the print impaired. Documents produced for the World Wide Web are gradually becoming more accessible and require less "massaging" by a post processor or other intermediary actions because some Web browsers contain access features that enhance the readability of a document to persons with disabilities.

Document Delivery

In this case, document delivery refers to the ability of an online viewer or browser to adequately display a document. Most browsers or viewers were created for temporarily able bodied persons. They do not contain accessible features or controls that make it easier for people with disabilities to use. Additionally, they are rarely designed to allow assistive product manufacturers to easily link their products to using software "hooks."

A classic example is pwWebSpeak (The Productivity Works). This GUI browser was designed

with synthetic speech and large text functionality built in. It also supports the HTML 2.0 specification, which includes the ICADD SGML Document Access attributes. The next section includes more information about pwWebSpeak.

Ensuring electronic document delivery through a browser could be significantly enhanced if developers included assistive preference options that allow a user to "turn on" captioning, descriptive video, sound cues, synthetic voice, keyboard mapping, screen magnification, and other accessibility features.

As noted earlier in this paper, people with disabilities are not completely unable to read or view electronic documents. Several solutions exist, which were designed to increase accessibility to information. The following sections provide manufacturer-supplied descriptions of each solution.

Successful Solutions

pwWebspeak Browser

The pwWebSpeak browser (The Productivity Works) is an Internet browser designed for users who wish to access the Internet in a non-visual manner. This includes users who cannot be tied to a keyboard or monitor, blind or visually impaired users, users with dyslexia or other learning disorders, and users who are learning new languages.

The intelligence built into pwWebSpeak understands the HTML constructs and automatically bypasses those constructs that have no relation to the information content of a document. Both speech and large character interpretation of the Web pages are provided so that all classes or users can use the software effectively.

pwWebSpeak is designed specifically to interact directly with the information on the Web pages and to translate the information content into speech. The user may navigate through the structure of a document based on its contents, paragraphs and sentences, rather than having to deal with scrolling and interpreting a structured screen display.

"Bobby" Accessibility Verifier

Bobby is a program that finds common accessibility problems on Web sites. It was created to help Web designers insure the greatest possible audience for their Web sites and especially to highlight common accessibility problems for those with disabilities. When Bobby analyzes a page, it provides detailed information on:

- Problem HTML tags and constructs that make it difficult for people with a variety of disabilities to access a Web page.

- Image and document load times to ensure quick page access on slow modems.

- A comprehensive analysis of how the page's HTML might be incompatible with those versions of HTML implemented by the major Web browsers (including Netscape Navigator, Internet Explorer, Mosaic, and AOL).

- Common problems with image maps.

- A variety of other important tests including looking for missing ALT text in image tags.

HTML-to-Braille Transformation Service

Both UCLA (*http://www.ucla.edu/ICADD/html2icadd-form.html*) and the University at Dresden (*http://elvis.inf.tu-dresden.de/html2brl/*) provide an HTML-to-braille transformation service. These services allow anyone who has an HTML-coded document to send that document to the server which then:

- Converts the document to the ICADD DTD, which may then be easily converted to braille, large text, or voice ready file format.

- Converts the document to the ICADD DTD and then converts that instance to a braille formatted file. This resulting file may then be sent to a braille printer or refreshable braille display for the blind user.

University of Toronto

SoftQuad together with the University of Toronto are presently engaged in a project to make SGML and HTML authoring and browsing tools accessible to people with disabilities and to guide SGML and HTML authors in creating accessible documents. The user who is reading hyperlinked multimedia documents using access technology such as screen readers, braille displays, or screen magnifiers, faces three challenges:

- Obtaining an overview of the document.

- Moving to specific sections or elements in the document.

- Retrieving alternative descriptions or labels of graphic or audio objects.

The user with sight can get a good sense of the content and scope of a document at a glance. Formatting and layout allow the user to quickly find a specific part of a document. This is not the case when using screen readers, braille displays, or screen magnifiers. SoftQuad and the University of Toronto are exploiting the structure inherent in SGML to allow users to efficiently navigate and obtain an overview of the document.

Available Resources

Several resources were relied on to develop this paper and are available to users, publishers, and software product manufacturers interested in information accessibility for people with disabilities. Following is a brief list of resources, including URLs.

Environment Canada's Adaptive Computer Technology Centre: Accessible Web Page Design

Environment Canada's Adaptive Computer Technology Centre (*http://www.igs.net/~starling/acces.htm*) was one of the first Web sites to include guidelines and online examples of accessible Web pages and HTML implementations.

Adaptive Technology Resource Centre at the University of Toronto

The purpose of the ATRC (*http://www.utoronto.ca/atrc/*) is to:

- Develop and share creative solutions to the challenges faced by users of adaptive technology.

- Foster the effective use of adaptive technology in education.

- Promote the integration of alternative access systems throughout the information technology infrastructure at this and other educational institutions.

Recordings for the Blind and Dyslexic

Providing services for nearly half a century, Recording for the Blind & Dyslexic (RFB&D, *http://www.rfbd.org*) is a national nonprofit organization that serves people who cannot read standard print because of a visual, perceptual, or other physical disability. RFB&D is recognized as the nation's leading educational lending library of academic and professional textbooks on audio tape from elementary through post-graduate and professional levels.

Trace Research & Development Center's Designing an Accessible World

The Trace R&D Center (*http://www.trace.wisc.edu/world/world.html*) is one of the leading assistive technology research facilities in the world. Their Web page is a classic example of accessible design. Additionally, Trace provides several online reference documents.

WGBH National Center for Accessible Media

NCAM (*http://www.wgbh.org/ncam*) develops strategies and technologies to make media accessible to millions of Americans, including people with disabilities, minority language users, and those with low literacy skills. For 85 million Americans with little or no access to media's sights and sounds, the CPB/WGBH National Center for Accessible Media (NCAM) is working to remove the barriers to communication by:

- Developing strategies and technologies to make all public media accessible at home, work, school, and in the community.

- Retrofitting existing television, radio, print, and theatrical movies with access technology.

- Designing access into emerging telecommunications such as Advanced Television (ATV) and the National Information Infrastructure.

Yuri Rubinsky Insight Foundation

The Yuri Rubinsky Insight Foundation (*http://www.yuri.org*) is dedicated to bringing together workers from a broad spectrum of disciplines to stimulate research and development of technologies that will ensure equality of access to information of all kinds. The YRIF is dedicated to commemorating the genius of the late Yuri Rubinsky.

The YRIF is also the new home of the WebABLE! disabilities information repository (*www.yuri.org/webable/*). ∎

References

1. Ingram, Ray. "Universal Accessibility—A Matter of Design," The Productivity Works, Inc., Princeton, New Jersey. *http://www.prodworks.com/ua_9606.htm*

2. Gunderson, Jon. "World Wide Web Browser Access Recommendations," Mosaic Accessibility Project, Usability Access Chair, University of Illinois at Urbana/Champaign. *http://www.staff.uiuc.edu/~jongund/access-browsers.html*

3. Gunderson, Jon. "World Wide Web Accessibility to People with Disabilities: A Usability Perspective," Mosaic Accessibility Project, Usability Access Chair, University of Illinois at Urbana/Champaign. *http://www.staff.uiuc.edu/~jongund/access-overview.html*

4. Nielsen, Jakob. "Top Ten Mistakes in Web Design," SunSoft, Inc.

5. Vanderheiden, Gregg C., Wendy A. Chisholm, Neal Ewers, "Design of HTML Pages to Increase Their Accessibility to Users With Disabilities: Strategies for Today and Tomorrow," Trace R&D Center, University of Wisconsin, Madison. *http://www.trace.wisc.edu/TEXT/GUIDELNS/HTMLGIDE/htmlgide.html*

About the Author

Mike Paciello
131 D.W. Highway #618
Nashua, NH 03060
paciello@ma.ultranet.com

Michael Paciello is Executive Director of the Yuri Rubinsky Insight Foundation. The Foundation is dedicated to stimulating research and development of technologies that will ensure equality of access to information for all people.

Mr. Paciello currently serves as Chairman of the Electronic Industries Association's Assistive Devices Division (EIA/ADD). Mr. Paciello also serves as the W3C's Disabilities Guest Editor, is co-founder of the International Committee for Accessible Document Design (ICADD), and creator of WebABLE!, one of the world's largest Web sites dedicated to people with disabilities.

USER INTERFACES WITH HTML AND JAVASCRIPT

David Flanagan

HTML provides two very important components of user interfaces (UIs). First, it provides the primitive elements (also known as "controls" or "widgets") that make up any user interface. These are push buttons, radio buttons, checkboxes, lists, text input fields, and so on. Figure 1 shows a complete set of the UI elements provided by HTML. In addition to these elements, of course, HTML also provides formatted text, images, hypertext links, and client-side image maps, all of which can serve as part of a UI.

Figure 1 also illustrates another important UI component provided by HTML—the ability to arrange the primitive elements of a UI on the page. In this case, it is done by placing the elements within an HTML table, but elements can also be arranged with less sophisticated HTML layout.

Despite the fact that HTML provides the building blocks of user interfaces and allows them to be laid out in pleasing ways within a Web page, this is not enough to produce a fully functional user interface. In fact, two very important features of user interfaces are not provided by HTML. The first, and perhaps the most obvious, is the ability to handle events—to respond when the user

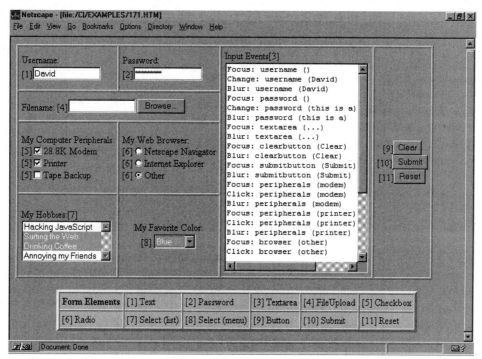

Figure 1   User interface elements provided by HTML

interacts with the UI. For example, if the user clicks on a particular checkbox in a UI, you might like to display a default value in some related text input field. Similarly, you might like to display a message in the browser's status line when the user moves the mouse over an image map, or when the user clicks a button.

Performing actions in response to user events is the most crucial feature of any kind of interactive user interface. Unfortunately, HTML provides only two possible actions:

- Reset form elements to their default state.
- Submit the values of form elements to a CGI script.

These actions are further limited by the fact that they must be triggered by special-purpose elements in the UI: forms can be reset only through Reset buttons and can be submitted only through Submit buttons.

In addition to their lack of event handling, HTML user interfaces also suffer from poor response time. It would be possible, for example, to create an HTML form that contained a number of different Submit buttons, each of which had some non-default label other than "Submit." Whenever the user clicked one of these buttons, the Web browser would contact the Web server, which could send a new HTML form that represented the updated state of the user interface. Even with a very fast network connection between browser and server, however, the delay required for this kind of update would make the interface awkward to use. Over a slower connection the interface would probably not be worth using at all.

Because of the paucity of actions that HTML can perform, and because of the delay imposed by the client/server model of the Web, user interfaces created purely with HTML can never have the richness that is possible on traditional desktop platforms. In fact, it is probably stretching the truth to refer to HTML forms as "user interfaces." In the 1990s, the term user interface implies a highly interactive dialog between user and computer. Because the traditional model of the Web involves a passive client and requires all "executable content" to be executed on the server, it is not possible to implement this kind of interactivity in pure HTML. The user interface provided by HTML forms is in fact a form of batch processing that harkens back to an earlier era of mainframes and 3270 dumb terminals.

Client-Side Executable Content with JavaScript

This discussion isn't meant to criticize the batch processing model of HTML forms. Given the limited bandwidth and typically high latency of the Internet, batch processing is the only viable model. It would not make sense to implement a highly interactive user interface over the Internet; this would require every user event to be transmitted from client to server, and the server's action to be transmitted back to the client. As any Unix user who has attempted to run a complex X Window System application over the Internet can attest, this model does not result in usable UIs.

This is where JavaScript comes in. By embedding executable content into HTML pages, it allows event handling and interaction between the user and the computer to take place on the client side, making round-trips to the server unnecessary. Of course, for many applications, a user's interaction with a Web page will still ultimately result in the submission of an HTML form to the server. The difference is that JavaScript allows the client to handle many intermediate events before the form is submitted, and these provide a much richer, more interactive interface for the user. Note that the addition of client-side JavaScript to HTML provides both of the UI features that HTML alone is missing: it allows event handling with a rich set of possible actions and provides rapid response time.

JavaScript makes true user interfaces possible through several of its capabilities. First, it is a general purpose programming language, which means that you can embed "executable content" of arbitrary complexity into Web pages. Second, JavaScript has a rich set of capabilities, such as the ability to read and write the contents of HTML forms, which allow JavaScript interfaces to perform interesting actions in response to user interaction. And third, JavaScript is notified of various events that occur when a user interacts with the elements of an HTML form, and can execute arbitrary code to "handle" those events.*

JavaScript Calculators

As mentioned above, JavaScript has the ability to read the user's input from HTML form elements and to set the value displayed within these elements. For this reason, the canonical example of a user interface that would not be possible without JavaScript is a calculator. A JavaScript calculator may be a program that simulates a traditional scientific calculator, or it may be a more specialized application for a particular purpose. What all JavaScript calculators have in common is that they read user input from a form, perform computations on that input, and display the results in the form. In almost all cases, everything takes place on the client—no communication with the server is required. Figure 2 shows a JavaScript calculator that helps you estimate your 1996 federal income tax. When you fill in information

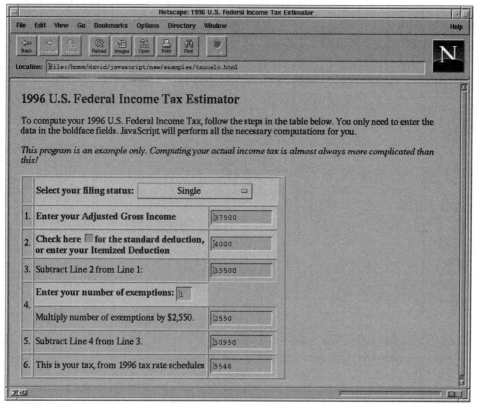

Figure 2   A JavaScript calculator that can estimate federal income tax

---

* This paper makes no attempt to document JavaScript. Refer to a book such as *JavaScript: The Definitive Guide* from O'Reilly & Associates for complete documentation.

about your filing status, income, exemptions, and deductions, it computes and displays the tax you owe.

If you understand how a JavaScript calculator program works, you'll understand how just about any JavaScript UI can be implemented. There are two requirements to make our tax estimator program work:

- We need to be notified when the user enters a value.
- We need to be able to read and write values from the form.

We'll see how to meet both of these requirements in the sections that follow.

Event Handlers

JavaScript event handlers are implemented through an extension to HTML. HTML tags that create objects the user can interact with (such as buttons, text input fields, and hypertext links) are given new HTML attributes (such as onClick, onChange, and onMouseOver). The value of these attributes is a string of JavaScript code; this code is executed when the appropriate event occurs for that object. Thus, in our tax calculator example, the income field is created with the following line of HTML:

```
<INPUT TYPE=text NAME="income"
    SIZE=12 onChange="compute()">
```

The onChange attribute specifies the code to be executed when the user enters a new income value. In this case, it will invoke the function compute(), which is defined elsewhere in the JavaScript program. Had we been writing a calculator that performed arithmetic, we might have a "plus" button defined with HTML code like this:

```
<INPUT TYPE=button NAME="plus"
    VALUE="+" onClick="add()">
```

Note that in this case we use the onClick event handler instead of onChange. HTML buttons invoke this event handler when they are clicked on.

Quite a few event handlers are supported by JavaScript. They are listed, along with the objects that invoke them, in Table 1. Note that the names of all JavaScript event handler attributes begin with "on."

Reading and Writing Form Values

We've seen how event handlers can be defined so that arbitrary JavaScript code can be run when the user enters a value, clicks on a button, or interacts with an interface in some other way. In order for these event handlers to be useful, they must be able to perform interesting actions. In our tax calculator example, the interesting action we want to perform is to read the user's income and other input from the form, compute the user's tax based on that input, and then display that computed value in the form. We saw that when the user enters an income value, the input field will invoke its onChange event handler, which will call the compute() function. Example 1 shows an abbreviated listing of that function, with some lines removed for simplicity. The example is heavily commented; the comments point out how the function reads and writes values of form elements, and they also draw your attention to some of the basic syntactic features of the JavaScript language.

Other Capabilities of JavaScript

In addition to reading user input from form elements and displaying computed values within form elements (as shown in Example 1), JavaScript also has a number of other capabilities that are useful for UIs. These are described in the sections that follow.

Form Verification

One common use of JavaScript is for form verification. While this uses the same techniques for reading form values as we saw previously, it also uses the onSubmit event handler of the <FORM> tag. This event handler is invoked just before a form is submitted. It can examine each of the

Object	Supported event handlers				
Area	onClick()†	onMouse-Over()	onMouse-Out()		
Button	onBlur()*	onClick()	onFocus()*		
Checkbox	onBlur()*	onClick()	onFocus()*		
FileUpload	onBlur()	onChange()	onFocus()		
Form	onReset()	onSubmit()			
Frame	onLoad()	onUnload()			
Image	onAbort()	onError()	onLoad()		
Link	onClick()	onMouse-Out()	onMouse-Over()		
Radio	onBlur()*	onClick()	onFocus()*		
Reset	onBlur()*	onClick()	onFocus()*		
Select	onBlur()*	onChange()	onFocus()*		
Submit	onBlur()*	onClick()	onFocus()*		
Text	onBlur()	onChange()	onFocus()		
Textarea	onBlur()	onChange()	onFocus()		
Window	onBlur()	onError()	onFocus()	onLoad()	onUnload()

Table 1   JavaScript event handlers

*Not supported in Navigator 3.0 on Unix platforms.
†Not supported in Navigator 3.0 on Windows platforms.

fields of the form to check that appropriate values have been entered. If any of the values is not properly entered, this event handler can cancel the form submission and notify the user of the error. The onSubmit handler cancels form submission by returning the JavaScript value false. If it returns any value other than false, or if it returns no value, form submission will proceed as normal.

Built-in Dialogs

JavaScript features three built-in dialog boxes that can be displayed with three simple functions. The alert() function displays a specified message in a dialog box.

- The confirm() function displays a yes-or-no question in a dialog box and waits for the user to click Okay or Cancel.

- It returns true if the user clicks Okay or false otherwise.

- The prompt() method displays a simple question and an optional default response and waits for the user to enter a string.

Figure 3 shows each of these dialog boxes. They can come in quite handy in JavaScript user interfaces. For example, the alert() method provides a useful way to notify the user when a form submission was canceled because of invalid input.

Dynamically Created and Dynamically Loaded Documents

One of the most important features of JavaScript is the ability to dynamically generate HTML text using the write() method of the Document object. This capability is most powerful when used in a Web site that contains multiple frames. In this scenario, events in one frame may trigger event handlers that output HTML text into another frame, effectively overwriting the document in that frame with a new one. Note that this

Example 1

```
function compute()
{
    // We'll be working with a form named "taxcalc" in the current
    //    document.
    // Note use of "var" statement to declare untyped variables.  Also note
    // the use of "." as in C++ and Java to access the fields of an object.
    var f = document.taxcalc;

    // Read the user's the filing status from a form element named "status"
    // within the form referred to by the variable f. Note that we read the
    // value of a form element as a field of an object.
    var status = f.status.selectedIndex;

    // Read the user's income from the form element named "income"
    // and convert the string value of that element to a number.
    // Again, we read the user's input as a field of an object.
    var income = parseFloat(f.income.value);

    /*
     * Intermediate code omitted here.
     * Based on the income and other input the omitted code computes a
     *    variable
     * named "line5" that contains income minus deductions and exemptions.
     * The code below computes tax based on this "line5" variable.
     */

    // Determine which tax schedule to use, based on filing status
    // Note the array syntax.  This array is defined elsewhere.
    var schedule = Schedules[status];

    // Determine which tax bracket to use within that schedule
    // Note the C++ and Java-style for loop.
    for(var i = 0; i < 5; i++) if (line5 >= schedule[i].cutoff) break;
    var bracket = schedule[i];

    // Compute the tax based on that bracket.  Note that "bracket" is a
    // data structure we've defined elsewhere.  It has fields like a Java
    // or C++ object might have.
    var tax = (line5 - bracket.cutoff) * bracket.percentage +
     bracket.base;

    // Round the tax to an integer number of dollars and store that value
    // into the form element named "tax".  Note that we set the value
    // displayed by a form element simply by setting the value of an
    //    object.
    f.tax.value = Math.round(tax);
}
```

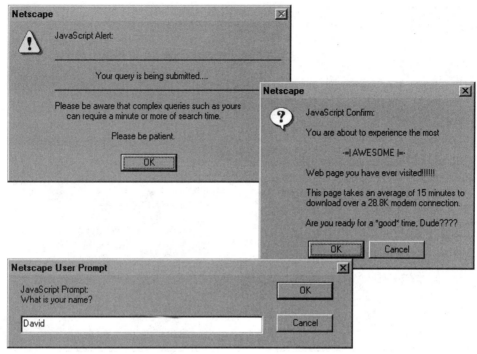

Figure 3   Built-in JavaScript dialog boxes

technique is essentially an extension to the calculator example we studied earlier. Instead ofcomputing a new value to display within an HTML form, however, this technique computes a completely new HTML document to display. This is a powerful technique precisely because HTML is such a powerful language for the presentation of text and graphics.

Instead of generating a new HTML document from scratch, an event handler can also force an existing document to be loaded into a frame. It does this by assigning the URL of the desired document to the location property of the Window object for that frame. Similarly, JavaScript can use the back() and forward() methods of the History object of a window or frame to load documents that have been previously viewed in that window or frame.

Dynamically Created Windows

It is possible to take this technique of dynamically creating HTML documents one step further and dynamically create browser windows in which those documents should be displayed. The open() method of the Window object creates a new browser window and allows you to specify the size for the window and the features (menu bar, tool bar, status line, etc.) that should be displayed in the window. Having created a new window, you can use JavaScript to output arbitrary HTML to it. One important use for this technique is to create dialog boxes that are more complex than those provided by the alert(), confirm(), and prompt() methods. Figure 4 shows just such a dialog box in a custom browser window. The window shown in this figure was created by a function invoked from the onError event handler of a Window object. The function created the window at a specific size and then

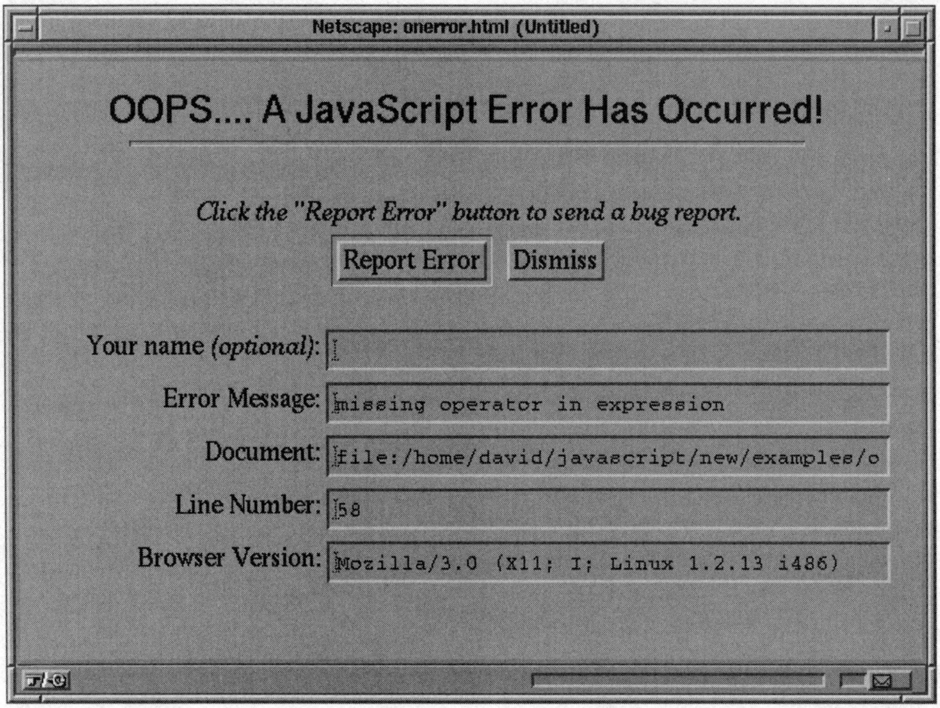

Netscape: onerror.html (Untitled)

OOPS.... A JavaScript Error Has Occurred!

Click the "Report Error" button to send a bug report.

Report Error   Dismiss

Your name *(optional)*: [

Error Message: missing operator in expression

Document: file:/home/david/javascript/new/examples/o

Line Number: 58

Browser Version: Mozilla/3.0 (X11; I; Linux 1.2.13 i486)

Figure 4   A dynamically created window browser

dynamically generated the HTML form that appears in the window. Although the result is a fairly complex dialog box, the code is really quite monotonous: after opening the new window, it consists simply of a series of **write**() method calls.

Controlling the Status Line

Another common use of JavaScript is to display messages in the browser status line. The **status** and **defaultStatus** properties of the Window object allow you to specify transient and persistent messages for display in that line. Perhaps the most common use of these properties is in conjunction with the **onMouseOver** event handler of hypertext links. By default, when you move the mouse over a hyperlink, most browsers display the URL of that link. For most users this is not particularly relevant or readable information.

With JavaScript, you can use code like the following to replace this machine-readable URL with a human-readable description:

```
<A HREF="../../../index.htm"
   onMouseOver="status = 'Go Back
   to My Home Page'; return true;"
>
Home
</A>
```

The **onMouseOver** event handler instructs the browser to display a helpful message in the browser status line. Note that the handler returns the value **true**. This instructs the browser not to perform its default action of displaying the URL of the link.

In Netscape Navigator 3.0, this technique also works with client-side image maps—the **<AREA>** tag supports the **onMouseOver** event handler in that release. This technique can be particularly useful with image maps, where it can serve as a kind of context-sensitive help for the user interface.

Image Replacement

One of the very powerful new JavaScript capabilities introduced in Navigator 3.0 is the ability to dynamically replace one image in an HTML document with another (of the same size, of course). This opens up a whole field of creative graphic design possibilities for user interfaces. For example, a client-side image map might replace itself with a new image when the mouse passes over it, thus providing feedback that the image is "activated" and available to be clicked. It also makes it possible to use images to simulate the behavior of checkboxes and radio buttons, allowing designers to replace the boring default look of those buttons with their own bold graphics. (Whether this is a good idea from the user interface design standpoint is an issue I'll leave to the individual designers.)

This image replacement technique has even been used to implement arcade-style games with animated graphics. For example, Tomer Shiran has used image replacement to implement a version of Tetris entirely in JavaScript. You can find his game at *http://www.geocities.com/SiliconValley/9000/netrisdeluxe.html.*

It is also worth noting, as an aside, that just as JavaScript can dynamically generate HTML documents with the `write()` method, so too can it generate documents with other MIME type data formats. Images are simply another type of data format, and JavaScript in Navigator 3.0 can in fact dynamically generate images. The current version of the `write()` method does not allow the NUL character (character 0) to be output, however, so only XBM images, which use an ASCII rather than a binary format, can be generated in practice. While the user interface implications of this technique are not clear, it is worth noting that Bill Dortch has implemented a simple drawing editor in JavaScript using this technique. You can try it out at *http://www.hidaho.com/doodlepad.* Note

however that you'll need a fast machine to achieve acceptable response times, since the requisite XBM images are large and thus slow to generate.

Miscellaneous JavaScript Capabilities

Besides the JavaScript capabilities we've seen above, a number of other capabilities can be useful in full-featured user interfaces. All form elements support a `focus()` method that you can use to set the keyboard focus to them. This allows JavaScript interfaces to provide custom focus management and guide the user through the process of filling out a form.

The JavaScript Window object also has a `focus()` method. When called, it raises the specified browser window to the top of the desktop and gives it the keyboard focus. The corresponding `blur()` method sends a browser window to the bottom of the desktop stacking order. The `scroll()` method of a window allows a JavaScript program to dynamically scroll the document displayed in a window to specified X and Y coordinates. Unfortunately, because it uses absolute pixel coordinates, this method is not particularly portable, although it may become more useful in the next release of Navigator, which should contain HTML tags for absolute positioning of elements.

JavaScript can use the `setTimeout()` method to specify a string of JavaScript code that is to be executed after a specified number of milliseconds have elapsed. This is useful for performing repetitive or periodic actions, such as simple animation.

Finally, another major new JavaScript feature in Navigator 3.0 is what Netscape calls "LiveConnect"—the ability to interact with Java applets and plug-ins from JavaScript. This is an extremely powerful new feature. Because applets can draw their own graphics and display their own user-interfaces, the ability to communicate with and control applets opens many UI possibilities for JavaScript programs. The ability to control Navigator plug-ins is also quite powerful. If you embed sound files in a document, for example, you can use the LiveAudio plug-in bundled with Navigator 3.0 to play those sounds. And because JavaScript can control LiveAudio, you can play those sounds in response to user events. Thus, it is possible to create buttons that provide aural feedback when you click on them and hyperlinks that draw attention to themselves by making a sound when the mouse passes over them.

faces—these are some of the actions that can be triggered by event handlers. The secret to creating powerful user interfaces with HTML and JavaScript is nothing more than combining these three pieces:

- Create HTML form elements

- That use JavaScript event handlers

- To trigger appropriate JavaScript actions ■

Summary

HTML provides the form elements, hypertext links, and other primitive building blocks that form the basis of user interfaces. JavaScript extends HTML by adding event handlers that are invoked when the user interacts with the primitive elements of a UI. These event handlers are listed in Table 1. The paragraphs following that table explored and explained some of the capabilities of JavaScript that pertain to user inter-

About the Author

David Flanagan
212 St. Margaret St., Apt D
Charleston, SC 29403
david@ora.com

David Flanagan is a freelance writer, trainer, and programmer. He has written five books for O'Reilly & Associates including *JavaScript: The Definitive Guide* and *Java in a Nutshell.*

GIF ANIMATION

Richard Koman

The face of the Web is changing. Take a look around. It's a far cry from the text-and-graphics medium it was a year or so ago. Today, the Web is moving, making sounds, constantly grabbing your attention, raising the noise level. GIF animation is a part of that process.

On one hand, it's an exciting, attention-grabbing, multimedia world, full of entertainment and interactivity.

On the other hand, what many people see is a Web littered with huge blank spaces surrounding puzzle pieces. That's the mark of content that requires some Netscape plug-in you don't have. To which you might say, "Never mind!"

Or you might click away, visiting a Netscape page that points you to another vendor's page, which directs you to the plug-in download page, where you download (in Windows) a self-extracting archive, which creates a setup program that you run to install the actual software. Unfortunately, the setup program asks you where you want to install the software (*Netscape\Program\Plug-ins* is usually the right answer). And if you've done all that correctly, you still need to note the URL you were trying to view, quit and restart Netscape, and re-enter the URL.

Compared to that process, li'l ol' GIF animation starts to look pretty nice. If you're using Netscape Navigator 2.0 or higher, or Microsoft Internet Explorer 3.0, GIF animation just works. GIF animation has clearly established itself as a core part of the Web language. You see them not just on experimental or amateur pages, but on the sites of the most button-down outfits in existence. The Dole '96 page. AT&T. Microsoft. c|net. MSNBC. Honda.

There are so many positives about GIF animation that I just have to make a list.

- *Users need no special software.* As I just noted, all they need is a browser that supports GIF animation.

- *Standard file format.* GIF is the graphics format for online images. Every Internet and online service application supports some version of the GIF standard, so it should be relatively easy for them to support the animation part of the standard. And since the animation is a GIF file, programs that don't support animation will still display a static image (usually the first frame but sometimes the last frame), not a question mark or a puzzle piece.

- *Ease of creation.* At least on the Macintosh there are several good programs for creating animated GIFs. Creating simple animations is rather easy with programs like GIFBuilder and GIFmation, although it's more difficult with available Windows software.

- *No server configurations.* You don't have to configure your server software (or, worse, ask your ISP or system administrator to do it for you) to serve a new data type, as you do with plug-ins.

- *Streaming technology.* Users don't have to wait for the entire animation to download before they see something as they do with technologies like Macromedia Shockwave for Director. As soon as each frame is done, it displays. Even though that makes for a somewhat choppy animation effect on slower connections, it satisfies the user's demand to know that something is happening.

- *Easy on servers.* Unlike server-push animation, in which a bunch of images are placed in a directory on a server and the server sends one to the user, waits for a signal that the first image has been received, then sends down the next one, and so on, a GIF animation delivers exactly one hit to the server. The browser takes care of everything else.

Of course GIF animation isn't the be-all and end-all. It does have limitations.

- *No sound.*

- *No interactivity.* Nothing lights up when you move your mouse around the image. You can't click in the animation to make something happen. Actually there is something in the GIF spec that lets you pause an animation until the user gives some input (presumably a click) but Netscape and Internet Explorer don't support that function.

- *Hard-disk crunching.* This was a problem with earlier versions of Netscape. Netscape stored the GIF in your disk cache and every time it looped, it had to call it off the disk. This appears to be much less of a problem in Netscape 3.0 and Internet Explorer 3.0.

The GIF Story

GIF animation is a real grassroots Net story. Netscape implemented support for GIF animation but didn't tell anyone. Individuals investigating the GIF standard who discovered that Netscape had implemented GIF animation and put the word out about how to create GIF animation.

Andrew Leonard told the story in a February 1996 column in *Web Review* (*http://webreview.com/96/02/09/tech/edge/index.html*). Here's an excerpt:

> *Last December, a guy in New York discovers a hitherto unknown way to create animations for Web pages. He posts the news to a couple of newsgroups in the comp.www.infosystems.* hierarchy. Some discussion ensues.*
>
> *In mid-January, the discussion catches the attention of a trolling bystander who happens to be the chief technical officer*

> *of a well-regarded, San Francisco-based Web production house. He checks out the hack, decides it's a marked improvement over how his company has previously been handling animations, and alerts his colleagues with an in-house email message, giving it his seal of approval.*
>
> *One of the recipients of the message is a Unix specialist who has been irritated that there is as of yet no Shockwave implementation for Unix—so he can't see all the cool Shockwave animations currently sprouting about the Net. He reposts his boss' alert to a closed Shockwave mailing list, letting everyone there know that there is an alternative.*
>
> *A subscriber to that mailing list copies the message over to a topic devoted to Netscape in the Web conference of the online service The Well. A number of Web developers regularly check this topic for the latest news, and one such developer decides to act. Within 24 hours, he's incorporated the animation technology on his own personal Web page.*
>
> *And that's how the VRML logo on Jim Race's VRML page suddenly came to life two weeks ago—a stunning example of the Net at its best. No PR blitzes, no press releases, no orchestration of hype whatsoever required. Just the Net in all its circuitous, word-of-digital-mouth glory—a case study of grassroots action in the information age.*
>
> *Royal Frazier is the man who got the animated ball rolling in December. But real credit for the GIF animation breakthrough belongs to Heiner Wolf, a German programmer at the University of Ulm.*
>
> *In February of 1995, Wolf and some colleagues were experimenting with a project aimed at putting a model rail-*

road on the Web. A key goal, says Wolf via email, was finding a way to animate the pages.

"[We wanted] some method to overwrite images on pages by newer ones. You can imagine my surprise when we looked into the GIF89a specification from CompuServe. It contained all we needed. Multiple images, difference images, and infinite image sequences. We just had to encode a sequence of GIF subimages on the fly."

But back then, no available browser supported the full GIF specification. So Wolf, a regular attender of Web-related conferences, decided to get the word out.

"I told my GIF story in '95 anytime someone asked about inline animation," he says.

Finally, Netscape bit. Scott Furman, a programmer responsible for imaging-related code, told Wolf that he would make sure Netscape Navigator supported the full range of possibilities for GIF89a.

Netscape did not decide, however, to make the news public. So despite Wolf's efforts, the greater Net community still remained in the GIF animation dark. Enter Royal Frazier.

One night in December, while playing around with the shareware program GIF Construction Set, Frazier (independently of Wolf) discovered the animation possibilities built into the GIF89a spec. And when he peered at his creation through the lenses of a few popular browsers, he found that only Netscape 2.0b3 ran the animation.

Lucky for the Web. Because although there's no shortage of animation action on the Web right now—Shockwave, of course; a new arrival, Sizzler from Totally Hip software, which allows "streaming animation"; and good old Java, continuing to plod its way along—there are some good reasons to embrace GIF animation.

First, in a single stroke, GIF89a animations transform the old way of doing low tech animations, "server push," into a moribund technology—roadkill on the info highway. Frazier argues that Web server administrators are bound to prefer GIF89a animations over server-push animations.

With a server-push animation, the server is constantly pushing out new images to the client—creating a steady stream of data going back and forth that sucks energy away from other concurrent processes such as FTP downloads. With a GIF89a animation, all the relevant information is downloaded to the client right at the beginning, forcing the client to do all the work. The speed of the animation is then determined by the size of its individual GIFs and how many horses the client processor has working.

Second, anybody can do it. You don't need a $1,000 Director program from Macromedia to create the animation, or have the years of experience in C++ programming necessary to hack a decent Java applet. Jim Race created his VRML logo animation (borrowing the GIFs from digital artist and all-around tech god Kevin Hughes) in half an hour.

Third, no special software or configuration is necessary to see a GIF89a animation. No plug-ins required. All you need is a recent version of Netscape. So Web crawlers can expect to see GIF animation springing up everywhere, without having to lift a finger.

As the Web races toward commercialization and high tech, proprietary software *formats, it's refreshing to see that the core grassroots energy of the Net still thrives. We can only wonder what's next?*

The Facts about GIFs

Before we jump into creating animations, it's helpful to understand a few concepts.

What Makes Them Animated?

GIF animation is a lot like film, or cel, animation. In a real animation studio, images are painted on clear plastic sheets called *cels*. Some images are backgrounds for the scene; most of the cels are of characters moving. When the animation is filmed, cels are overlayed so that background layers show through.

You can think of GIF animation in similar terms. The file contains a number of frames that are layered on top of each other. In simple animations, each frame is a complete scene. In more sophisticated animations, the first frame provides the background and subsequent frames just provide the changing image. This is similar to the way cel animation works.

A GIF animation consists of a number of images and a "control block" that specifies the length of delay before the next frame is displayed, as well as other attributes like transparency, palettes, and so on.

GIFs Use Palettes

Every GIF file contains a palette of the available colors for the image (or all of the images) in the file. The palette defines what colors will show up in the image. It's not quite as simple as that, though, because there's a global palette—sort of a default palette that all images will use unless otherwise noted—and local palettes, which are the palettes for each individual image.

GIFs are 8 bit or less. The absolute maximum number of colors in a palette is 256 (8 bit),

although they can have fewer colors, which reduces file size.

What About Unisys?

GIF uses a compression scheme called LZW (Lempel-Ziv-Welch), which is patented by Unisys. Although the GIF format was developed by CompuServe and everyone thought for years that it was completely public domain, Unisys let it be known about two years ago that they own the patent on the compression scheme and that they would collect royalties from software programs that use it. You don't have to worry about paying the royalty just for creating GIF files. Only software developers have to pay the royalty.

Browser Weirdness

As with most Web technologies, GIF animators have to be concerned with how the various Web browsers handle GIF animation. As we said, Netscape was the first browser to support GIF animation, but that doesn't mean they did it right. In fact, there are a number of problems with Netscape's implementation. Microsoft's support for GIF animation in Internet Explorer 3.0 is much better than Netscape's, but it's still not without problems.

A vast majority of Web users utilize one of these two browsers, but there are still the online services' browsers to worry about. The nice thing about GIF animation files is that they're still GIF files and every browser knows how to do something with them. Some browsers display the first frame and some the last frame.

This can be a problem if your first frame can't stand by itself. If you're building a name letter by letter, for instance, it won't look very good to have just the first letter displayed. If you keep this in mind, you can design around these limitations—by briefly displaying a complete image as the first frame, for instance.

But as GIF animation catches fire across the Web, this is increasingly a non-issue. America Online users will soon have access to both Internet Explorer, and Netscape, and between Netscape, Internet Explorer and AOL users, you're reaching just about everyone.

Tools

There are several software programs for creating GIF animation and many more coming out all the time. Here's a list of the programs we knew about at press time:

GIFBuilder

Macintosh only. GIFBuilder by Yves Piguet is the dominant Macintosh program for GIF animation. It's freeware that's easy and intuitive to use and boasts some super features like frame optimization.

GIF Construction Set

Windows only. GIF Construction Set is not terribly easy to use or intuitive. It does have some nice modules for automatically creating generic animations, creating rolling text, and applying special effects to an image.

GIFmation

Macintosh only. This is commercial software from BoxTop Software. It features a more visual interface than GIFBuilder and sophisticated palette handling options. We worked from a beta version of the software. A release version was not ready for inclusion on the CD, but you can download a demo version of GIFmation from BoxTop's Web site at *http://www.boxtopsoft.com.*

WebPainter

Macintosh only. WebPainter from Totally Hip Software is a general image-editing program that creates GIF animation as well as several other formats. It has a whole bunch of 2D painting tools and various animation features like onion skinning, multiple cel editing, and foreground/background drawing cels. It also includes several pre-designed animations. WebPainter supports PICS, Quick-Time, and GIF.

GifGifGif

Mac and Windows. Published by Pedagoguery Software, GifGifGif is a specialized program for creating an animation of screen activity. GifGifGif records all your screen activity—typing, pulling down menus, dragging icons, etc.—and builds a GIF animation. It's a great application for software instruction and demonstration.

Ulead PhotoImpact GIF Animator

Windows 95/NT only. An intuitive, easy to use Windows program that boasts superior co palette management and file compression schemes.

VideoCraft GIF Animator

Windows 3.x and 95/NT. Andacraft has taken an existing video effects progam and added GIF output capability to make a GIF animation program preloaded with special effects capabilities.

Andatech Animated Banner Maker

A free animation-creation utility on the Web. Just enter some type, choose an effect, and the software cranks out a GIF for you. On the Web at *http://www.andatech.com/vidcraft/banners.html*

GIFWizard

From Raspberry Hill Publishing, GIFWizard is a very useful free online utility to check the efficiency of your GIF file, animated or not. GIFWizard generates multiple versions of your GIF using increasingly smaller colors and tells you how many bytes are saved at different levels. It will create a GIF for you with unused colors discarded and generate a palette of those colors, with information about usage of each color, hexadecimal values, and more. If you really want an inside look at your GIF file, check the detailed analysis for a line-by-line look at the guts of your file.

Microsoft Animator

Windows 95/NT only. Another capable GIF animation program, complete with "style sheets" and various special effects.

Principles of GIF Animation

The principles of GIF animation are the same, no matter which program you're using. Some programs make it easier or more intuitive; some programs don't support all the features in the spec.

One of the most popular programs is GIFBuilder for the Macintosh, a freeware program for the Macintosh by Yves Piguet. Invariably most GIF-Builder users say something like, "I just dragged my GIFs into GIFBuilder and—boom—it was done."

GIFBuilder is actually that simple, but it's also a lot more complex. Making animations that are as small as possible, that look good on both Windows and Macintosh, and that don't needlessly repeat bytes is slightly more complex than "drag-drop, you're done."

The latest version of the software, GIFBuilder 0.4.1, boasts several advanced features such as:

- The ability to import QuickTime movies, PICT files, and Adobe Premiere FilmStrip files.

- A frame optimization option that throws out parts of frames that have already been used.

- The ability to save individual frames as GIF files.

- The color palette window, with drag'n'drop of palette files from and to the Finder.

- The ability to load the global palette of GIF files directly.

First Steps on the Macintosh

Figure 1 is an incredibly simple animation used by illustrator John Hersey on his home page. This example shows the basics of creating an animation. There are only three frames to the whole animation.

The baby face belongs to John's son Cole, now 2-1/2 years old. "It's the perfect image for me because I feel like a kid most of the time anyway," says Hersey.

As you can see from the images above, the animation simply builds a series of concentric circles around the baby's face and loops forever.

When you start up GIFBuilder, the program opens a window called `Frames`, which is where all the animation work occurs, and a frame called `Animation`, which shows the image for each frame as you select it.

You import pictures simply by dragging them from your desktop (if your Mac supports drag-and-drop) to the Frames window. Or you can choose `File/Add Frame` to add frames one at a time. Drag-and-drop is standard in System 7.5 and makes life a lot easier when you're dealing with an animation of dozens of frames.

Figure 1   A basic three-part animation that builds concentric circles around the baby's face and loops

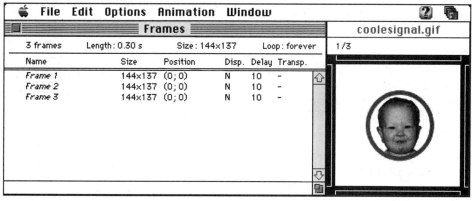

Frames						coolesignal.gif	

Figure 2   The Frames settings for the three images that make up the animation in Figure 1

It's good practice to put all your images for an animation into their own folder and to name the files alphanumerically, which is how they are loaded as frames in GIFBuilder. Let's say the files are named *baby1.gif, baby2.gif,* and *baby3.gif.* When we drag them over to GIFBuilder, the images will already be in the correct order. If you want to rearrange the order of images, simply select the filename, and drag it to the desired position in the list.

Figure 2 shows what the Frames window looks like when we import John's three images. If you just want to accept the default settings, select **File/Save** to write the new GIF file. Select a location for the file, click OK, and you're done.

The next step is to create the HTML that you'll put on your page. Select **Edit/Copy Image Tag.** This copies the IMG tag, with the correct HEIGHT and WIDTH tags, to the clipboard. You can then paste this line into your HTML editor, using the Macintosh Paste command (Command-V). Of course, if you're not serving the GIF from the same directory as the HTML file, you may have to edit the HTML to reflect this.

Now just put the file on your server, and you're serving the animation. There's no need to serve the component GIFs; all the images are contained in the new GIF file.

Changing the Frame Delay

The only change John made to these default settings was to change the interframe delay from the default of 10/100ths of a second to 20/100ths of a second.

To do this he selected Frame 1 in the Frames window and then selected **Options/Interframe Delay.** In the dialog box (Figure 3), he

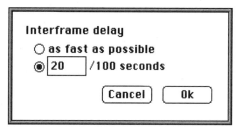

Figure 3   The Interframe Delay dialog box

entered the number 20 and pressed OK. He did the same thing for Frame 2 and Frame 3.

The delay on Frame 1 gives a 20/100ths second delay between Frame 1 and Frame 2; the delay on Frame 2 puts a 20/100ths second delay between Frame 2 and Frame 3. But what about the delay on Frame 3? Since the animation loops, the delay on Frame 3 specifies the amount of time before Frame 1 reappears.

Since those are the only changes we're making, we can save the final GIF file. Just choose `File/Save As`, enter a filename (ideally ending with *.gif*), and click OK.

Changing the Disposal Method

This animation uses three full-frame images. The disposal method is Unspecified, which means that the entire frame will be replaced by the next frame. If you want to see the effects of changing the disposal method, select a frame and choose `Options/Disposal Method`. This brings up a pop-up menu with the four possible options: `Unspecified`, `Do Not Dispose`, `Restore to Background`, and `Restore to Previous`.

Optimizing Your Animation

GIFBuilder 0.4 contains a fantastic feature that can dramatically reduce the size of your file. The command is `Options/Frame Optimization`. Just select this option before you write the file, and chances are you'll see great savings in file size.

How much savings depends on the nature of the images. If you're repeating the same pixels in frame after frame, you could reduce file size by one-half or more, simply by choosing the frame optimization method.

Frame optimization works very well when you are simply adding more information to your first frame. Without frame optimization, you would have to isolate each part of the image in a separate frame and then position each frame by hand.

A good example of the power of frame optimization is a flashing lights animation Bob Schmitt and I put together for a tutorial on the *Web Review* Web site.

Figure 4 gives a decent representation of what happens in the animation. Basically we're creat-

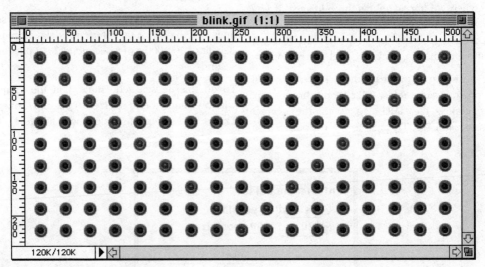

Figure 4   A flashing lights animation

Frames

9 frames	Length: 0.90 s		Size: 500x15			Loop: forever
Name	Size	Position	Disp.	Delay	Transp.	
Frame 1	500x15	(0; 0)	N	10	-	
Frame 2	500x15	(0; 0)	N	10	-	
Frame 3	500x15	(0; 0)	N	10	-	
Frame 4	500x15	(0; 0)	N	10	-	
Frame 5	500x15	(0; 0)	N	10	-	
Frame 6	500x15	(0; 0)	N	10	-	
Frame 7	500x15	(0; 0)	N	10	-	
Frame 8	500x15	(0; 0)	N	10	-	
Frame 9	500x15	(0; 0)	N	10	-	

Figure 5   The Frames window settings for the flashing lights animation without frame optimization

ing a pattern of lights by lighting the two light bulbs on the end of an array and then lighting successive inner pairs of lights.

The first frame is the blank array. The second frame lights the two end lights. The third frame turns off the end lights and lights the next innermost lights. And so on until the last frame, when only the center bulb is lit

Figure 5 shows the Frames window from GIF-Builder for this file, which weighs in at 14K. Every frame is the same size, 500 × 15, and is full-frame, positioned at 0,0. Note also that the disposal method is set to Do Not Dispose.

In Figure 6, take a look at what happens when we turn on frame optimization (Options/Frame Optimization) and save a new file. All the settings for Frame 1 remain the same, but look at the rest of the frames. GIFBuilder has resized and repositioned all the subsequent frames so that they contain a rectangle with just the image that's changed from the previous frame.

Figure 7 shows Frame 1. It's full size, 500 × 15, and positioned at 0,0—the top left corner.

In the second frame (Figure 8), GIFBuilder has trimmed the edges of the image away, so that just the lightbulbs remain. The image height has been reduced from 15 pixels to 8 and the width from

Frames

9 frames	Length: 0.90 s		Size: 500x15			Loop: forever
Name	Size	Position	Disp.	Delay	Transp.	
Frame 1	500x15	(0; 0)	N	10	-	
Frame 2	489x8	(5; 4)	N	10	-	
Frame 3	429x8	(35; 4)	N	10	-	
Frame 4	369x8	(65; 4)	N	10	-	
Frame 5	308x8	(95; 4)	N	10	-	
Frame 6	248x8	(125; 4)	N	10	-	
Frame 7	188x8	(155; 4)	N	10	-	
Frame 8	128x8	(185; 4)	N	10	-	
Frame 9	68x8	(215; 4)	N	10	-	

Figure 6   The Frames window settings for the flashing lights animation with frame optimization

Figure 7   The image in frame 1 of the flashing lights animation is full size

Figure 8   In the frame optimization process, the image in frame 2 of the flashing lights animation has been trimmed

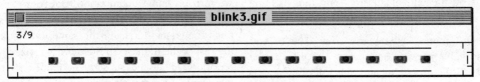

Figure 9   The frame optimization process continues with further trimming of the image

Figure 10   In the last frame of the flashing lights animation, only the center bulb is lit

500 pixels to 489. Now take a look at the position for Frame 2 in the Frames window. The value is 5,4. That is, this image is positioned 5 pixels to the right (X axis) and 4 pixels down (Y axis).

The process continues with the next frame. In Frame 3 (Figure 9), we've trimmed away the entire far left and far right bulbs, since they're not needed anymore, and we've trimmed the second lights down to the bulbs. The height of the image is still 8 pixels, and that won't change in subsequent frames. The width, however, is now 429. And the position is now 35,4.

The process continues that way, trimming about 60 pixels from the width of the graphic and mov-

ing the position over 30 pixels. Then we get to the last frame (Figure 10), in which only the center bulb is lit.

Although it took a while to explain what happened here, the work was all done by the program. And look at the results: our 14K file is now only 6K!

Disposal Methods

Next let's look at a somewhat mysterious option, the disposal method. This is set by highlighting one or all of the frames in the Frames window and choosing one of the options—Do Not Dispose, Dispose to Background, Dispose to Previous, or Unspecified.

The important thing to realize about disposal methods is that they are related to the transparency mode. That is, if your frames don't have transparency, you don't have to worry much about disposal methods. But if you are using transparency, it's critical to set the right disposal mode.

What is disposal method? It is simply the answer to the question: What do you do with the previous frame?

The choices are:

Unspecified

Use this option to replace one full-size, non-transparent frame with another.

Do Not Dispose

In this option, any pixels not covered up by the next frame continue to display. This is the setting used most often for optimized animations. In the flashing light animation, we wanted to keep the first frame displaying, so the subsequent optimized frames would just replace the part that we wanted to change. That's what Do Not Dispose does.

Restore to Background

The background color or background tile—rather than a previous frame—shows through transparent pixels. In the GIF specification, you can set a background color. In Netscape, it's the page's background color or background GIF that shows through.

Restore to Previous

Restores to the state of a previous, undisposed frame. Figures 11 and 12 show the effect of this option. Figure 11 shows the three component frames of the animation. The first frame is a full-frame image of the letter "A." For the second frame, we took just

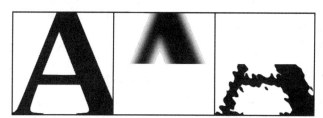

Figure 11   The first frame on the left is a full-frame image of the letter "A"; in the second frame, Photoshop's Gaustian blur effect has been applied to the top half of the letter; in the third frame, Photoshop's Ripple filter has been applied to the bottom half of the letter.

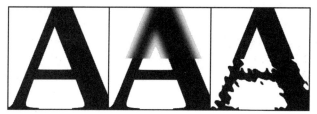

Figure 12   The effects of Disposal Method settings on the frames in Figure 11

the top half of the letter and applied a Gaussian blur in Photoshop. For the third frame we took just the bottom half of the letter and applied Photoshop's Ripple filter.

The first frame is set to `Do Not Dispose`, while the other two frames are set to `Restore to Previous`. Figure 12 shows the effect of these settings. The second frame displays the blurred top of the letter, while the bottom of the normal A from the first frame is displayed on the bottom. The third frame displays the rippled bottom of the A with the normal A from Frame 1 showing through the top.

The thing to remember about `Restore to Previous` is that it's not necessarily the first frame of the animation that will be restored, but the last frame set to `Unspecified` or `Do Not Dispose`. And the most important fact is that Netscape doesn't correctly support `Restore to Previous`. It treats `Restore to Previous` as `Do Not Dispose`, so the the last frame—not the last undisposed frame—shows through empty or transparent areas. Microsoft Internet Explorer 3.0 does handle `Restore to Previous` correctly.

Transparency Settings

Now let's look at transparency. The first thing to know is that although you can set transparency in a variety of programs—such as Adobe's GIF89a and BoxTop's PhotoGIF plug-ins for Photoshop—GIFBuilder discards these transparency settings. To make transparent animations, you must set transparency in GIFBuilder.

To do this, select one or all of your frames in the Frames window, and choose `Options/Transparent Background`. This brings up another menu with the following options:

No
> No transparency.

White
> White pixels are transparent. (The RGB values for white are 255,255,255.)

Based on first pixel
> The color of the first pixel of the animation—that is, the top left pixel, the one at coordinates 0,0—is transparent. This is a handy option since often you'll have an image in the center and the four corners will be transparent.

Other
> This option brings up a color picker so you can select a color for transparency.

Putting It All Together

In the quest for the most efficient graphics, it makes sense to use transparency, optimization and disposal method together. Take a simple example: a spinning globe on a blue background.

Many designers will include the blue background as part of every frame and replace the entire image with each frame. But if you set the blue background to transparent (`Options/Transparency/Based on First Pixel`) and set disposal method to `Revert to Background`, you'll reduce the file size of each frame and improve the performance of the animation.

Since Web browsers use the background color of the page for the `Revert to Background`, you can set the background of the animation using the BGCOLOR tag. This has the advantage of divorcing the animation's background from the GIF file. If you decide you want a yellow background on your page, the animation's background changes automatically. But `Revert to Background` isn't always the right answer.

If you've optimized your animation, `Revert to Background` would only display each optimized image surrounded by the background color. In this case, `Do Not Dispose` is the right choice.

Let's look at an example that puts all of these concepts together. Figure 13 shows a page from the SiteSpecific site.

Figure 13   A page from the SiteSpecific site

Let's look at the tower animation in depth. SiteSpecific actually put this animation up as a full-frame animation without transparency or optimization. Optimizing the animation in GIF-Builder reduced file size from 20K to 16K. The full images are shown in Figure 14 and the optimized images are shown in Figure 15.

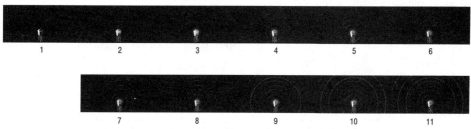

Figure 14   Full, unoptimized images of the SiteSpecific tower animation

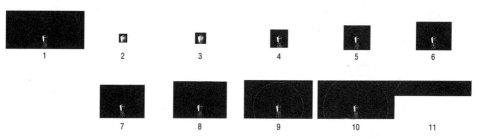

Figure 15   Optimized images of the SiteSpecific tower animation

With the animation optimized, the disposal method needs to be set to Do Not Dispose so underlying images continue to display. The transparency setting is Based on First Pixel. It's certainly possible to leave transparency off (since it does little to affect file size). If the background color is also used in the image, leave transparency off. In this case, however, there are clean divisions between black and white, and transparency works fine. Figure 16 shows the Frames window for the optimized, transparent animation.

Other Options

This section specifies most of the other commands in GIFBuilder's Options menu.

Interlaced

This is a toggle switch to set whether the GIF will be interlaced or non-interlaced. Interlacing involves the progressive rendering of images, rather than waiting for the entire image to be downloaded before display. When interlacing is on, the first frame will display progressively, with the image divided into lines—some of which will display at first, while others display later. Interlacing can affect either the entire animation or a single image.

While interlacing is somewhat helpful for static GIF images, it doesn't help much with animations since each frame is on screen for a short amount of time.

Colors

This option selects the palette you will use for the file. Every GIF image has a palette, a list of up to 256 colors that can be used in the image. The issue with palettes is simply which colors should be used so the image will look as good as possible no matter which computer system it's being viewed on.

The options under the Color menu are shown in Figure 17.

Before we get into the details here, let's just get this out front. Your best option is the 6x6x6 Palette, otherwise known as the Netscape palette. This is the palette that Netscape uses in Windows. On the Mac, Netscape uses the Mac system palette. Thus if you confine yourself to the colors in the Netscape palette, you can't go wrong. Everyone in the world will see pretty much the same colors.

The Netscape palette, a 216-color palette, is a subset of the Macintosh system palette, which is 256 colors. So it's not too much worse than designing with your system set to 8-bit color. But

11 frames	Length: 1.75 s		Size: 350x168		Loop: forever
Name	Size	Position	Disp.	Delay	Transp.
Frame 1	350x168	(0; 0)	N	60	1
Frame 2	37x38	(156; 101)	N	5	1
Frame 3	49x49	(150; 95)	N	10	1
Frame 4	79x79	(134; 80)	N	15	1
Frame 5	123x108	(113; 60)	N	15	1
Frame 6	159x125	(95; 43)	N	15	1
Frame 7	202x145	(73; 23)	N	15	1
Frame 8	240x161	(54; 7)	N	15	1
Frame 9	306x168	(21; 0)	N	10	1
Frame 10	350x168	(0; 0)	N	10	1
Frame 11	350x66	(0; 0)	N	5	1

Figure 16   The Frames window for the optimized, transparent tower animation

of course it is limiting—this palette contains virtually no grays and it also cuts out some of the darker reds and greens available on the Mac. So you may not be able to stick with the pure Netscape palette. In that case you should still keep the Netscape palette in mind, trying to deviate as little as possible to reduce dithering.

System Palette
> Uses the standard 8-bit Macintosh system palette.

Gray Shades
> Uses 256 shades of gray, which are all that are required to show the full range of a grayscale image. Remember, though, that the Netscape palette contains very few grays, so a full-blown grayscale image won't look very good on Windows machines.

Best Palette
> GIFBuilder looks at the images and uses just the colors from the Mac system palette that you use in your image.

6x6x6 Palette
> The Netscape palette, discussed above.

Load Palette
> Lets you specify a palette file to use with the image. Use this option to load your custom palettes.

Remove Unused Colors
> When this option is selected, GIFBuilder removes unused colors from your palette, reducing file size.

Save Palette
> Saves the palette of your image.

Depth

You don't have to use all 8 bits if you don't need them. The Depth option lets you specify whether you want to limit the image to some number of bits less than 8. To do this, select System or Grayscale palette from the Colors menu, then select Bit Depth from the Depth menu. For a black and white (not grayscale) image, select 1 bit.

It's probably better, however, to use the 6×6×6 Palette and have GIFBuilder remove unused colors. The 6×6×6 Palette requires the full 8 bits, so if you select that palette from the Colors menu, you'll see the other bit depths grayed out.

Dithering

Dithering is a way to simulate intermediate color shades. It should be used with continuous-tone images. You should use the 6×6×6 Palette with dithering so Windows doesn't try to dither the image a second time.

Image Size

When Minimum Size is on, the size is calculated so that the animation's bottom right corner corresponds to the lowest right-hand frame. Frames are always cropped to fit in the animation bounding box.

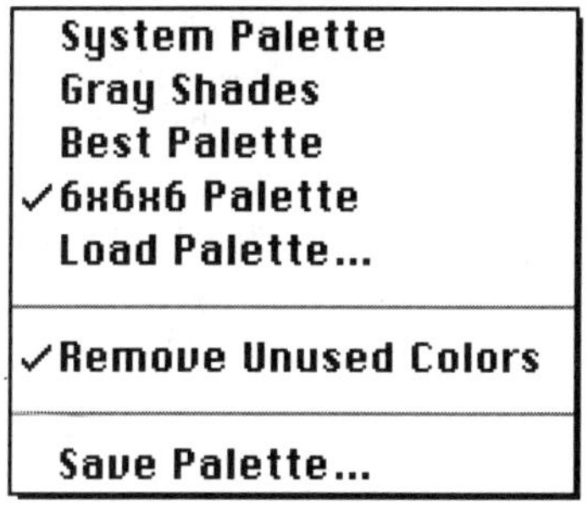

```
┌─────────────────────────────┐
│      System Palette         │
│      Gray Shades            │
│      Best Palette           │
│   ✓ 6н6н6 Palette           │
│      Load Palette...        │
├─────────────────────────────┤
│   ✓ Remove Unused Colors    │
├─────────────────────────────┤
│      Save Palette...        │
└─────────────────────────────┘
```

Figure 17   The options under the Color menu in GifBuilder

Background Color

Regardless of what color you select in the background color option, Netscape and Internet Explorer display the background color or image you specify in your HTML page. So this option doesn't affect the display of the GIF in Netscape, only in GIFBuilder itself (or any other program that properly implements the GIF spec). The above-mentioned problem with the color pickers applies here as well.

Loop

In GIFBuilder, you can specify the number of times an animation loops—none, forever, or any number you specify. In reality, Netscape doesn't recognize the fact that you've asked for five loops, or whatever. It only loops the animation or not. Internet Explorer 3.0, however, does recognize the number of loops you've specified.

One workaround to this problem is to build the looping right into the file by repeating the frame sequence a number of times. This of course increases the file size quite a bit and prolongs downloading.

Starting Points

These settings are a good starting point for creating animations in GIFBuilder.

Color Palette
6×6×6 (Netscape)

Interlacing
Off

Dithering
On for photographic images, Off for drawings with few colors

Image Size
Minimum Size

Background Color
Black

Looping
None or Forever

Transparency
Off

Disposal Method
Varies

Future Directions

While the GIF animation *per se* is well defined, we are already seeing a second generation of programs that go beyond the workmanship of merely constructing GIF files, *a la* GIF Construction Set and GIFBuilder. It should be relatively trivial for full-strength animation and video editing programs to add GIF as an export format, thus allowing much more sophisticated imagery than is possible when making individual frames by hand in Photoshop. The first in this wave is probably Andatech's VideoCraft GIF Animator, but Adobe Premiere and After Effects are hopefully not too far behind. Finally, we hope to see support for animated GIFs in Java, so that advanced Java applets can take advantage of the efficiency of GIF animation. ∎

About the Author

Richard Koman
Songline Studios
101 Morris St.
Sebastopol, CA 95472
rkoman@songline.com

The author of GIF Animation Studio, Richard Koman is the former managing editor of *Web Review*—the critically acclaimed Web magazine—and technology editor of *Communication Arts.* He has covered computers and graphic design since 1990 and co-authored *The Mosaic Handbook* for O'Reilly & Associates. As a book editor at Songline Studios, he edits books in the Web Review Studio Series.

MNG

A MULTIPLE-IMAGE FORMAT IN THE PNG FAMILY

Glenn Randers-Pehrson

Introduction

The Portable Network Graphics (PNG) [1] format for bitmapped images was recently approved by the World Wide Web Consortium (W3C) as a W3C Recommendation. MNG (Multiple image Network Graphics), a proposed addition to the PNG family, is for storing and transmitting multiple image animations and composite frames and is now being designed by the PNG developers.[2]

Because the images making up a MNG are in PNG format, MNG shares the good features of PNG:

- It is unencumbered by patents.

- It is streamable.

- It has excellent, lossless compression.

- It stores up to 16 bits per channel.

- It provides transparency and an alpha channel.

- It provides platform-independent rendition of colors by inclusion of gamma and chromaticity information.

- It provides early detection of common file transmission errors and robust detection of file corruption.

- Single-image GIF (Graphical Interchange Format) files can be losslessly converted to PNG.

In addition, MNG has the following features:

- It provides animation with loops and variable interframe delays.

- It allows composition of frames containing multiple images.

- It facilitates the use of images as "sprites."

- It capitalizes on frame-to-frame similarities to reduce the amount of data that must be included in the datastream.

- It provides "restart" points at which an animation can be resumed in case of data loss or corruption.

- A "frame priority" chunk allows authors to indicate which frame should be displayed by single-image viewers and a subset of frames that should be displayed by slow viewers.

- Multiple image GIF files can be losslessly converted to MNG.

A Simple MNG Datastream

The simplest form of MNG is an 8-byte MNG file signature, a MNG header chunk (MHDR), plus a series of one or more PNG datastreams (less their 8-byte signatures), followed by a MEND chunk, as shown in Example 1. MNG is more powerful than that, however. It is frequently true that the images will be similar, and data from the first image are reused in the second image to conserve on the amount of data that must be stored or transmitted.

When only a smaller rectangle within the second image has pixels that are different from those in the first image, the DHDR chunk can specify that only a smaller rectangle of pixels (sometimes called a "change box") be transmitted. Whether the pixels for the full image or for a smaller rectangle are changed, the data can be presented as new values that replace the old ones or as deltas (differences) from the corresponding pixels in the previous image. Usually the data in delta form is much more compressible. Several movies of

Example 1

```
138 M N G CR LF 26 LF# MNG 8-byte signature
MHDR maxwidth maxheight ... # MNG Header Chunk IHDR width height ...# PNG Header
    Chunk
gAMA 50000# PNG Gamma chunk
cHRM ...# PNG Chromaticity Chunk
PLTE ...# PNG Palette
IDAT ...# PNG Pixel data
IEND# End of first PNG datastream
DHDR 0 1 0# Delta-PNG Header
IDAT ...# Delta-PNG Pixels
DEND# End of Delta-PNG
MEND# End of MNG datastream
```

finite-element calculational results by the U.S. Army Research Laboratory required only about a quarter of the file space when converted from a simple series of PNGs to delta-encoded PNGs.

It is possible to change just the alpha samples in the image or, in selected parts of it, to fade an image in or out against a background image.

Further dramatic savings in the size of the datastream can be achieved when an image or a portion of one is merely relocated. MNG provides a LOCA chunk in which the new coordinates of the image are transmitted instead of having to retransmit the entire image. A CLIP chunk is also available, to make it possible to show only a portion of a previously transmitted image. The LOCA chunk can be used for scrolling or panning across an image that is larger than the display area.

Loops

MNG has a simple loop structure that can be used for repeating images. In Example 2, five images are defined and displayed in order 0-1-2-3-4 and then played ten times in order 3-2-1-0-1-2-3-4.

Composite Frames and Sprites

In addition to the simple single-image frames described thus far, MNG can also describe composite images that are built up of two or more PNG images. For example, one image could be a

full-screen background while others could be small sprites that are moved around by means of the LOCA chunk. Examples that demonstrate these capabilities and others (including scrolling, tiling, storing 3D tomographic data, and converting GIF animations to MNG format) are given as appendices in the MNG proposal [2].

MNG provides several framing modes that can be used with composite images. The modes are designed to work with either "draw mode" or "sprite mode" viewers. "Draw mode" viewers composite the frames by drawing the images in order as they are encountered. "Sprite mode" viewers accumulate the images and composite them all at once. Such viewers can take advantage of hardware acceleration if present. The framing modes include:

- Each image is a separate frame (as in the two examples shown previously).

- A group of images makes up a "draw mode" frame. All images are initially invisible and are made visible with explicit directives.

- A group of images makes up a series of "draw mode" frames. All images are initially invisible and are made visible one at a time, like cards being dealt.

- A group of images forms a "sprite mode" frame, in which the images retain their visibility status from the previous frame.

Example 2

```
138 M N G CR LF 26 LF# MNG 8-byte signature
MHDR maxwidth maxheight ...# MNG Header Chunk
IHDR width height ...# PNG Header Chunk
gAMA ... PLTE ... IDAT ... IEND # Define Image 0 CLON 0 1 DHDR 1 1 1 IDAT ...
    IEND # Define Image 1 CLON 1 2 DHDR 2 1 1 IDAT ... IEND # Define Image 2 CLON
    2 3 DHDR 3 1 1 IDAT ... IEND # Define Image 3 CLON 3 4 DHDR 4 1 1 IDAT ...
    IEND # Define Image 4 LOOP 0 0 10# Begin Loop
SHOW 3 1 SHOW 0 4# Show images 3-1, 0-4
ENDL 0# End Loop
MEND# End MNG
```

- A group of images forms a "draw mode" frame, but image identifiers are reused to conserve memory.

The MNG proposal explains how to render a "draw mode" frame with a "sprite mode" viewer, and vice versa.

Status of MNG

The MNG proposal is being designed by the PNG developers and is being discussed in the *mpng-list@dworkin.wustl.edu* mailing list. Interested persons can subscribe by sending a message to *majordomo@dworkin.wustl.edu* that contains the line "subscribe mpng-list" (and nothing else) in the body.

The MNG format specification has not yet been frozen, but it has reached a state where test implementations are possible. There has been discussion of MNG since the completion of the PNG design in March 1995, and the first informal MNG drafts appeared on June 25, 1996. As of November 1, 1996, 22 drafts had been produced and reviewed by the PNG group.

Several prototype MNG datastreams have been written, and a viewer has been written that is able to process a subset of MNG datastreams (simple movies without composite frames), including delta-encoded images. These have already been used by the U.S. Army for real presentation work. The prototype MNG files and viewer ("viewpng," written at the U.S. Army Research Laboratory for use on SGI workstations running IRIX 5.3) and the latest version of the

MNG proposal from the PNG Development Group are available at *ftp://swrinde.nde.swri.edu/pub/mng/*.

Request for Comments

Comments on the proposed MNG format are welcome and should be addressed to *mpng-list@dworkin.wustl.edu.* ■

References

1. PNG (Portable Network Graphics) Specification, version 1.0, *http://www.w3.org/pub/WWW/TR/REC-png-multi.html.*

2. MNG (Multiple-image Network Graphics) Proposal, *ftp://swrinde.nde.swri.edu/pub/mng/documents/*

About the Author

Glenn Randers-Pehrson
U.S. Army Research Laboratory
ATTN: AMSRL-WM-TD
Aberdeen Proving Ground, Maryland 21005-5066
glennrp@ARL.MIL
http://www.rpi.edu/%7Erandeg/

Glenn Randers-Pehrson, a research physicist at the U.S. Army Research Laboratory, is a 1964 graduate of Rensselaer Polytechnic Institute and has Master's degrees in Mechanical Engineering and Computer Sciences from Stevens Institute of Technology and Rutgers University. Glenn has been involved in computer graphics for 30 years, is one of the developers of the PNG format, and is leading the MNG development effort.

New Metrics for New Media

Toward the Development of Web Measurement Standards

Thomas P. Novak, Donna L. Hoffman

Introduction

The advertiser-supported Web site is one of several business models vying for legitimacy in the emerging medium of the World Wide Web on the Internet [10]. Currently, there are three major types of advertiser-supported sites:

- *Sponsored content* sites like HotWired, ESP-NET Sportszone, and ZD Net.

- *Sponsored search agents and directories* like InfoSeek, Excite, and Yahoo.

- *Entry portal* sites like Netscape.

At present, these three classes of sites are split at about 55 percent, 36 percent, and 19 percent, respectively, in terms of advertising revenue [14].

The sponsorship model is attracting increasing management attention because advertising is expected to be an increasingly significant source of revenues in this new medium [25]. Sponsored sites are attractive because they are well suited to the Web environment [11], yet retain important parallels to existing media in the physical world. In theory, institutional advertising practices and metaphors can be borrowed from traditional media environments to assist initial commercial efforts. Additionally, as it becomes apparent that commercial viability of the online storefront model is years away [17], many Web managers are beginning to place more importance on advertising revenue streams as a source of profitability for online ventures [25].

Against this backdrop, firms are trying to understand what makes a sponsored site successful. As advertisers and marketers debate the best ways to measure and track visits and usage on commercial Web sites, most firms remain largely in the dark about how many customers exist online for their offerings. Because the industry currently lacks standards for what to measure and how to measure it, the Web is having difficulty being accepted as an advertising medium, and there is no assurance that firms will be successful in generating significant revenues from advertising in the future. Ultimately, the lack of standardization will limit the long-term viability of the sponsorship model [18].

This lack of standardization exists on several fronts. First, there are no established principles for measuring traffic on commercial Web sites that seek to generate revenues from advertising sponsorship. Second, there is no standard way of measuring consumer response to advertisements. Third, there are no standards for optimal media pricing models. Finally, the complexity of the medium in general hinders the standardization process.

From an advertising perspective, the Web medium shares some similarity to radio: there are many different markets, and they are clearly (at least in theory) segmented. But standardization in the radio medium eases the process of the media buy. In contrast, the Web presents a "nightmare" buy for agencies and their clients [6]. For example, Focalink's database of over 600 commercial Web sites [9] shows that there are more than 90 sizes for Web ad banners, that sites use many different metrics to price advertising, that there is no consistency in definitions even among the same or similar metrics, and that consumer demographic information is virtually nonexistent.

Despite the lack of information in this chaotic emerging environment, there is no dearth of

Table 1   1995 Advertising Expenditures in Various Media

Advertising Medium	Total U.S. Expenditures (billions of dollars U.S.)	Comments
Direct Response—Mail	31.2	
Direct Response—Phone	82.7	Telemarketing
Outdoor—Traditional	1.83	Billboards
Outdoor—Out of home	3.00	Transit, bus, airport, etc.
Print—Magazine	12.5	
Print—Newspaper	37.7	
Radio	11.1	
Television	38.1	
Web	.312	Estimate for 1996 [13]
Other	21.3	

activity. AdSpend [14] estimates advertising revenues for the first half of 1996 at $71.7 million, already at the level of a previous estimate of $74 million by Forrester Research for all of 1996 [6]. However, advertising revenue remains highly concentrated, with two thirds of all revenues going to the top ten of 600 advertiser-supported Web sites [14]. Estimates of Web advertising expenditures in the year 2000 range from $1.7 billion (Bear Sterns) to $1.9 billion (SIMBA) to $5 billion (Jupiter) [6].

Despite these heady forecasts, the perception persists that Web-based advertising efforts are not (and may never be) "serious." In part this may be because traditional advertising spending easily dwarfs current Web advertising efforts. For example, the price of a single 30-second television spot on prime-time's top show, "Seinfeld," is currently $550,000 [1]. As Table 1, compiled from the Direct Marketing Association (1996) and the Outdoor Advertising Association of America (1996) shows, Web advertising expenditures represent a medium in its infancy.

Yet the skepticism can more importantly be traced to the fact that few have specified conclusively just how advertising on the Web can and should further a firm's strategic marketing objectives. Clearly, *standardizing the Web measurement process is a critical first step on the path toward the successful commercial development of the Web.*

Therefore, the objectives of this white paper are to:

- Review practices for advertising measurement in traditional media.

- Examine current practices for advertising measurement on the Web, drawing comparisons to methodologies.

- Propose standardized terminology and methodology for Web advertising measurement.

- Offer preliminary recommendations for Web advertising research.

- Address the policy and strategic considerations that affect the development of Web advertising standards.

We believe that metrics based solely on impressions are necessary in the Web measurement process but cannot and should not form the basis of a Web measurement system. Therefore, in addition to proposing a set of "basic constructs" and "exposure metrics" that define the consideration set of possible measures, we also introduce a set of "interactivity metrics" that we believe must be included in any complete program for Web measurement. We take care to identify what data are required in order to calculate a particular metric and remain cognizant of the link between Web metrics and media pricing models.

We hope our preliminary measurement proposal stimulates rigorous discussion and debate. Our intention is to encourage the competitive marketplace to adopt specific metrics from each set. Research is necessary to identify which metrics are most useful for judging the effectiveness of advertising, for determining where and how ads should be placed, and for determining optimal pricing schemes for efficient media buys.

Advertising Measurement Terminology in Traditional Media

There is considerable confusion regarding the terminology currently in use for Web advertising; the first step is to ensure that all are working with the same vocabulary. We propose that if there is terminology from traditional media that is appropriate to use in the context of Web-based advertising, it should be used to avoid confusion and ease the adoption process of standards formation. Thus, we begin by providing a glossary of the standard definitions for key measures in print and broadcast vehicles. Such measures are used in most media audience evaluations and for intermedia comparisons in media planning in traditional mass media.

Gross impressions/impressions

The gross sum of all media exposures (numbers of people or homes) without regard to duplication [28].

Reach

The number of [unduplicated] people or households that will be exposed to an advertising schedule at least once over a specified period of time [3].

Effective reach

The number or people who are exposed to an ad at the "effective frequency."

Frequency

The number of times that an individual is exposed to a particular advertising message in a given period of time.

Effective frequency

The number of exposures needed for an ad to become "effective." In mass media models, effective frequency stipulates that a certain amount of exposure is necessary before it is effective and is used interchangeably with effective exposures. Research indicates that less than three exposures will not allow adequate recall. However, too many exposures are inefficient in that incremental recall after 7, 8, or 10 exposures during a purchase cycle is very small.

CPM

Cost per 1,000 impressions (exposures). The cost per 1,000 people (or homes) delivered by a medium or media schedule [28].

Duplication

The number or percentage of people who see an advertisement or campaign in two or more vehicles.

Gross Rating Points

GRPs are a measure of scheduling impact calculated on a weekly or monthly basis. GRP for mass media can be calculated as multiplying the reach (expressed as a percentage of prospects in the target market exposed to television and/or magazine vehicles carrying the ad) by frequency. The GRP level for a particular schedule can also be calculated by summing the ratings of the individual show carrying the commercial (assuming one commercial per show).

Share

"Share of audience" is the percentage of HUT (or PUT, PUR, PVT [people viewing television]) tuned to a particular program or station. "Share of market" is the percentage of advertising impressions generated by all brands in a category accounted for by a particular brand, but often also refers to share of media spending [28].

Ratings

The percentage of a given population group consuming a medium at a particular moment. Generally used for broadcast media but can be used for any medium. One rating point equals one percent [28].

HUT, PUT, HUR, PUR (homes/people using TV/radio)

The percentage of {homes/people} tuned in to {TV/radio} at a particular time [28].

Composition

The mixture of audience characteristics found in the audience for a medium or vehicle. This term also refers to the percentage of some medium's total audience made up of the target segment.

Cost per inquiry

The cost to generate an inquiry in direct-response advertising. Calculated by the total cost of the direct-response advertising divided by the number of inquiries it generates (*www.infi.net/powerhouse/glossary.html*).

Current Practice for Advertising Measurement on the Web

Types of Ads

We focus on the form of advertising referred to as "banner ads" and "target ads." This primitive form of Web-based advertising may ultimately not be the most effective, but since it is the current dominant form, we feel it is appropriate to propose a set of standards for its measurement. At a minimum, using banner and target ads, whatever the limitations might turn out to be, provides a concrete example to work with. Although we expect Web-based advertising efforts to evolve, the problem with making more general recommendations that could encompass other types of yet to be developed Web-based advertising is that they would be too broad and diffuse to be practically useful.

A *banner ad* is a small, typically rectangular, graphic image that is linked to a target ad. Banner ads come in a variety of sizes, with 90 percent of banner ads ranging from 120 to 500 pixels wide (with a median of 460 pixels) and from 45 to 120 pixels high (with a median of 60 pixels) [9]. Banner ads typically provide little information other than the identification of the sponsor and serve as an invitation for the visitor to click on the banner to learn more. Figure 1 shows a few examples of banner ads.

Figure 1   Banner ads

Target ads, on the other hand, can be fairly involved, ranging from a single Web page with basic HTML, to a Web page enhanced by Java applets, audio, or forms, to a series of linked pages, or to a complete corporate "Internet presence," "content," or "online storefront" site [10].

Chatterjee [5] considers banner ads to be a form of *passive advertising exposure,* in that the consumer does not consciously decide to view the banner ad. Rather, the banner ad is presented as an outcome of accessing a particular Web content page or as the outcome of entering a series of keywords into a search engine. Conventional market segmentation theory would lead us to predict that the more targeted the banner ad, the higher the click rate. Thus, ads placed on home pages of general interest sites or on the entry page of a search engine would have lower click rates than ads that are consistent with the content of a narrowly targeted Web site or banner ads presented by a search engine in response to specific keywords (e.g., ads for Lionel trains presented every time a visitor searches for "model railroad" or for "Neil Young").

Paid links are a different form of passive advertising and may be most simply viewed as a text version of a banner ad. Paid links are often incorporated in directories, which may contain large numbers of such paid links.

Chatterjee considers target ads, on the other hand, to be a form of *active advertising exposure,* since the consumer actively decides to access the target ad (i.e., by clicking on the banner ad) only after being passively exposed to the banner. *Active ad exposure is under the consumer's control; passive ad exposure is under the marketer's control.* Thus, the distinction between passive and active advertisements implies a crucial difference between banner and target ads. Further, the concept of an active advertisement is a feature that differentiates Web advertising from advertising in traditional media.

To date, most of the focus in Web advertising measurement has been upon banner advertise-

ments. This is most likely because their passive nature means banner ads have many more parallels with traditional media planning than do active ads. The factors that affect perceptual selection (i.e., that the consumer will pay attention to an advertisement he or she comes across) in print media should also impact perceptual selection of banner ads. These factors are closely tied to the "creative" function in advertising and include size, position, directionality, motion, color, intensity, contrast, and novelty (e.g., Wilkie 1990), all of which we would expect to be useful for predicting the likelihood that a visitor will click on a banner ad.

Pricing Models

Currently, exposure models, based upon CPM (cost per thousand) or flat fees applied to site exposure or banner ad exposure are the dominant approach to Web media pricing. Fees based upon actual click-throughs are also in use, where the advertiser pays for actual clicks on a banner ad that lead to the advertiser's target ad. In the following section, we consider these and other possible pricing models. While we believe it is premature to recommend any one media pricing model, it is important to understand the relative strengths and limitations of methods currently in use or that have been proposed.

Exposure models
(CPM and flat fee)

Flat fee pricing consists of a fixed price for a given period of time. Flat fees were the earliest Web advertising pricing model to appear. Flat fee pricing can be implemented either with or without traffic guarantees. Naturally, it would be advantageous to the advertiser to request guarantees of traffic level. The earliest ad pricing approaches on the Web simply used flat fees (e.g., ad cost per month) without clear specification of the traffic delivered in that period of time. At a minimum, accurate information on site traffic must be made available to the advertiser so that the advertiser can evaluate alternative Web media vehicles.

Assuming accurate traffic information, flat fee prices can be readily converted into a CPM (cost per thousand exposures) model. CPMs can also be enhanced by providing "guarantees" of the number of impressions in a given period of time. Thus, we consider the flat fee and CPM models to be interchangeable if traffic information specifying the number of (possibly unique) visitors to a Web site is available. If traffic information is not available, flat fee pricing can still be used, although its value is then impossible to evaluate.

Ninety percent of CPMs for Web advertising sites [9] range from $10 to $150, with a median of $60. This compares with CPMs of $6–$14 for national television, $8–$20 for magazine, and $18–$20 for newspaper advertising [13].

The ultimate challenge is to determine the business models that will be effective in this new environment. At present, the advertiser-supported business model is being largely driven by a broadcast paradigm that has initially gravitated toward CPMs as the appropriate unit of measure. In this model, the belief is that exposure-based pricing takes into account different advertisers' response functions and represents a rational way to price advertising on the Web.

But in fact, impression/exposure models go only part of the way because the Web is different from traditional broadcast media. The Web is based on a many-to-many communication model, and traditional media are based on a one-to-many communication model. Thus, in addition to exposure metrics, we also need interactivity metrics. The CPM approach places too much emphasis upon the banner ad and essentially no emphasis upon the target ad, which is the "real" marketing communication that the advertiser wishes the visitor to see and interact with.

In the CPM model, larger numbers are bigger winners because the one-to-many model seeks a mass audience for its message. The dangers of relying solely on exposure models means that interactive managers will be driven to scale their sites to larger, mass audiences with more homogeneous tastes in order to attract more advertising revenue. This is in contrast with solving the more difficult problem of how to measure interactivity and price advertising according to the value of a consumer's interactive visit to the advertiser.

CPM and flat fee models do nothing more than simply count the number of visitors exposed to a particular banner advertisement on a particular site. But because consumer behavior on the Web depends upon a whole host of measurable factors, including the type of site and the consumer's motivation for visiting it [11], a simple counting of visits is not sufficient to demonstrate value to the advertiser of their advertising expenditures. We believe it is meaningless to compare directly the number of visitors exposed to banner ads across pages without taking these factors into account.

Click-through

Ad pricing based upon click-through is an attempt to develop a more accountable way of charging for Web advertising. The payment for a banner ad is based on the number of times a visitor actually clicked on it; this currently runs about $0.25 per click [13]. A relatively small proportion of those exposed to a banner ad actually click on the banner; DoubleClick (1996) reports that 4 percent of visitors who are exposed to a banner ad the first time click on the ad. The top 25 percent performing ads in the DoubleClick Network had an average click rate of 8 percent, with some click rates as high as 12 to 15 percent. Click-through rates drop off after the first exposure, falling to 2 percent for the second and third exposures and 1 percent or less at four exposures. Thus, payment based upon click-through guarantees not only that the visitor was exposed to the banner ad but actively decided to click on the banner and become exposed to the target ad. Click-through payment can be viewed as payment for target ad exposures.

However, the practice is not without controversy. In April 1996, Yahoo! agreed to let Procter &

Gamble pay only for the click-through, rather than for gross impressions [2]. Some Internet publishers feel that this pricing strategy is unfair, arguing that the click-through is at least partially a function of the "creative" and not under the publisher's control. On the other hand, as we argued above, applying only traditional media exposure models to the Web does not take into account its unique, interactive nature. Additionally, the Internet is the first commercial medium in which it is actually possible to measure consumer response, not just assume it. Thus, although the click-through model may not represent the optimal approach to measuring the value of interactivity, it offers a departure point from which to proceed.

Interactivity

While payment based upon click-through guarantees exposure to target ads, it does not guarantee that a visitor liked the ad or even spent any substantial time viewing the ad. *We propose that a further measure of the value of an advertisement should be based upon the degree to which the visitor interacts with the target ad.* Such an interactivity metric could be based upon duration time spent viewing the ad, the depth or number of pages of the target ad accessed, or the number of repeat visits to the target ad.

Recently, a member of the Online Advertising Discussion List (1996) announced to the list that Modem Media, the interactive advertising agency, had developed a pricing model in which its clients will pay, not for exposures or click-through, but only for activity at the client's Web site. This has raised anew the controversy surrounding the best Web media pricing models, with Web publishers arguing that the problem with activity-based measures like click-through or interactivity is that the Web publisher cannot be held responsible for the activity related to an advertisement. An analogy is drawn with print, in which the Web publisher would argue that the print medium charges for ads whether or not they lead to sales.

Not surprisingly, advertisers and their agencies argue that since the Web medium allows for accountability, models can and should be developed that measure consumer behavior. In the long run, the solution will probably be found by accepting the reality that the medium and the advertisement interact and that all parties share responsibility for outcomes.

Outcomes

Ultimately, marketers are interested in outcomes, and the ultimate outcome is purchase. As Stephen Klein of I/Pro stated, "One hundred thousand people going to a site is worth something, but a site that only five people visit can be worth more if they are the right five people" [18].

The metrics discussed thus far relate to early stages of the purchase process. Banner ads affect the consumer's awareness, and interaction with the target ad affects the consumer's comprehension and understanding. Beyond these initial stages are the marketing objectives of attitude change, purchase intention, and ultimately, purchase.

An outcome-based approach to pricing Web advertising begins by specifying exactly what the marketer would like the target ad to do. Examples of typical outcomes include influencing attitudes, motivating the consumer to provide information about him or herself, or leading the consumer to purchase. Whatever the marketing objective, the Web provides a vehicle for integrated marketing campaigns that allows the marketer to track and measure the advertisement's effectiveness.

A current example is PI (per inquiry) ads. These ads pay a royalty on actual product sales but require no upfront payment. Consider the Associates Program (*www.amazon.com/exec/obidos/subst/assoc-invitation.html*) offered by *amazon. com*, a million-title Web-based book store. Thus far, over 300 Web sites have joined the Associates Program. In this program, Associates advertise books sold by *amazon.com* that they feel are appropriate to the content of their Web site. If a visitor accesses *amazon.com* through the Associate's Web site and purchases the book advertised on the Associate's site, the Associate receives a referral fee of up to 8 percent of the purchase price of the book.

The next step is to develop a set of integrated response measures (over time and possibly over sites) that relate exposure and interactivity metrics to consumer response. This may take the form of, for example, purchase behavior in an online storefront, attitude change, number of visitors who request further information, and so on. However, the development of such metrics requires two things:

- Identified visitors.

- Multi-site data on every Web site involved in the integrated marketing campaign.

Until these data are available, the measurement of outcome remains elusive.

Industry Players

In this section, we categorize the competitors in the Web measurement business. This categorization proceeds by organizing firms' offerings according to the functions each serves. These functions include Measurement and Analysis, Auditing, Advertising Support, and Standards. We define each function briefly below.

Our intent is not to review in detail what each product does or how (or even how well) it does it, but instead to summarize the competitors and their alliances in terms of the markets in which they compete. Every effort has been made to sketch these relationships accurately, but the fast moving nature of the Web measurement industry means that some inaccuracies are possible. In Tables 2 through 5 that follow, we list firms within each category in alphabetical order, list the products each firm offers within that category, table its strategic partners, and then offer any relevant observations. Partners are classified according to whether they are investors, owners, or involved in a strategic alliance. As the tables make clear, there is an enormous amount of activity in this emergent industry.

Table 2   Industry Players: Visitor Measurement and Analysis

Firm	Products	Partners	Comments
Allen Marketing Group, Inc. *www.allen.com*	Guest Track		Registration program that builds profiles of registered users and links them with log file to enable customized presentations.
Andromedia *www.andromedia.com*	Aria Web Recording and Reporting SystemVisiTrac (cobranded version of Aria with K2 Design)	Draper Richards, LP (investor) K2 Design (strategic alliance) Platinum Ventures (investor) Softbank Corporation (investor)	
Bien Logic *www.bienlogic.com*	Surf Report		

Table 2 *(continued)* Industry Players: Visitor Measurement and Analysis

Firm	Products	Partners	Comments
Clickshare *www.clickshare. com/clickshare*	Clickshare Access and Payment System		Registration program that tracks consumers via unique ID enabling multi-site user authentication, microtransaction billing and settlement, and cross-site access measurement; Newshare Corp. spinoff.
Everyware *www.everyware. com*	Bolero		
Group Cortex, Inc. *www.cortex.com/ sitetrack*	Site Track		
Interse *www.interse.com*	Market Focus	Arbitron New Media (strategic alliance)	Meets ABVS standards.
I/PRO *www.ipro.com*	I/CODE Nielsen I/PRO I/COUNT	CyberAtlas (acquisition) DoubleClick (strategic alliance) Hearst Corporation (investor) NetGravity (strategic alliance) Nielsen Media Research (strategic alliance) Softbank Corporation (investor) Verifone (strategic alliance)	I/CODE is a registration program.
Logical Design Solutions *www.lds.com/prod-serv/prodserv.html*	LDS WebTrac	Save the Children (strategic alliance)	Can match log file data to external databases.
NetCount *www.netcount.com*	NetCount Basic NetCount Plus NetCount HeadCount	Price Waterhouse (investor)	Spinoff of Digital Planet; products will be marketed under the NetCount/Price Waterhouse name.
net.Genesis *www.netgen.com*	Net.Analysis		
The NPD Group, Inc. *www.npd.com*	PC Meter		Household panel provides demographic data on home PC usage patterns, including time spent on specific pages of the World Wide Web, in departments of online services and in desktop applications.

Table 2 *(continued)* Industry Players: Visitor Measurement and Analysis

Firm	*Products*	*Partners*	*Comments*
Open Market *www.openmarket. com/omi/products /webreport.html*	WebReporter		
Software, Inc. *www.webtrends. com*	WebTrends		Inexpensive product targeted to small and mid-size Web sites.
Webthreads *www.webthreads. com*	Webthreads 1.01		
WebWatch *www.webwatch. com*	WebWatch		
W3.Com *w3.com*	Web Site Toolkit		Tracking system used to modify the site for different users based on profiles and browsing behavior.

Visitor measurement and analysis

The Web measurement process involves counting and summarizing the visitor transactions on a Web site. Measurement and analysis products tell managers who is accessing their site, when, and what is being accessed. Different products perform these tasks at different levels of specificity and with different degrees of accuracy.

Auditing

Traditionally, the auditing process (Table 3) involves the objective evaluation of transaction counts by an independent agency. The purpose of the audit is to produce validated data that permits advertisers to compare Web sites in the context of the media buy. A "trusted" third party is sought to avoid any potential or actual conflicts of interest. In the Web medium, the auditing function is served both by traditional media auditors and firms that engage in the measurement process.

Table 3   Industry Players: Auditing

Firm	*Products*	*Partners*	*Comments*
Audit Bureau of VerificationServices (ABVS) *www.accessabvs. com*	Interactive Auditing Service	Audit Bureau of Circulations (wholly owned subsidiary) Interse (strategic alliance)	Working with MarketArts WebFacts (formerly WebTrack).
Business Publication Association (BPA)			
Interse *www.interse.com*	Interse/ABVS Daily Report Interse/ABVS Monthly Report		

Table 3 *(continued)* Industry Players: Auditing

Firm	Products	Partners	Comments
I/PRO *www.ipro.com*	Nielsen I/PRO I/AUDIT	Nielsen Media Research (strategic alliance)	Can a measurement and analysis company also do independent, third party auditing?
MarketArts *www.marketarts.com*	WebFact WebStat		Collaborating with Audit Bureau of Circulations (ABC) through a subsidiary known as Audit Bureau of Verification Services; beta-testing its auditing service at CondeNet, Atlantic Monthly, TimesFax, and Adfinder WSJ.
WebWatch *www.webwatch.com*			
NetCount *www.netcount.com*	NetCount Rate and Ranking Service		Can a measurement and analysis company also do independent, third-party auditing?

While prevailing industry wisdom is that independent third party audits are necessary for potential advertisers to trust traffic claims of Web sites, there are some dissenting viewpoints. Rick Boyce, vice president and director of advertising sales at HotWired, has been quoted as saying, "No one has come up to me yet and said, 'We won't buy your site because you haven't had an independent audit. We built our own tools that allow us to measure impressions and click-throughs. But, we're different because our brand name indicates quality'" [18]. Thus, the key issue is advertiser trust, and it remains to be seen whether independent third party auditing is the only method for securing such trust.

Advertising support

Recently, the industry has seen the emergence of firms dedicated to supporting the advertising function (see Table 4). These firms offer products that aid the advertiser, the agency, and/or the Web publisher, in the various aspects of the online media buy.

Table 4 Industry Players: Advertising Support

Firm	Products	Partners	Comments
Competitive Media Reporting	AdLab	USAData (strategic alliance)	
DoubleClick *www.doubleclick.net*		I/PRO (strategic alliance)	"On demand" advertising; Poppe Tyson spinoff; specializes in customized ad delivery.
Focalink *www.focalink.com*	MarketMatch SmartBanner		Customized ads. SmartBanner matches ads to visitors and tracks ad volume. Market-Match provides database for agencies to assist in media buy.

Table 4 *(continued)* Industry Players: Advertising Support

Firm	*Products*	*Partners*	*Comments*
Jupiter Communications *www.jup.com*	AdSpend		Formerly WebTrack
NetCount *www.netcount.com*	NetCount AdCount		Measurement of the performance and effectiveness of online advertisements.
NetGravity *www.netgravity.com*	AdServer	I/PRO (strategic alliance)	Management of online advertising; ad inventory management, dynamic ad targeting, real-time information, and sales process automation; AdServer schedules and tracks ads across Web pages (e.g., Yahoo! uses it to schedule and track 12,000 banners across 200,000 pages).
PointCast Network *www.pointcast.com*	SmartAd Broadcast System (SBS)	ABVS Interactive auditing (strategic alliance)	

Standards

Numerous firms and organizations have signaled their intent to set measurement standards for Web advertising (see Table 5). The point of such standards is to facilitate the measurement process (what should be measured and how should it be measured?) and define universal criteria for verification of visitor measurements claimed by commercial Web sites.

Numerous strategic and policy issues affect the standards-setting process, including whether trust of the auditing function requires an independent third party in the measurement process, and how to protect consumer privacy in the face of extensive "clickstream" data collection efforts.

Current Industry Terminology Used in Web Advertising Measurement

What do people do on the Web? Why are they doing it? Since most would agree that hits are meaningless as comparative measures of visitor behavior on the Web, Web sites now tend to report visits. But, what exactly does a "visit"

mean? Can Web publishers provide even the most basic descriptive statistics about their sites, including how many unique visitors are coming, how often users visit, where they tend to come from, how long they stay, the average number of pages per visit, the four or five most popular navigation patterns through the site, the most popular pages, the least popular pages, and so on?

Clear, standardized terminology and measurement procedures are needed to:

- Define visits to Web sites.

- Describe consumer behavior during a visit.

- Relate visits to interactivity and outcomes.

Such standards are critical to demonstrate the viability of the Web as a commercial medium and provide mechanisms for tracking usage as well as measuring investment opportunities and business success.

The following sections provide organized definitions currently used by the Web advertising industry. These definitions were compiled from the following five sources:

Table 5 Industry Players: Standards

Firm	Products	Partners	Comments
Audit Bureau of Verification Services (ABVS) *www.accessabvs.com*	Interactive Auditing Service		Subsidiary of Audit Bureau of Circulations (ABC); working with MarketArts WebFacts (formerly WebTrack).
Better Business Bureau *www.bbbonline.org*	BBBOnLine	AmeriTech (founding sponsor) AT&T (founding sponsor) Eastman Kodak (founding sponsor) Federal Trade Commission (strategic alliance) GTE (founding sponsor) Hewlett Packard (founding sponsor) Netscape (founding sponsor) Sony (founding sponsor) Visa (founding sponsor)	Online program (1997 launch), operates as a seal of approval for Web sites in compliance with traditional BBB standards for customer service and marketplace ethics (BBB Code of Advertising).
BPA International *www.bpai.com*	BPA Interactive		International board of directors comprised of advertisers, agencies, and publishers.
CASIE *www.commerce-park.com /AAAA/bc/casie/ guide.html*	CASIE Guiding Principles of Interactive Media Audience Measurement		Joint project of the Association of National Advertisers and the American Association of Advertising Agencies with the support of the Advertising Research Foundation.
Interactive Alliance *www.arbitron.com/ nmcmi.html*	Cyber Measurement Index	Audit Bureau of Circulations (strategic alliance) Clickshare (member) Interse (member) McCollum Spielman Worldwide (member) MarketCast (member) 40 other "alliance advisors"	Founders: Arbitron Company (Arbitron NewMedia) and Next Century Media, Inc.

Table 5 *(continued)* Industry Players: Standards

Firm	Products	Partners	Comments
Internet Advertising Bureau *iab@edelman.com*	No proposal to date		Formerly the Internet Advertising Council and the Web Advertising Bureau organization for ad-supported Web site and online services. Will work with Coopers & Lybrand to measure ad revenues on the Internet. First public accounting is due to be released in early 1997.
Magazine Publishers of America (MPA) *www.magazine.org /mpainfo/mpainfo. html*	Proposed Standards for Internet Advertising Measurement		
Newspaper Association of American (NAA) *www.naa.org*	The Conaghan Report: Tracking Audience and Advertising on the Web		
World Wide Web Consortium (W3C) *www.w3.org*	No proposal to date	INRIA (host) Keio University (host) MIT (host)	Funded by dues from member organizations; additioov-ided by DARPA and European Community. Darpa provided seed funding. EC provides financial support.

IPRO
   www.ipro.com/faq.html

CASIE
   www.commercepark.com/AAAA/bc/casie/ guide.html

TRAFFIC RESOURCE
   www.trafficresource.com/glossary.html

Interse
   www.interse.com/ourproducts/faq.html

NetCount
   www.netcount.com/glossary.html

Unfortunately, these definitions do not always agree. Nevertheless, they provide a good starting point for developing clearer definitions. We organize the current terminology according to three categories:

Definitions
   Hits, visitor/user, visit/session, ad/page

Exposure measures
   Ad views, page views, site visits

Interactivity measures
   Ad clicks/click through, duration time

The "Definitions" category includes basic terminology necessary to construct advertising measures. The advertising measures include exposure andteractivity measures.

Definitions of hits

Hits have been widely criticized as a measure of Web traffic. While the definitions of hits are quite consistent, the weakness of hits as a valid measure of traffic to a Web site is quite evident. Since hits includes all units of content (images, text, sound files, Java applets) sent by a Web server when a particular URL is accessed, hits are inherently noncomparable across Web sites. The definitions are presented here only for completeness, not because we believe there is any validity to reporting hits. The only reason a Web site would report numbers of hits, other than ignorance of the meaningless of hits, is that this is typically a large and very impressive sounding number.

hits

1. When a visitor reaches a Web site, their computer sends a request to the site's computer (server) to begin displaying pages. Each element of a requested page (including graphics, text, interactive items) is recorded by the site's Web server log file as a "hit." Because page designs and visit patterns vary from site to site, the number of hits bears no relationship to the number of pages viewed or visits to a site. (I/PRO)

2. The number of pages and/or graphic files requested by visitors. A single page with multiple graphics can be counted as multiple hits since each graphic is counted as a separate hit. (TRAFFIC)

3. The equivalent of advertising impressions here defined as "the gross number of files accessed from x site or domain during y time." There are variable numbers of deeper files attached by hyperlinks to each page in cyberspace, making this a "rubber yardstick." As explained previously, a "clickable element" is a hyperlink allowing a one-click movement to the deeper file behind the page functioning as a menu for that deeper file. Hits implies that the user has been exposed to the deeper material, which may never have been selected for display on the screen. As an example, a one-second visit to a home page containing 35 hyperlinks counts as 35 hits within the current Hypertext

Transfer Protocol (CASIE). Note: actually a visit measure, not a definition.

request

A request is a connection to an Internet site (i.e., hit) that successfully retrieves content. Unlike a hit, a request doesn't include client or server "errors." Requests counts are conservative because browser software and many Internet gateways intercept some requests before they reach the server, and these cached requests are never logged. (Interse)

request

A request occurs when a browser asks a Web server for some unit of content. Common units of content include: images, text, pages, sound clips, video files, Shockwave files, and Java applets. (NetCount)

transfer

A transfer occurs when a browser completely receives a unit of content from a Web server. (NetCount)

NOTE

Streamed content (such as RealAudio or Streamworks) is measured differently and does not require a complete download in order to be considered successfully transferred.

qualified hits

A further refinement of hits, qualified hits exclude less important information recorded in a log file as hits such as error messages, etc. While qualified hits provide a better idea of traffic volume, it is not an accurate assessment of the actual number of users. (IPRO)

click

NetCount has resolved the hit dilemma by not counting hits at all, instead reporting page information requests (PIRs) and successful page information transfers (PITs). PITs are a true measurement of page deliveries going beyond page requests. (NetCount)

Definitions of visitors/users

With the exception of the CASIE definitions, visitors or users represent individuals who visit Web sites. The definitions differ according to how much is known about an individual visitor/user.

Note that CASIE defines "users" as the *number* of users. This is less precise than the other definitions, which define a user or visitor as a person who visits a Web site. When reporting numbers of visitors, we prefer to use the metrics of exposures, reach, and frequency discussed later in the section "Exposure Metrics.'

visitor

> An individual that visits a Web site. (TRAFFIC)

user

> 1. An uniquely identifiable person. An accurate count of users is not possible without some form of registration or authentication. (NetCount)
> 2. A user is anyone who visits the site at least once. (Interse)

users

> "The number of different people visiting x site or domain during y time." (Reach) (CASIE) Note: actually a visit measure, not a definition.

unique visitor

> A visitor that can be qualified as a unique individual within a given period of time. The period of time can vary but is usually between a half hour and an hour. (TRAFFIC)

unique user

> 1. The number of different individuals who visit a site within a specific time period are called unique users. To identify unique users, Web sites rely on some form of user registration or an identification system such as I/CODE. (I/CODE)
> 2. A user is anyone who visits the site at least once. Interse market focus goes

through a series of attempts to recognize unique users. If an extended log file contains persistent cookie data, the software uses this data to recognize unique users. If no cookie data is available, the software uses a registered username to recognize users. If no registration information is available, the software uses, as a last resort, users' Internet hostnames. Many organizations use Internet gateways, which mask the real Internet hostnames, so user counts may be conservative for those users determined through their Internet hostnames. (Interse)

identified user

> 1. A user for whom demographics are known and available. (NetCount)
> 2. "Demographic measures of visits or users relating to X site or domain during Y time." (Demographics) (CASIE)

Definitions of visits and sessions

Visits and sessions are defined in this section. Again, CASIE defines a visit as the number of visits, while we favor the other definitions that simply say what a visit is. This is because there are a variety of ways visits to a site can be counted (i.e., site exposure vs. site reach), and the definition of the method of counting visits should be independent of the definition of a visit itself.

The ability to clearly define a visit depends upon whether a visitor can be uniquely identified. If not, heuristics, such as the 30-minute timeout incorporated in the IPRO and Interse definitions, must be used to define a visit.

visit

> 1. A visit is commonly defined as a sequence of requests made by one user. Once a visitor stops making requests from a site for a given period of time, called a timeout, the next hit by this visitor is considered a new visit. To simplify comparisons, I/PRO uses a 30-

minute timeout to determine the start of a new visit. I/PRO determines site visits by adding visits from single-user Internet addresses that can be tracked and identified to a count of multi-user addresses. I/PRO uses a proprietary algorithm to convert multi-user hits into discrete visits. (I/PRO)

2. A visit is a series of consecutive requests from a user to an Internet site. If a log file includes referrer data, new visits begin with referring links external to the Internet site. Regardless of whether or not you have referrer data, if a user doesn't make a request for 30 minutes, the previous series of requests is considered a completed visit. (Interse)

3. A series of transactions performed by a user at a single Web site. This differs from a "session." (NetCount)

4. "The gross number of occasions on which a user looked up x site or domain during y time." (Gross Exposures) (CASIE)

session

A series of transactions performed by a user that can be tracked across successive Web sites. For example, in a single session, a user may start on a publisher's Web site, click on an advertisement, then go to an advertiser's Web site, and make a purchase. (NetCount)

Definitions of ads and pages

Note that the definitions of "banner" and "advertisement" in this section are very similar, with both referring to what we have previously called the passive "banner ad."

banner

An image on a sponsorable site that functions as a link to the advertiser's site. Banner size is usually measured in pixels: width × height. (I/PRO)

advertisement

Typically a clickable image or a Java applet on a publisher's Web site, an advertisement is usually hyperlinked to a page on the advertiser's Web site. (NetCount)

Web page

All Web sites are collections of electronic "pages." Each Web page is an HTML (Hypertext Markup Language) document that may contain text, images, or media objects. A page can be either static or dynamically generated. The best known page is the "home page," which is usually a visitor's point of entry and which usually features an index to a Web site. (I/PRO)

Exposure measures: ad views, page views, and site visits

The section presents definitions of various "exposure measures" that have been proposed. For a page that contains a banner ad, ad view, page view, exposure, and impression are equivalent.

ad view

Number of times an banner ad is downloaded and presumably seen by visitors. If the same ad appears on multiple pages simultaneously, ad views may understate the number of ad views, due to browser caching (see definition below). Corresponds to net impressions in traditional media. (I/PRO)

ad view/exposure/impression

Number of times that a banner has been presented to visitors (equivalent to exposures or impressions). (TRAFFIC)

exposure

An exposure is counted each time an advertisement is delivered by a Web server. Exposures can be used by Web publishers to validate the number of "impressions" that were delivered at their Web site. Exposures can be reported for stationary ads as well as for ads that rotate throughout a site. (NetCount) *page view*

1. Number of times a user requests a page that may contain a particular ad. Indicative of the number of times an ad was potentially seen, or "gross impressions." Page views overstate ad impressions when users turn Auto Load Images off to speed browsing. (I/PRO)
2. Number of times a particular Web page has been presented to visitors. (TRAFFIC)

weekly visit

Number of visitors to a Web site in a given week. Multiple visits may be generated by one person. (TRAFFIC)

Interactivity measures: ad clicks and click-throughs

This section and the following one present various "interactivity measures." The measures in this section are primarily definitions of the click-through rate. Some definitions of click-through rates that have appeared in the business press lack common sense. For example, *Marketing News* (1996) offers the following definition: "The click-through rate divides the number of click-throughs by the number of hits to measure interest in an individual hot-linked ad." Considering our earlier discussion of hits, division by number of hits will make the resulting quantity completely meaningless.

The definitions in the next section ("Interactivity measures: duration time") introduce the idea that interactivity can be captured through the measurement of duration time. The theoretical rationale for this notion is discussed in Hoffman and Novak [11]. Empirical support for the principle is offered by Resnick (1996).

ad click

The number of times users "click" on an ad banner to request additional information from the advertiser. Typically, users are directed (hot-linked) to the advertiser's Web site. (I/PRO)

ad click rate

Sometimes referred to as "click-through rate," this is the number of ad clicks as a percentage of ad views. (I/PRO)

click/ad click

The number of times that an ad has been clicked by visitors. A measure of response to an ad placement. (TRAFFIC)

click rate

The percentage of visitors that view an ad and click on it. (TRAFFIC)

inquiry

An inquiry is counted each time a user clicks on an advertisement. Inquiries can be used by Web advertisers to gauge the response to their ads. By monitoring the number of inquiries generated by an advertisement on a regular basis, advertisers can experiment with content and placement to see how changes affect response rates. The immediacy of AdCount's reporting allows an advertiser to quickly respond to declining inquiry rates by changing a banner and then watching to see if rates improve. (NetCount)

click-through rate

To complete the equation, AdCount watches to see how many inquiries result in successful click-throughs to the advertiser's Web site. A click-through is an accurate count of the number of times that a user left a publisher's Web site and successfully arrived at an advertiser's Web site. This provides a reconciliation for the times when a user clicks on an advertisement but receives a "server busy" error instead of arriving at the advertiser's Web site. (NetCount)

Interactivity measures: duration time

This section contains definitions of duration time measures.

average time on page

The average amount of time spent by a user on a single Web page. (NetCount)

Table 6   Current Metrics Used in Web Measurement

	Vehicle Level	Page Level	Ad Level
Unit of analysis	Web site	Site section or page	Sponsor's ad page
Traditional media analogs	Reach/frequency Circulation ratings	Frequency Gross impressions	Recall Recognition
Current exposure metrics	Number of site accesses/visits per day Site access/visit based ratings	Number of page accesses/ visits per day	Number of ad page accesses/ visits per day

NOTE

Since users have the ability to temporarily leave a Web site and then return to the same page via the Back button in their browser, the average time spent on a page will not be 100 percent accurate. However, for a highly viewed page, the average time on page will be nearly 100 percent accurate.

Proposed Standardized Terminology for Web Advertising Measurement

Overview

There are three distinct levels of analysis for Web advertising measurement:

- Vehicle level

- Page level

- Ad level

By linking the various measures to consumer outcomes, the ultimate objective is to quantify the value of a visit to commercial sponsors.

For each level of analysis, there are *exposure metrics* and *interactivity metrics*. Exposure metrics are based upon the one-to-many communication model underlying traditional media and indicate that a visitor has been exposed to (i.e., has had the opportunity to view) a Web site, a Web page, or an advertisement. Interactivity metrics are based upon the many-to-many communication

model underlying the Web and indicate the extent to which the visitor actively engages with the Web content or advertisement.

Exposure metrics can be behavioral (i.e., reach and frequency) or cognitive/attitudinal (i.e., recall and recognition). Similarly, interactivity metrics can be behavioral (i.e., duration time) or cognitive/attitudinal (i.e., flow [10]). In this paper, we focus exclusively upon behavioral exposure and interactivity metrics for Web advertising measurement.

Considering these three levels of analysis, Table 6 presents traditional media analogs and examples of currently used exposure metrics.

Summary of Metrics

Now consider Table 7, which summarizes our proposed behavioral exposure and interactivity metrics. All of these metrics are defined in detail subsequently.

Definitions of Metrics

Table 8 summarizes the basic constructs needed to construct the various exposure and interactivity metrics. The table is followed by definitions of the basic constructs, exposure metrics, and interactivity metrics.

For example, to obtain "banner ad exposures," one needs unidentified, session, tracked, or identified visitors, plus information concerning whether the visitor was exposed to the banner ad.

Table 7 — Summary of Proposed Metrics for Web Measurement

	Vehicle Level	Page Level	Ad Level
Exposure metrics	Site exposures Site exposure Duplication Site reach Site frequency	Page exposures Page reach Page frequency	Banner ad exposures Target ad exposures Banner ad reach Target ad reach Banner ad reach duplication Banner ad frequency Target ad frequency Banner ad visit frequency Target ad visit frequency
Interactivity metrics	Visit duration time Intervisit duration time Raw visit depth Visit depth	Page duration time	Ad click-through Ad click-through reach Ad click-through frequency Ad click-through duplication Banner ad duration time Target ad duration time

Table 8 — Basic Constructs Used to Derive Exposure and Interactivity Metrics

Basic Constructs

Exposure Constructs	Unidentified Visitor	Session Visitor	Tracked Visitor	Identified Visitor	Banner Ad	Target Ad	Web Page	Visit	Duration Time	Multi-Site Data
Banner ad exposures	X	X	X	X	X	X				
Target ad exposures	X	X	X	X		X				
Page exposures		X	X	X				X		
Site exposure duplication			X	X				X		X
Banner ad reach			X	X	X					
Target ad reach			X	X		X				
Page reach			X	X			X			
Site reach			X	X				X		
Banner ad reach duplication			X	X				X		X
Banner ad frequency			X	X	X					
Target ad frequency			X	X		X				
Page frequency			X	X			X			
Site frequency			X	X				X		
Banner ad visit frequency		X	X	X	X			X		
Target ad visit frequency		X	X	X		X		X		

Table 8 *(continued)* Basic Constructs Used to Derive Exposure and Interactivity Metrics

Basic Constructs

Interactivity Metrics	Unidentified Visitor	Session Visitor	Tracked Visitor	Identified Visitor	Banner Ad	Target Ad	Web Page	Visit	Duration Time	Multi-Site Data
Banner ad effective frequency			X	X	X	X		X		
Banner ad effective reach			X	X	X	X		X		
Banner ad effective visit frequency		X	X	X	X	X		X		
Banner ad effective visit reach		X	X	X	X	X		X		
Ad click-through		X	X	X	X	X				
Ad click-through reach			X	X	X	X				
Ad click-through frequency			X	X	X	X				
Ad click-through duplication			X	X	X	X				X
Banner ad duration time	X	X	X	X	X				X	
Target ad duration time	X	X	X	X		X			X	
Web page duration time	X	X	X	X			X		X	
Visit duration time		X	X	X				X	X	
Intervisit duration time			X	X				X	X	
Session duration time			X	X				X	X	X
Raw visit depth/visit depth	X	X	X				X	X		

The following sections present formal definitions of Basic Constructs, Exposure Metrics, and Interactivity Metrics.

Basic constructs

Visitors

Unidentified visitor

A visitor is an individual who visits a Web site. An "unidentified visitor" means that no information about that visitor is available.

Session visitor

A session ID is available (e.g., cookie or token) or inferred (e.g., incoming IP address plus browser type), which allows a visitor's responses to be tracked within a given visit to a Web site.

Tracked visitor

An ID is available (e.g., cookie), which allows a user to be tracked across multiple visits to a Web site. No information, other than a unique identifier, is available for a tracked visitor.

Identified visitor

An ID is available (e.g., cookie, voluntary registration), which allows a user to be tracked across multiple visits to a Web site. Other information, possibly supplied voluntarily by the visitor (e.g., name, demographics) can be linked to this ID. Another way to obtain an identified visitor is to develop a Web gateway or panel (e.g., WebTV or PC Meter) that captures a complete record of a visitor's behavior.

Web Content

Banner ad

A simple advertisement whose purpose is to attract a visitor's attention so that the visitor will click on the banner ad and be exposed to the target ad. One or more banner ads appear on a Web page.

Target ad

The full advertisement, which may range from a single Web page to an entire corporate Web site.

Web page

Any HTML document, either static or dynamically generated, that contains text, images, or media objects.

Visit

A series of consecutive Web page requests from a visitor to a Web site. Once a visitor stops making requests from a site for a given period of time (e.g., 30 minutes), the next request by the visitor is considered a new visit.

Session

A series of consecutive visits made by a visitor to a series of Web sites.

Other

Duration time

The length of time between two events, such as successive requests to one or more Web pages (page duration) or visits to a given Web site (intervisit duration).

Multi-site data

IDs are available, which allow tracked or identified visitors to be followed across multiple Web sites.

Exposure metrics

Exposures

Banner ad exposures

Total number of times visitors were exposed to a banner ad in a time period, without regard to visitor duplication (passive exposure).

Target ad exposures

Total number of times visitors were exposed to a target ad in a time period, without regard to visitor duplication (active exposure).

Page exposures

Total number of times visitors were exposed to a Web page in a time period, without regard to visitor duplication (active exposure).

Site exposures

Total number of visitor sessions at a Web site in a time period, without regard to visitor duplication (active exposure).

Site Exposure Duplication

The number/percentage of unique visitors to a set of Web sites who visit more than one of the Web sites in a time period.

Reach

Banner ad reach

Total number of unique visitors exposed to a banner ad in a time period.

Target ad reach

Total number of unique visitors exposed to a target ad in a time period.

Page reach

Total number of unique visitors exposed to a Web page in a time period.

Site reach

Total number of unique visitors at a Web site in a time period.

Banner ad reach duplication

The number/percentage of unique visitors to a set of Web sites who are exposed to the same banner ad at more than one of the Web sites in a time period.

Frequency

Banner ad frequency

The distribution of the number of times unique visitors were exposed to a banner ad in a time period.

Target ad frequency

The distribution of the number of times unique visitors were exposed to a target ad in a time period.

Page frequency

The distribution of the number of times unique visitors were exposed to a Web page in a time period.

Site frequency

The distribution of the number of times unique visitors came to a Web site in a time period.

Banner ad visit frequency

The distribution of the number of times visitors are exposed to a banner ad during a single visit, without regard to visitor duplication across visits.

Target ad visit frequency

The distribution of the number of times visitors are exposed to a target ad during a single visit, without regard to visitor duplication across visits.

Interactivity metrics

Effective Reach and Frequency

Banner ad effective frequency

The optimal number of prior exposures to a banner ad, in one or more visits, required for a visitor to click on the banner and be exposed to the target ad. This must be empirically determined from the available data.

Banner ad effective reach

Total number of unique visitors exposed to a banner ad a sufficient number of times (i.e., at an *effective frequency*) in one or more visits in a time period.

Banner ad effective visit frequency

The optimal number of exposures to a banner ad, within a single session, required for a visitor to click on the banner and be exposed to the target ad. This must be empirically determined from the available data.

Banner ad effective visit reach

Total number of unique visitors exposed to a banner ad a sufficient number of times (i.e., at an *effective visit frequency*) in a single visit.

Click-through

Ad click-through

The percentage of time visitors who were exposed to a banner ad clicked on the banner and were then exposed to the target ad in a time period, without regard to visitor duplication.

Ad click-through reach

Total number of unique visitors who clicked on a banner ad and were exposed to the target ad in a time period.

Ad click-through frequency

The distribution of the number of times unique visitors clicked on a banner ad and were exposed to the target ad in a time period.

Ad click-through duplication

The number/percentage of unique visitors to a set of Web sites who clicked on a banner ad and were exposed to the target ad at more than one of the Web sites in a time period.

Duration Time

Banner ad duration time

The length of time a visitor is exposed to a Web page containing a banner ad. Can be reported as an average or distribution in a given time period, without regard to visitor duplication. (If tracked/identified visitors are present, banner ad duration can also determine the total length of time unique visitors are exposed to a banner ad in a time period.)

Target ad duration time

The length of time a visitor is exposed to a target ad. Can be reported as an average or distribution in a given time period,without regard to visitor duplication. (If tracked/identified visitors are present, target ad duration time can also determine the distribution of the total length of time unique visitors are exposed to a target ad in a time period.)

Web page duration time

The length of time a visitor is exposed to a Web page. Can be reported as an average or distribution in a given time period, without regard to visitor duplication. (If tracked/identified visitors are present, Web page duration time can also determine the distribution of the total length of time unique visitors are exposed to a Web page in a time period.)

Visit duration time

The length of time of a visit to a Web site. Can be reported as an average or distribution in a given time period, without regard to visitor duplication. (If tracked/identified visitors are present, visit duration time can also determine the distribution of the total length of time unique visitors spent at a Web site in a time period.)

Intervisit duration time

The length of time between successive visits to a Web site. Can be reported as an average or distribution in a given time period for unique visitors.

Session duration time

The length of time of a series of consecutive visits to a series of Web sites (i.e., session length). (If tracked/identified visitors are present , session duration time can also determine the distribution of the total length of time unique visitors spent on the Web, across sites, in a time period.)

Depth

Raw visit depth

Total Web pages exposure/session. The total number of pages a visitor is exposed to during a single visit to a Web site. Can be reported as an average or distribution in a given time period, without regard to visitor duplication.

Visit depth

Total unique Web page exposures/session. The total number of unique pages a visitor is exposed to during a single visit to a Web site. Can be reported as an average or distribution in a given time period, without regard to visitor duplication.

Additional Measurement Constructs

Besides the measures we have described in the section "Definitions of Metrics," additional statistics could and should be considered in the context of Web advertising measurement. While we do not discuss these additional measures in this paper, they include:

- Primary navigation patterns through the Web site

- Cross-site navigation patterns

- Demographic, psychographic, and behavioral characteristics of visitors to a Web site, and to specific pages within a Web site

- Cognitive and attitudinal measures, including flow

- Visitor loyalty and repeat visits

Outcome metrics

In addition to the behavioral and psychological measures considered above, outcome metrics must be developed. Although the models most frequently applied to the Web are based on traditional, mass media models, it makes sense to consider the direct response paradigm. Consider the following definition of direct marketing [7]:

> . . . any direct communication to a consumer or business recipient that is intended to generate a response in the form of an order (direct order), a request for further information (lead generation), and/or a visit to a store or other place of business for purchase of a specific product(s) or service(s) (traffic generation).

The concepts of "direct order," "lead generation," and "traffic generation" are immediately and obviously applicable in the many-to-many environment underlying the Web. Consider the DMA's (1996) definitions of these "intended purposes."

Direct order

Includes all direct response advertising communications, through any medium, that are specifically designed to solicit and close a sale. All of the information necessary for the prospective buyer to make a decision to purchase and complete the transaction is conveniently provided in the advertisement.

Lead generation

Includes all direct response advertising communications, through any medium, that are designed to generate interest in a product or a service, and provide the prospective buyer with a means to request and receive additional information about the product or service.

Traffic generation

Includes all direct response advertising communications conducted, through any medium, that are designed to motivate the prospective buyer to visit a store, restaurant, or other business establishment to buy an advertised product or service.

We believe that outcome definitions and metrics developed from considering the Web as a unique hybrid of direct response and traditional communication media will lead to the optimal set of models for measurement and pricing.

Recommendations for Web-Based Advertising Measurement Standards

Figure 2 organizes many of the exposure (rectangular boxes) and interactivity (boxes with rounded corners) metrics and relates them to consumer outcomes. Consumer outcomes are defined in terms of a standard hierarchy of effects model [30]. This is a very preliminary diagram, and it is intended to suggest research hypotheses that can be tested.

Figure 2 also highlights the fact that both exposure and interactivity metrics may have (possibly different) contributions to various stages in the hierarchy of effects model. For example, we implied earlier that banner ad reach/frequency/exposure will be related to awareness, while target ad duration time and depth will be related to comprehension.

Research Hypotheses

The next step is to generate testable hypotheses based upon Figure 2. For example, Chatterjee (1996) has proposed the following hypotheses:

1. Greater number of passive exposures will be positively associated with higher probabilities of active sponsor ad exposure.

2. Greater passive exposure duration should be associated with lower probabilities of active sponsor ad exposure.

3. Greater number of prior visits to the Web site will be associated with higher probabilities of occurrence of active sponsor ad exposure.

4. Shorter intervisit times will be associated with higher probabilities of occurrence of active sponsor ad exposure.

The practical purpose of generating and testing such hypotheses is twofold. First, we will gain a better understanding of what factors influence

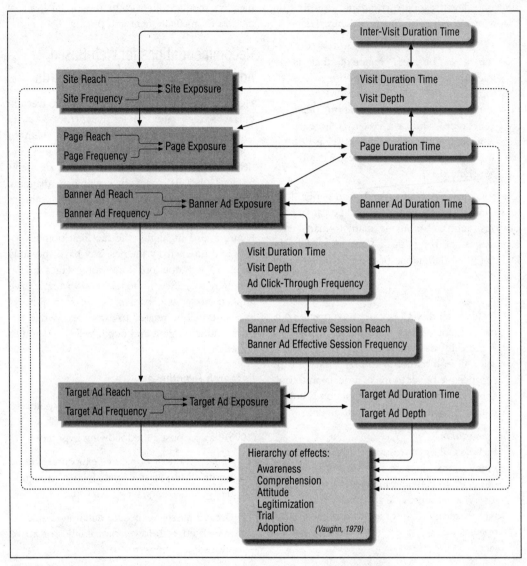

Figure 2   Relationships among exposure, interactivity, and consumer response

measures such as the ad click-through rate or the target ad duration time. What are the benchmark values for effective reach and frequency, and what affects these?

By understanding the influencing mechanisms, we can then take action to increase ad click-through rates, for example. Response functions, such as the optimal number of exposures to a

banner ad within and across visits, must be determined and have clear implications for dynamic placement of banner ads based upon a visitor's previous history of exposure to the ad.

Second, we are ultimately interested in identifying the exposure and interactivity metrics that should determine advertising prices. This will be a function of the degree to which the metric is related to influencing the stage in the hierarchy of effects model that the advertiser is focusing upon.

Currently, most of the focus seems to be upon paying for banner advertising that simply delivers exposures to target ads. It is not clear that this is necessarily money well spent. If the marketing objective is to increase consumer comprehension of a firm's product line offerings, it would make sense for the advertiser to pay more for visitors who spent more time viewing the target ad and who viewed more pages (greater depth) of the target ad.

Web Measurement in Practice

Within firms, publishers should start to measure their sites on all of the quantities listed in Table 8. These quantities should be assessed on a weekly basis, and the weekly period itself should be evaluated for strategic appropriateness in this new medium.

The industry should consider adopting the exposure and interactivity metrics proposed in this paper. Vendor and auditor reporting should include not just reach and frequency, but duration time metrics as well. This action requires an industry concurrence on the definition of a visit. Currently, 30 minutes is used by at least one firm as the timeout period, but this measure must be validated with observational data.

Finally, since tracked or identified visitors are required for the medium to reach its potential as a revolution in communication between firms and their customers, the industry must work to establish a mechanism for customer identification that is developed in the context of the policy and strategic considerations raised below.

Policy and Strategic Considerations

Policy Considerations

A number of policy issues must be considered when developing Web measurement standards. These include:

- Privacy

- Rights of consumer data ownership

- Ethics

Policy considerations are particularly important, because issues such as consumer protection, fraud, and deceptive claims are potential points of entry for government regulators into the Web marketplace.

Privacy

Although a thorough analysis of privacy issues is beyond the scope of this white paper, it is important to raise the issue in the context of Web measurement. Networked, distributed computing environments like the Internet offer unprecedented opportunities for the invasion of privacy. This is because information about individuals is now more accessible and more easily combined and integrated than in the physical world. Thus, it is not so much that we can learn things about consumers that we could not learn before, but rather that we can gain access to such information that might have been too expensive, too time-consuming, or too difficult to traditionally gather.

In addition, it is not clear who would be able to have access to such consumer information, or what they might do with the information. In a different context, serious privacy issues have arisen regarding patient mental health information that has been entered into computer networks at the insistence of insurance companies [15, 27]. This information can be accessed by a class of "health information trustees" whose inappropriate use of this information in some cases has had serious and damaging consequences for consumers. A parallel class of "marketing information trustees" could potentially have access to vast databases of consumer transaction data.

In the context of Web measurement for marketing and advertising purposes, the specific issues are what information we are gathering from consumers, whether they know we are gathering it, and what we plan to do with it. There is a tension between the marketer's need to know information about individual consumers for the purposes of targeted marketing efforts and the consumer's right to privacy. We believe the ultimate solution to this tension is to enter into a full partnership with consumers in which they control ownership of their demographic and behavioral data and determine how and when (and if) it will be used. This solution respects the many-to-many model underlying the World Wide Web in which consumers can also be providers to the medium and allows consumers to remain active participants in the interactive communication process.

For a demonstration of the type of information available to marketers about visitors to Web sites, visit *anonymizer.cs.cmu.edu:8080/prog/snoop.pl*. The Anonymizer site demonstrates what sort of information about the visitor is available to the Web site. Depending upon the platform we have accessed the Anonymizer URL from, the information ranges from simply stating that we are accessing the site from a particular hardware/browser platform (i.e., "a 680×0-based Macintosh running Netscape") to the deeply troubling statements, "Your name is probably Tom Novak, and you can be reached at *novak@moe.ogsm.vanderbilt.edu.* You're located around Nashville, TN. Your computer is a Unix box running SunOS. Your Internet browser is Netscape."

The industry, consumers, and regulators have only just begun to discuss these issues. In the months to come, managers need to be prepared to address the issue of consumer privacy in online environments.

Rights of consumer data ownership

Closely related to privacy is the issue of who should possess the rights to consumer navigation and transaction data. Peppers (1996) has proposed that online marketers should act as "hosts" for consumer data. In this model, identifying information is kept secret, but nonidentifying information is remarketed. Because the consumer gets communications targeted to her interests in

an explicit bargain between the consumer and the marketer, such a policy, Pepper argues, can work to the mutual advantage of both consumer and marketer. Peppers (1996) also proposes that marketers develop a "privacy bill of rights" in which marketers do the following:

- State *why* they need consumer information, including an argument of the ways in which collecting this information will improve consumers' lives.

- Agree what they will *never* do with consumer data.

- Detail what options the consumer has regarding the data and these policies.

- Indicate what events on the part of the marketer require *notification* of the consumer.

Many marketers feel that privacy is a "commercially valuable benefit" [23] and that protecting consumer privacy is actually consistent with customization to customer needs in the online environment.

We believe that the overriding principle that must guide efforts to negotiate explicit contracts between marketer and consumer is the one of "opt-in" in which the consumer is informed about the privacy consequences of their online behavior prior to engaging in such behavior. This is in stark contrast to the more common "opt-out" policy prevalent in the physical world in which consumers may never know that data is being collected about them and possibly resold to others without their knowledge.

The approaches to privacy that are most likely to attract the attention of government regulators are those that ignore consumers' rights and fail to enter into explicit agreements with consumers about their demographic and behavioral data.

The recent Graphics, Visualization, and Usability Center study [24] found that Web users value their privacy, particularly as expressed by visiting sites anonymously or by adopting various aliases depending upon the circumstances of the visit.

Further, users desire "complete control" over whether a particular Web site should receive any information on them. While users recognize that marketers require demographic and behavioral data on visits for business purposes, users do not feel that marketers have the right to sell these data to other firms. Web users seemed willing to provide demographic information if marketers would tell them what was being collected and how it would be used. Pitkow and Kehoe (1996) conclude "that respondents are more concerned with their right to control demographic information, than any compensation they might receive for revealing it. Only 5.9 percent reported that they would not give a site demographic information under any condition." These findings suggest that privacy policies in this emerging medium should be driven by the unique characteristics of the medium (e.g., interactivity) and the desires of its users (e.g., control) as they experience that medium [12].

Ethics

Researchers are beginning to address what constitutes ethical behavior in the conduct of online research [4, 8, 29]. A key result of this research, that "informed consent" is a critical component of ethical research in many online environments, has general implications for the way marketers may approach gathering data from Web visitors. However, much more specific consumer research is necessary to determine the best ways to develop and implement such policies in commercially oriented Web environments.

"Disguised ads" are another potential ethical concern. Suppose that an advertiser-supported search agent site presented links to an advertiser's Web site at the beginning of a list produced by a search request for a set of keywords. In this case, while the requestor may believe a link appears at the beginning of the list because it is the most *relevant* to his/her keyword request, the top position of the link may be due to sponsor payments. Such practices must be made clear to users of the search agent, as they have the

potential to deceive consumers and undermine trust in search agent sites.

Strategic Considerations

Numerous strategic considerations must also be addressed when developing advertising measurement standards, including:

- Target marketing
- Comparability
- Isolated versus coordinated ad placement
- Depth versus breadth
- Viability of the advertising sponsorship model

Target marketing

Web sites facilitate one-to-one marketing by permitting customization and tailoring of content and user interface. For example, Group Cortex's Site Track product generates customized Web content, so that the navigating experience can be tailored to a user's preferences. Focalink and DoubleClick provide customized placement of ads, so that different visitors see advertisements most appropriate to their interests. Intelligent agents also provide means to build a relationship between the visitor and the marketer. However, most current practice in Web advertising measurement ignores the fact that Web content and ads can be tailored to segments of respondents or groups of respondents.

Comparability

The CASIE (1995) principles recommend that "audience estimates covering a particular interactive vehicle be directly comparable to estimates covering another interactive vehicle within the same interactive medium." This is a sensible recommendation, if taken to mean that common metrics should be used when evaluating comparable Web sites. However, is a Web site that does not incorporate user-driven customization comparable to a Web site that does incorporate customization? One would expect that a certain number of ad exposures at a site that targeted ads according to user preferences or demographics would be more effective than the equivalent number of exposures at a site that presented a single ad to all visitors. Thus, while it is necessary to begin with comparable metrics to compare Web sites, there must also be some adjustment for the inherent noncomparability of Web sites along dimensions that impact the functional relationship of the given metric with advertising effectiveness.

The CASIE principles further state that "comparability to measurements taken of traditional media is also desirable whenever practical. However, this is not a mandatory requirement for interactive media measurement when the behavioral characteristics of the new media themselves demand new dimensionality of measurement." Again, we believe this is a reasonable position. However, we would add that where it is possible to do so, *terminology* used in traditional media (e.g., exposures, reach, frequency, etc.) be used in Web advertising. This does not mean that one can or should directly compare such measures across interactive and traditional media. It simply means that the same construct is being measured. It also does not mean that traditional metrics are the only metrics applicable to Web media measurement. On the contrary, due to the interactive nature of the Web and the underlying many-to-many communications model, new metrics for advertising measurement will be useful.

Isolated versus coordinated ad placement

A media plan will typically involve a set of Web sites, based upon decision rules that take into account cost and effectiveness of placing ads on various Web sites. As noted, some firms, such as Focalink and DoubleClick have developed ad placement products that facilitate this media planning process. However, in these initial states of Web-based advertising, it should be expected that much of the current state of the art of Web ad placement is based upon isolated, rather than

coordinated, media buying strategies. Effective Web measurement needs to recognize that coordinated, rather than isolated, ad placement is more desirable, and that measures of visitor duplication across Web sites are necessary.

There has been inordinate interest, possibly motivated by a desire to draw analogies with traditional media, in identifying the "top" Web sites, in terms of traffic (e.g., NPD's PC Meter) or advertising revenue (e.g., Jupiter's AdSpend). A focus of attention upon the "largest Web sites" will likely lead to a suboptimal media plan. Carried to the extreme, the vast majority of ads will be placed upon the largest Web sites, which by definition will have more heterogeneous visitor populations than smaller, more targeted Web sites.

The strategic issue of isolated vs. coordinated ad placement relates to the diffusiveness of payment for Web advertising. On one hand are large sums for ads placed on relatively small numbers of sites viewed by large numbers of visitors, while on the other hand are micropayments for ads placed on large number of sites each viewed by relatively small number of visitors.

A logical extension of this idea is what we term "transclusive advertising." Nelson [20] describes transclusion as "hyper-sharing: all instances and copies are resolved to the simulation of one cosmic original, which is omnipresent, a canonical address somewhere on the network." One practical application is the "transcopyright" [19], which is "permission to republish . . . material in any context, under the condition that only the address is distributed by the republisher."

For example, anyone could use a transcopyrighted GIF format image by including a link on one's Web page to the *original* GIF image, as well as a link to an original permission page that specifies the exact terms of use of the image. Thus, in advertising placement, when one considers the continuum from isolated to coordinated ad placement, a logical extension is to end-user placement of advertising. By taking Nelson's idea and substituting advertising for copyright, one can imagine a scenario in which any Web site can, on its own volition, place an advertisement for company X and be compensated by company X based on an agreed-upon measure of advertising response. One example of a similar approach is used by the *amazon.com* Associates Program (*www.amazon.com/exec/obidos/subst/assoc-invitation.html*). In this program, any Web site can place a link to one of 300,000 books sold by *amazon.com* and receive a royalty for all sales that occurred as a result of a visitor accessing *amazon.com* via that link.

These examples illustrate the array of possibilities in selecting vehicles in a Web-based media plan. In all cases, in order to develop a rational measure of the cost for placing an ad, we need a standardized and appropriate methodology for advertising measurement.

Depth versus breadth

There are two complementary approaches to collecting visitor data for advertising measurement. Server access logs focus upon *depth* and, in theory, provide a complete record of all traffic to a given Web site. Of course, caching by the user's browser and caching of Web pages by Internet service causes the server access log to be an incomplete record and an underestimate of true traffic. Given mandatory registration (e.g., I/PRO) or tracking via cookies (see, for example, *http://www.netscape.com/newsref/std/cookie_spec.html*), one can combine in-depth data across multiple Web sites. However, the number of Web sites that can be combined will be a small fraction of all available Web sites.

The *breadth* approach is characterized by panels of Web users (e.g., PC Meter) whose navigation behavior is tracked over the complete set of sites they visited in a given period of time. The panel consists of a sample of Web users who are representative of a larger target population.

Thus, the tradeoff is between information on (nearly) all visitors to a small fraction of all Web sites in the depth approach, and information on (nearly) all Web sites visited by a small fraction of all visitors in the breadth approach.

Viability of the advertising sponsorship model

Finally, an important strategic consideration is the long-term viability of the advertising sponsorship model. Advertising sponsorship is by no means the only viable method for supporting commercial Web sites. While advertising is currently the dominant business model on the Web, online store fronts, subscriptions, and micropayments (see, for example, *http://www.w3.org/pub/WWW/TR/WD-mptp*) provide alternative business models with considerable potential [25].

Conclusion

In this white paper, we have argued that standardizing the Web measurement process is a critical first step on the path toward the successful commercial development of the Web. To that end, we have provided an overview of current practice and considerations that affect the question of what the standards for Web advertising measurement should be. Given the ambiguity in current terminology for advertising measurement on the Web, we have proposed a series of definitions of basic constructs, exposure metrics, and interactivity metrics. We further proposed that if there is terminology from traditional media that is appropriate to the Web, that terminology should be used to avoid confusion and ease the adoption process of standards formation.

We identified two primary forms of Web-based advertising: banner ads and target ads. Active ad exposure of target ads is under the consumer's control; passive ad exposure to banner ads is under the marketer's control. This distinction has important implications for the measurement process.

In our discussion of current and emerging media pricing models, we observed that CPM and flat fee models do nothing more than count the number of visitors exposed to a particular banner ad at a particular site. Thus, we proposed a pricing model based on interactivity metrics. The rationale behind this argument is that the degree to which the visitor interacts with the target ad is a better measure of the value and effectiveness of an ad.

Ultimately, what is required is a set of integrated response measures that relate exposure and interactivity metrics to consumer response. We argued that it may be worthwhile to measure consumer outcomes in the context of direct response rather than solely in terms of mass media exposure.

Our primary objective in writing this paper is to stimulate further research and discussion and help facilitate the process of developing Web measurement standards. The preliminary diagram we proposed in Figure 2 organizes the measures introduced and relates them to consumer response in terms of a standard hierarchy of effects model. We offered a set of initial research questions and hypotheses to be pursued and an initial set of recommendations that we urge the industry to discuss, refine, and adopt. ∎

References

1. "Fall Prime-Time Pricing Survey," *Advertising Age,* September 16, 1966.

2. "Procter & Gamble World Wide Web Ad Strategy Raises Online Ire," Associated Press, April 28, 1966, San Francisco, *www2.nando.net/newsroom/ntn/info/042896/info5_380.html*

3. Batra, Rajeev, John G. Myers, and David A. Aaker. *Advertising Management,* 5th edition, Upper Saddle River, N.J.: Prentice Hall, 1996.

4. Boehlefeld, Sharon Polancic. "Doing the Right Thing: Ethical Cyberspace Research," *The Information Society* 12, 1996, pp. 141–152.

5. Chatterjee, Patrali. "Modeling Consumer Network Navigation in World Wide Web Sites: Implications for Advertising," dissertation proposal, Owen Graduate School of Management, Vanderbilt University, 1996.

6. CyberAtlas, 1996, *www.cyberatlas.com*

7. "DMA Report—Economic Impact: U.S. Direct Marketing Today," Direct Marketing Association, 1996, *www.the-dma.org*

8. Duncan, George T. "Is My Research Ethical?" *Communications of the ACM,* special issue on Internet in the home, December 1996, forthcoming.

9. Focalink, MarketMatch Database, 1996.

10. Hoffman, D.L., T.P. Novak, and P. Chatterjee. "Commercial Scenarios for the Web: Opportunities and Challenges," *Journal of Computer-Mediated Communication,* special issue on electronic commerce, December 1995.

11. Hoffman, D.L., and T.P. Novak. "Marketing in Hypermedia Computer-Mediated Environments: Conceptual Foundations" *Journal of Marketing,* July 1996.

12. Hoffman, Donna, and Thomas P. Novak. "A New Marketing Paradigm for Electronic Commerce," *The Information Society,* 1996, forthcoming.

13. "The Web in Perspective: A Comprehensive Analysis of Ad-Supported Web Sites," I/PRO Research, 1996.

14. "Web Ad Revenue Jumps 83 Percent in Second Quarter, According to Jupiter AdSpend Data," Jupiter Communications Press Release, September 3, 1996, *www.jup.com/jupiter/release/sept96/93adspend/*

15. Lewin, Tamar. "A Loss of Confidence: A Special Report. Questions of privacy roil arena of psychotherapy," *New York Times,* sect. A, p. 1, May 22, 1996.

16. "It's hit and click," *Marketing News* 30 (20), September 23, 1996, p. 38.

17. MIT Faculty/Industry Workshop. "Envisioning the Future of Internet Marketing: Research and Strategy Implications," Sloan School of Business, MIT, September 18–19, 1996.

18. Murphy, Ian P. "On-line ads effective? Who knows for sure?" *Marketing News* 30 (20), September 23, 1996, pp. 1, 38.

19. Nelson, Ted. "Transcopyright for .GIF pictures on the WWWeb," manuscript, Keio University Shonan Fujisawa Campus, June 1, 1996.

20. Nelson, Ted. "The Xantic Paradigm," manuscript, Keio University Shoan Fujisawa Campus, June 28, 1996.

21. Online Advertising Discussion List, volume 1, number 91, September 24, 1996, *www.tenagra.com/online-ads/*

22. Outdoor Advertising Association of America, Inc. "Growth in 1995 Outdoor Advertising Revenues is Largest in over a Decade," March 7, 1996, *www.oaaa.org/np/ht/revs.htm*

23. Peppers, Don. "The Business Case for Protecting Privacy," paper presented at Spotlight 1996, Marketing 1:1, Inc., Stamford, CT.

24. Pitkow, Jim, and Colleen Kehoe. "Fifth GVU WWW User Survey. High Level Summary and Trend Analysis: Data Privacy," GVU Center, College of Camputing, Georgia Institute of Technology, April 1996, *www.cc.gatech.edu/gvu/user_surveys/*

25. Rebello, Kathy. "Special Report: Making Money on the Net," *Business Week*, September 23, 1996, pp. 104–118.

26. Resnick, Paul. "Creating Value/Assisting the Visitor, " panel at the MIT Faculty/Industry Workshop, "Envisioning the Future of Internet Marketing: Research and Strategy Implications," Sloan School of Business, MIT, September 18–19, 1996.

27. Scarf, Maggie. "Keeping Secrets," *The New York Times*, sect. 6, p. 38, June 16, 1996.

28. Surmanek, Jim. *Introduction To Advertising Media*, NTC Business Books: Lincolnwood, Illinois, 1996. (Definitions from appendix can be found at *www.smartbiz.com/sbs/arts/iam13.htm*)

29. Thomas, Jim. "Introduction: A Debate about the Ethics of Fair Practices for Collecting Social Science Data in Cyberspace," *The Information Society*, 12, pp. 107–117, 1996.

30. Vaughn, Richard. "How Advertising Works: A Planning Model," *Journal of Advertising Research* 20, 5 October 1980, pp. 28–29.

31. Wilkie, William L. *Consumer Behavior,* 2nd Edition, New York: John Wiley & Sons, 1990.

Acknowledgments

We wish to thank Daimler-Benz, Interval Research Corporation, Netscape Communications Corporation, O'Reilly & Associates, and Yankelovich Partners for their generous sponsorship of this effort.

About the Authors

Thomas P. Novak
Owen Graduate School of Management
Vanderbilt University
Nashville, TN 37203
novak@moe.ogsm.vanderbilt.edu

Thomas P. Novak (A.B. Oberlin College; M.A., Ph.D., L.L. Thurstone Psychometric Laboratory, University of North Carolina, Chapel Hill) is an Associate Professor of Management and Co-Director of Project 2000 at the Owen Graduate School of Management, Vanderbilt University. Prior to joining the faculty at Vanderbilt, Novak has been a member of the marketing faculties at Southern Methodist University, Columbia University, and New York University.

Novak and his colleague Professor Donna Hoffman started Project 2000 in 1994 to study the marketing implications of commercializing computer-mediated environments like the World Wide Web on the Internet. Project 2000's Web site may be found at *http://www2000.ogsm.vanderbilt.edu/*.

Novak is a noted Internet marketing expert, has published numerous scholarly articles in the major U.S. and European marketing and electronic commerce journals, and is a contributing writer to both *Wired* and HotWired. During the summer of 1995, Novak helped to debunk the Rimm study on marketing pornography on the Internet and the *Time* magazine cyberporn cover story. *Internet World* has named him an Internet Hero for 1995. In April 1995, Novak received the TLA/SIRS Intellectual Freedom Award for this work.

Donna L. Hoffman
Owen Graduate School of Managemen
Vanderbilt University
Nashville, TN 37203
hoffman@colette.ogsm.vanderbilt.edu

Donna L. Hoffman (A.B. University of California at Davis; M.A., Ph.D., L.L. Thurstone Psychometric Laboratory, University of North Carolina, Chapel Hill) is an Associate Professor of Management and Co-Director of Project 2000 at the Owen Graduate School of Management, Vanderbilt University.

Hoffman and her colleague Professor Tom Novak started Project 2000 in 1994 to study the marketing implications of commercializing computer-mediated environments like the World Wide Web on the Internet. The virtual office address for

Project 2000 is *http://www2000.ogsm.vanderbilt. edu/*.

Hoffman, a widely quoted authority on Internet marketing, has published numerous scholarly articles and book chapters and is a contributing writer to both *Wired* and HotWired. She serves on the editorial boards of *Journal of Consumer Research*, *Marketing Letters*, and *Marketing Science* and reviews for all the major journals in marketing and electronic commerce. Hoffman is a member of the founding editorial boards of the *Journal of Electronic Commerce* and *EC World*. Hoffman is currently serving a two-year elected term as president of the INFORMS Section on Marketing and is an active member of the Association for Consumer Research, the American Marketing Association, the Association of Computing Machinery, and the Internet Society.

In 1995, *Internet World* named her an Internet Hero and *Newsweek* named her one of the "Net 50 People Who Matter Most on the Internet."

More Titles from O'REILLY™

Developing Web Content

Building Your Own WebSite

By Susan B. Peck & Stephen Arrants
1st Edition July 1996
514 pages, ISBN 1-56592-232-8

This is a hands-on reference for Windows® 95 and Windows NT™ desktop users who want to host their own site on the Web or on a corporate intranet. This step-by-step guide will have you creating live Web pages in minutes. You'll also learn how to connect your web to information in other Windows applications, such as word processing documents and databases. Packed with examples and tutorials on every aspect of Web management. Includes highly acclaimed WebSite™ 1.1—all the software you need for Web publishing.

Web Client Programming with Perl

By Clinton Wong
1st Edition Fall 1996
250 pages (est.), ISBN 1-56592-214-X

Web Client Programming with Perl teaches you how to extend scripting skills to the Web. This book teaches you the basics of how browsers communicate with servers and how to write your own customized Web clients to automate common tasks. It is intended for those who are motivated to develop software that offers a more flexible and dynamic response than a standard Web browser.

JavaScript: The Definitive Guide

By David Flanagan
1st Edition Winter 1997
700 pages (est.), ISBN 1-56592-234-4

This definitive reference guide to JavaScript, the HTML extension that gives Web pages programming language capabilities, covers JavaScript as it is used in Netscape 3.0 and 2.0 and in Microsoft Internet Explorer 2.0. Learn how JavaScript really works (and when it doesn't). Use JavaScript to control Web browser behavior, add dynamically created text to Web pages, interact with users through HTML forms, and even control and interact with Java applets and Navigator plug-ins.

HTML: The Definitive Guide

By Chuck Musciano & Bill Kennedy
1st Edition April 1996
410 pages, ISBN 1-56592-175-5

A complete guide to creating documents on the World Wide Web. This book describes basic syntax and semantics and goes on to show you how to create beautiful, informative Web documents you'll be proud to display. The HTML 2.0 standard and Netscape extensions are fully explained.

Designing for the Web: Getting Started in a New Medium

By Jennifer Niederst with Edie Freedman
1st Edition April 1996
180 pages, ISBN 1-56592-165-8

Designing for the Web gives you the basics you need to hit the ground running. Although geared toward designers, it covers information and techniques useful to anyone who wants to put graphics online. It explains how to work with HTML documents from a designer's point of view, outlines special problems with presenting information online, and walks through incorporating images into Web pages, with emphasis on resolution and improving efficiency.

WebMaster in a Nutshell

By Stephen Spainhour & Valerie Quercia
1st Edition October 1996
378 pages, ISBN 1-56592-229-8

Web content providers and administrators have many sources of information, both in print and online. WebMaster in a Nutshell pulls it all together into one slim volume—for easy desktop access. This quick-reference covers HTML, CGI, Perl, HTTP, server configuration, and tools for Web administration.

For information: **800-998-9938**, 707-829-0515; **info@ora.com; http://www.ora.com/**
To order: **800-889-8969** (credit card orders only); **order@ora.com**

Security

Practical UNIX & Internet Security, 2nd Edition

By Simson Garfinkel & Gene Spafford
2nd Edition April 1996
1004 pages, ISBN 1-56592-148-8

This second edition of the classic *Practical UNIX Security* is a complete rewrite of the original book. It's packed with twice the pages and offers even more practical information for UNIX users and administrators. In it you'll find coverage of features of many types of UNIX systems, including SunOS, Solaris, BSDI, AIX, HP-UX, Digital UNIX, Linux, and others.

Contents include UNIX and security basics, system administrator tasks, network security, and appendixes containing checklists and helpful summaries.

Building Internet Firewalls

By D. Brent Chapman & Elizabeth D. Zwicky
1st Edition September 1995
546 pages, ISBN 1-56592-124-0

More than a million systems are now connected to the Internet, and something like 15 million people in 100 countries on all seven continents use Internet services. More than 100 million email messages are exchanged each day, along with countless files, documents, and audio and video images. Although businesses are rushing headlong to get connected to the Internet, the security risks have never been greater.

Some of these risks have been around since the early days of networking—password attacks (guessing them or cracking them via password dictionaries and cracking programs), denial of service, and exploiting known security holes. Some risks are newer and even more dangerous—packet sniffers, IP (Internet Protocol) forgery, and various types of hijacking. Firewalls are a very effective way to protect your system from these Internet security threats.

Building Internet Firewalls is a practical guide to building firewalls on the Internet. If your site is connected to the Internet, or if you're considering getting connected, you need this book. It describes a variety of firewall approaches and architectures and discusses how you can build packet filtering and proxying solutions at your site. It also contains a full discussion of how to configure Internet services (e.g., FTP, SMTP, Telnet) to work with a firewall, as well as a complete list of resources, including the location of many publicly available firewall construction tools.

PGP: Pretty Good Privacy

By Simson Garfinkel
1st Edition January 1995
430 pages, ISBN 1-56592-098-8

PGP is a freely available encryption program that protects the privacy of files and electronic mail. It uses powerful public key cryptography and works on virtually every platform. This book is both a readable technical user's guide and a fascinating behind-the-scenes look at cryptography and privacy. It describes how to use PGP and provides background on cryptography, *PGP*'s history, battles over public key cryptography patents and U.S. government export restrictions, and public debates about privacy and free speech.

Computer Crime

By David Icove, Karl Seger & William VonStorch
(Consulting Editor Eugene H. Spafford)
1st Edition August 1995
462 pages, ISBN 1-56592-086-4

This book is for anyone who needs to know what today's computer crimes look like, how to prevent them, and how to detect, investigate, and prosecute them if they do occur. It contains basic computer security information as well as guidelines for investigators, law enforcement, and system administrators. It includes computer-related statutes and laws, a resource summary, detailed papers on computer crime, and a sample search warrant.

Computer Security Basics

By Deborah Russell & G.T. Gangemi, Sr.
1st Edition July 1991
464 pages, ISBN 0-937175-71-4

Computer Security Basics provides a broad introduction to the many areas of computer security and a detailed description of current security standards. This handbook uses simple terms to describe complicated concepts like trusted systems, encryption, and mandatory access control, and it contains a thorough, readable introduction to the "Orange Book."

For information: **800-998-9938**, 707-829-0515; **info@ora.com; http://www.ora.com/**
To order: **800-889-8969** (credit card orders only); **order@ora.com**

Network Administration

Getting Connected: The Internet at 56K and Up

By Kevin Dowd
1st Edition June 1996
424 pages, ISBN 1-56592-154-2

Getting Connected is a complete guide for businesses, schools, and other organizations who want to connect their computers to the Internet. This book covers everything you need to know to make informed decisions, from helping you figure out which services you really need to providing down-to-earth explanations of telecommunication options, such as frame relay, ISDN, and leased lines. Once you're online, it shows you how to set up basic Internet services, such as a World Wide Web server. Tackles issues for PC, Macintosh, and UNIX platforms.

DNS and BIND, 2nd Edition

By Paul Albitz & Cricket Liu
2nd Edition Winter 1996
456 pages (est.), ISBN 1-56592-236-0

This book is a complete guide to the Internet's Domain Name System (DNS) and the Berkeley Internet Name Domain (BIND) software, the UNIX implementation of DNS. This second edition covers Bind 4.8.3, which is included in most vendor implementations today, as well as Bind 4.9.3, the potential future standard.

Using & Managing UUCP

By Ed Ravin, Tim O'Reilly, Dale Dougherty & Grace Todino
1st Edition September 1996
424 pages, ISBN 1-56592-153-4

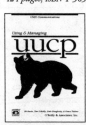

Using & Managing UUCP describes, in one volume, this popular communications and file transfer program. UUCP is very attractive to computer users with limited resources, a small machine, and a dial-up connection. This book covers Taylor UUCP, the latest versions of HoneyDanBer UUCP, and the specific implementation details of UUCP versions shipped by major UNIX vendors.

TCP/IP Network Administration

By Craig Hunt
1st Edition August 1992
502 pages, ISBN 0-937175-82-X

TCP/IP Network Administration is a complete guide to setting up and running a TCP/IP network for practicing system administrators. The book covers setting up your network, configuring important network applications including sendmail, and issues in troubleshooting and security. It covers both BSD and System V TCP/IP implementations.

Networking Personal Computers with TCP/IP

By Craig Hunt
1st Edition July 1995
408 pages, ISBN 1-56592-123-2

This book offers practical information as well as detailed instructions for attaching PCs to a TCP/IP network and its UNIX servers. It discusses the challenges you'll face and offers general advice on how to deal with them, provides basic TCP/IP configuration information for some of the popular PC operating systems, covers advanced configuration topics and configuration of specific applications such as email, and includes a chapter on NetWare, the most popular PC LAN system software.

sendmail, 2nd Edition

By Bryan Costales, with Eric Allman
2nd Edition Winter 1997
950 pages (est.), ISBN 1-56592-222-0

This second edition of the *sendmail* Nutshell Handbook covers sendmail version 8.8. This cross-referenced edition offers an expanded tutorial, solution-oriented examples, and new topics such as the #error delivery agent, sendmail's exit values, MIME headers, and how to set up and use the user database, mailertable, and smrsh.

Software

WebSite™ 1.1

By O'Reilly & Associates, Inc.
Documentation by Susan Peck & Stephen Arrants
2nd Edition January 1996
Four diskettes, 494-pg book, WebSite T-shirt
ISBN 1-56592-173-9; UPC 9-781565-921733

WebSite 1.1 makes it easier than ever for Windows NT 3.51 and Windows 95 users to start publishing on the Internet. WebSite is a 32-bit multi- threaded World Wide Web server that combines power and flexibility with ease of use. *WebSite 1.1* features include: HTML editor, multiple indexes, WebFind wizard, CGI with Visual Basic 4 framework and server push support, graphical interface for creating virtual servers, Windows 95 style install, logging reports for individual documents, HTML-2 and -3 support, external image map support, and Spyglass Mosaic 2.1 Web browser.

WebSite Professional ™

By O'Reilly & Associates, Inc.
Documentation by Susan Peck
1st Edition June 1996
Includes 3 books, ISBN 1-56592-174-7

Designed for the sophisticated user, *WebSite Professional™* is a complete Web server solution. *WebSite Professional* contains all of *WebSite's* award-winning features, including remote administration, virtual servers for creating multiple home pages, wizards to automate common tasks, a search tool for Web indexing, and a graphical outline fo Web documents and links for managing your site. New with *WebSite Professional:* support for SSL and S-HTTP, the premier Web encryption security protocols; the WebSite Application Programming Interface (WSAPI); Cold Fusion, a powerful development tool for dynamic linking of database information into your Web documents; and support for client and server-side Java programming.

WebSite Professional is a must for sophisticated users who want to offer their audiences the best in Web server technology.

WebBoard ™

By O'Reilly & Associates, Inc.
1st Edition February 1996
Includes 3 diskettes & a 98-pg book, ISBN 1-56592-181-X

WebBoard™ is an advanced multi-threaded conferencing system that can help attract users to your Web server. With *WebBoard*, people can use their Web browsers to participate in online discussions about any number of topics. *WebBoard* is ideal for use in business environments and in legal or educational organizations or groups—anywhere online discussions can help groups communicate and keep track of ongoing decisions and issues.

PolyForm™

Documentation by John Robert Boynton
1st Edition May 1996
Two diskettes & 146-pg book, ISBN 1-56592-182-8

PolyForm™ is a powerful 32-bit Web forms tool that helps you easily build and manage interactive Web pages. *PolyForm's* interactive forms make it easy and fun for users to respond to the contents of your Web with their own feedback, ideas, or requests for more information. *PolyForm* lets you collect, process, and respond to each user's specific input. Best of all, forms that once required hours of complicated programming can be created in minutes because *PolyForm* automatically handles all of the CGI programming for processing form contents.

Statisphere™

By O'Reilly & Associates, Inc.
1st Edition Winter 1996
2 diskettes & a 135-page book, ISBN 1-56592-233-6

Statisphere™ is a Web traffic analyzer that provides precise, graphical reporting on your Web server's usage. Easy-to-read, browser-based reports deliver real-time profiles and long-term trend analysis on who's visiting your site and what they're reading. Whether you're tracking traffic rates for advertising, or steering Web development efforts to where they'll have the most impact, Statisphere gives you the answers you need to make the right decisions about your Web site.

Web Server Administration

Apache: The Definitive Guide

By Ben Laurie & Peter Laurie
1st Edition Winter 1997
300 pages (est.), ISBN 1-56592-250-6

Despite all the hype about Netscape, Apache is far and away the most widely used Web server platform in the world. It runs on about half the world's existing Web sites and is rapidly increasing market share. *Apache: The Definitive Guide* is the only complete guide on the market today describing how to obtain, set up, and secure the Apache software. Officially authorized by the Apache Group, this book is the definitive documentation for the world's most popular Web server.

Contents include:

- The history of the Apache Group
- Obtaining and compiling the server
- Configuring and running Apache, including such topics as directory structures, virtual hosts, and CGI programming
- The Apache Module API
- Apache security
- The Apache manuals
- A complete list of configuration directives
- A complete demo of a sample Web site

UNIX Web Server Administration

By John Leavitt
1st Edition Winter 1997
325 pages (est.), ISBN 1-56592-217-4

With our increasing dependence on Web sites for our daily work, the Web server has emerged as one of the most crucial services a company can offer. When the server is slow, customers are frustrated. When the server or network is down, customers are turned away.

UNIX Web Server Administration tells Web administrators how to keep a server running smoothly. This book not only covers Apache, the most popular server on the Internet, but also the NCSA, CERN, and Netscape servers.

Managing Internet Information Services

By Cricket Liu, Jerry Peek, Russ Jones, Bryan Buus & Adrian Nye
1st Edition December 1994
668 pages, ISBN 1-56592-062-7

Managing Internet Information Services describes how to create services for the millions of Internet users. By setting up Internet servers for World Wide Web, Gopher, FTP, Finger, Telnet, WAIS (Wide Area Information Services), or email services, anyone with a suitable computer and Internet connection can become an "Internet Publisher."

Services on the Internet allow almost instant distribution and frequent updates of any kind of information. You can provide services to employees of your own company (solving the information distribution problems of spread-out companies), or you can serve the world. Perhaps you'd like to create an Internet service equivalent to the telephone company's directory assistance. Or maybe you're the Species Survival Commission, and you'd like your plans online; this book describes a prototype service the authors created to make SSC's endangered species Action Plans viewable worldwide. Whatever you have in mind can be done. This book tells you how.

Creating a service can be a big job, involving more than one person. This book separates the setup and maintenance of server software from tdata management, so that a team can divide responsibilities. Sections and chapters on data management, a role we call the Data Librarian, are marked with a special icon.

"Excellent book . . . carefully written, informative and readable . . . [well] organized. . . .I 'm enjoying it considerably. I picked it up to flip through—I'm a writer of Internet books myself, and I do a lot of 'been there, done that' when I approach an Internet book—and after an hour or so, I discovered I was actually reading the book. I have even taken the step of . . . using my post-it-notes tabs to mark the good stuff."
—Jill Ellsworth, Ph.D., Author of *The Internet Business Book, Education on the Internet, and Marketing on the Internet*

Stay in touch with O'REILLY™

Visit Our Award-Winning World Wide Web Site

http://www.ora.com/

VOTED

> "Top 100 Sites on the Web" —*PC Magazine*
> "Top 5% Websites" —*Point Communications*
> "3-Star site" —*The McKinley Group*

Our Web site contains a library of comprehensive product information (including book excerpts and tables of contents), downloadable software, background articles, interviews with technology leaders, links to relevant sites, book cover art, and more. File us in your Bookmarks or Hotlist!

Join Our Two Email Mailing Lists

LIST #1　NEW PRODUCT RELEASES: To receive automatic email with brief descriptions of all new O'Reilly products as they are released, send email to: listproc@online.ora.com and put the following information in the first line of your message (NOT in the Subject: field, which is ignored): **subscribe ora-news "Your Name" of "Your Organization"** (for example: **subscribe ora-news Kris Webber of Fine Enterprises)**

List #2　O'REILLY EVENTS: If you'd also like us to send information about trade show events, special promotions, and other O'Reilly events, send email to: **listproc@online.ora.com** and put the following information in the first line of your message (NOT in the Subject: field, which is ignored): **subscribe ora-events "Your Name" of "Your Organization"**

Visit Our Gopher Site

- Connect your Gopher to **gopher.ora.com**, or
- Point your Web browser to **gopher://gopher.ora.com/**, or
- telnet to **gopher.ora.com** (login: **gopher**)

Get Example Files from Our Books Via FTP

There are two ways to access an archive of example files from our books:

REGULAR FTP — ftp to: **ftp.ora.com** (login: **anonymous**—use your email address as the password) or point your Web browser to: **ftp://ftp.ora.com/**

FTPMAIL — Send an email message to: **ftpmail@online.ora.com** (write "help" in the message body)

Contact Us Via Email

order@ora.com — To place a book or software order online. Good for North American and international customers.

subscriptions@ora.com — To place an order for any of our newsletters or periodicals.

software@ora.com — For general questions and product information about our software.
- Check out O'Reilly Software Online at **http://software.ora.com/** for software and technical support information.
- Registered O'Reilly software users send your questions to **website-support@ora.com**

books@ora.com — General questions about any of our books.

cs@ora.com — For answers to problems regarding your order or our products.

booktech@ora.com — For book content technical questions or corrections.

proposals@ora.com — To submit new book or software proposals to our editors and product managers.

international@ora.com — For information about our international distributors or translation queries.
- For a list of our distributors outside of North America check out: **http://www.ora.com/www/order/country.html**

O'REILLY™

101 Morris Street, Sebastopol, CA 95472 USA
TEL 707-829-0515 or 800-998-9938 (6 A.M. to 5 P.M. PST)
FAX 707-829-0104

TO ORDER: **800-889-8969** (CREDIT CARD ORDERS ONLY); **order@ora.com; http://www.ora.com/**
OUR PRODUCTS ARE AVAILABLE AT A BOOKSTORE OR SOFTWARE STORE NEAR YOU.

Titles from O'REILLY™

INTERNET PROGRAMMING

CGI Programming on the
World Wide Web
Designing for the Web
HTML: The Definitive Guide
JavaScript: The Definitive Guide
Learning Perl
Programming Perl, 2nd Edition
Regular Expressions
WebMaster in a Nutshell
Web Client Programming with Perl
(Winter '97)
The World Wide Web Journal

USING THE INTERNET

Smileys
The Whole Internet User's Guide
and Catalog
The Whole Internet for Windows 95
What You Need to Know:
Using Email Effectively
What You Need to Know: Bandits on the
Information Superhighway

JAVA SERIES

Exploring Java
Java AWT Reference (Winter '97 est.)
Java Fundamental Classes Reference
(Winter '97 est.)
Java in a Nutshell
Java Language Reference (Winter '97 est.)
Java Threads
Java Virtual Machine (Winter '97)

SOFTWARE

WebSite™ 1.1
WebSite Professional™
WebBoard™
PolyForm™
Statisphere™

SONGLINE GUIDES

Gif Animation Studio
NetActivism
NetLaw (Winter '97)
NetLearning
NetResearch (Winter '97)
NetSuccess for Realtors
Shockwave Studio (Winter '97 est.)

SYSTEM ADMINISTRATION

Building Internet Firewalls
Computer Crime:
A Crimefighter's Handbook
Computer Security Basics
DNS and BIND, 2nd Edition
Essential System Administration,
2nd Edition
Getting Connected:
The Internet at 56K and Up
Linux Network Administrator's Guide
Managing Internet Information Services
Managing Usenet (Spring '97)
Managing NFS and NIS
Networking Personal Computers
with TCP/IP
Practical UNIX & Internet Security
PGP: Pretty Good Privacy
sendmail, 2nd Edition (Winter '97)
System Performance Tuning
TCP/IP Network Administration
termcap & terminfo
Using & Managing UUCP
Volume 8: X Window System
Administrator's Guide

UNIX

Exploring Expect
Learning GNU Emacs, 2nd Edition
Learning the bash Shell
Learning the Korn Shell
Learning the UNIX Operating System
Learning the vi Editor
Linux in a Nutshell (Winter '97 est.)
Making TeX Work
Linux Multimedia Guide
Running Linux, 2nd Edition
Running Linux Companion
CD-ROM, 2nd Edition
SCO UNIX in a Nutshell
sed & awk, 2nd Edition (Winter '97)
UNIX in a Nutshell: System V Edition
UNIX Power Tools
UNIX Systems Programming
Using csh and tsch
What You Need to Know:
When You Can't Find Your
UNIX System Administrator

WINDOWS

Inside the Windows 95 Registry

PROGRAMMING

Advanced PL/SQL
Applying RCS and SCCS
C++: The Core Language
Checking C Programs with lint
DCE Security Programming
Distributing Applications Across
DCE and Windows NT
Encyclopedia of Graphics File
Formats, 2nd Edition
Guide to Writing DCE Applications
lex & yacc
Managing Projects with make
Oracle Performance Tuning
Oracle Power Objects
Oracle PL/SQL Programming
Porting UNIX Software
POSIX Programmer's Guide
POSIX.4: Programming for
the Real World
Power Programming with RPC
Practical C Programming
Practical C++ Programming
Programming Python
Programming with curses
Programming with GNU Software
Pthreads Programming
Software Portability with imake,
2nd Edition
Understanding DCE
Understanding Japanese Information
Processing
UNIX Systems Programming for SVR4

BERKELEY 4.4 SOFTWARE DISTRIBUTION

4.4BSD System Manager's Manual
4.4BSD User's Reference Manual
4.4BSD User's Supplementary
Documents
4.4BSD Programmer's Reference
Manual
4.4BSD Programmer's Supplementary
Documents

X PROGRAMMING
THE X WINDOW SYSTEM

Volume 0: X Protocol Reference Manual
Volume 1: Xlib Programming Manual
Volume 2: Xlib Reference Manual
Volume. 3M: X Window System
User's Guide, Motif Edition
Volume. 4: X Toolkit Intrinsics
Programming Manual
Volume 4M: X Toolkit Intrinsics
Programming Manual,
Motif Edition
Volume 5: X Toolkit Intrinsics
Reference Manual
Volume 6A: Motif Programming
Manual
Volume 6B: Motif Reference Manual
Volume 6C: Motif Tools
Volume 8 : X Window System
Administrator's Guide
Programmer's Supplement for Release 6
X User Tools (with CD-ROM)
The X Window System in a Nutshell

HEALTH, CAREER, & BUSINESS

Building a Successful Software Business
The Computer User's Survival Guide
Dictionary of Computer Terms
The Future Does Not Compute
Love Your Job!
Publishing with CD-ROM

TRAVEL

Travelers' Tales: Brazil (Winter '96)
Travelers' Tales: Food (Fall '96)
Travelers' Tales: France
Travelers' Tales: Gutsy Women
(Fall '96)
Travelers' Tales: Hong Kong
Travelers' Tales: India
Travelers' Tales: Mexico
Travelers' Tales: San Francisco
Travelers' Tales: Spain
Travelers' Tales: Thailand
Travelers' Tales: A Woman's World

TO ORDER: **800-889-8969** (CREDIT CARD ORDERS ONLY); **order@ora.com; http://www.ora.com/**
OUR PRODUCTS ARE AVAILABLE AT A BOOKSTORE OR SOFTWARE STORE NEAR YOU.

International Distributors

Customers outside North America can now order O'Reilly & Associates books through the following distributors. They offer our international customers faster order processing, more bookstores, increased representation at tradeshows worldwide, and the high-quality, responsive service our customers have come to expect.

EUROPE, MIDDLE EAST AND NORTHERN AFRICA *(except Germany, Switzerland, and Austria)*

INQUIRIES
International Thomson Publishing Europe
Berkshire House
168-173 High Holborn
London WC1V 7AA, United Kingdom
Telephone: 44-171-497-1422
Fax: 44-171-497-1426
Email: **itpint@itps.co.uk**

ORDERS
International Thomson Publishing Services, Ltd.
Cheriton House, North Way
Andover, Hampshire SP10 5BE,
United Kingdom
Telephone: 44-264-342-832 (UK orders)
Telephone: 44-264-342-806 (outside UK)
Fax: 44-264-364418 (UK orders)
Fax: 44-264-342761 (outside UK)
UK & Eire orders: **itpuk@itps.co.uk**
International orders: **itpint@itps.co.uk**

GERMANY, SWITZERLAND, AND AUSTRIA

International Thomson Publishing
Königswinterer Straße 418
53227 Bonn, Germany
Telephone: 49-228-97024 0
Fax: 49-228-441342
Email: **anfragen@oreilly.de**

AUSTRALIA

WoodsLane Pty. Ltd.
7/5 Vuko Place, Warriewood NSW 2102
P.O. Box 935, Mona Vale NSW 2103
Australia
Telephone: 61-2-9970-5111
Fax: 61-2-9970-5002
Email: **info@woodslane.com.au**

NEW ZEALAND

WoodsLane New Zealand Ltd.
21 Cooks Street (P.O. Box 575)
Wanganui, New Zealand
Telephone: 64-6-347-6543
Fax: 64-6-345-4840
Email: **info@woodslane.com.au**

ASIA *(except Japan & India)*

INQUIRIES
International Thomson Publishing Asia
60 Albert Street #15-01
Albert Complex
Singapore 189969
Telephone: 65-336-6411
Fax: 65-336-7411

ORDERS
Telephone: 65-336-6411
Fax: 65-334-1617

JAPAN

O'Reilly Japan, Inc.
Kiyoshige Building 2F
12-Banchi, Sanei-cho
Shinjuku-ku
Tokyo 160 Japan
Telephone: 81-3-3356-5227
Fax: 81-3-3356-5261
Email: **kenji@ora.com**

INDIA

Computer Bookshop (India) PVT. LTD.
190 Dr. D.N. Road, Fort
Bombay 400 001
India
Telephone: 91-22-207-0989
Fax: 91-22-262-3551
Email: **cbsbom@giasbm01.vsnl.net.in**

THE AMERICAS

O'Reilly & Associates, Inc.
101 Morris Street
Sebastopol, CA 95472 U.S.A.
Telephone: 707-829-0515
Telephone: 800-998-9938 (U.S. & Canada)
Fax: 707-829-0104
Email: **order@ora.com**

SOUTHERN AFRICA

International Thomson Publishing Southern Africa
Building 18, Constantia Park
240 Old Pretoria Road
P.O. Box 2459
Halfway House, 1685 South Africa
Telephone: 27-11-805-4819
Fax: 27-11-805-3648

O'REILLY™